CASUALTY OF SILENCE

CASUALTY

OF

SILENCE

BY

ERNESTINE MOORE

Lyons & Grant
Multimedia LLC
New York

Copyright © 2012 by Ernestine Moore

All rights reserved. Except as permitted under the U.S. Copyright Act of 1976, no part of this book may be reproduced in any form or by any electronic or mechanical means including information storage and retrieval systems, without permission in writing from the publisher. The only exception is by a reviewer, who may quote short excerpts in a review.

Published by Lyons & Grant Multimedia LLC
New York

visit our website at www.LGMmedia.net

Printed in the United States of America

Library of Congress Control Number: 2013933178

ISBN-13: 978-0-9837172-7-0

ISBN-10: 0-9837172-7-3

I want to thank and praise God, giving Him all the glory. Without Him, this book would not be possible. I want to thank Him for allowing me to experience everything that I have experienced and still experience. I endured, and survived and continue to survive a lot of traumatic situations. This book is to help educate others, as well as myself about the effects of abuse and how to handle it, and how every individual handles abuse differently.

This book is dedicated to the memory of my father, the kindest and most gracious, loving man I've known, Samuel Williams, and to my lovely godmother, Claudine Hodges, who was a mother to me during my darkest days. She opened her heart and loved and cared for me, making me a part of her family. She did what she could do to rescue me from much of the abuse in my life.

I also dedicate this book to my mother and to all my other abusers. Without them afflicting me with the countless, heartless acts, I wouldn't be who I am today—a survivor.

I want to say a special thanks to my sisters, Angela Ross and Amy Moore and to all my brothers, and to my kids, daughters Womp, Montoya Moore, Chrissy Moore and my sons Emmanuel Moore, Jyvon Moore (and to my two future sons, Rayvon Moore and Vondale Moore), who I love and cherish and who hold a special place in my heart.

This book is also dedicated to all of you to show you what you can accomplish when you don't give up and believe that God will make a way.
Finally, this book is also dedicated to all the people who have been and who are continuing to be victims of abuse. Seek help. Don't use what happened to you as an excuse and give up on yourself, you too can survive.

"Beating the hand I was dealt"

Odds were against me from the day I was born; but even then I proved to be a survivor.

Years ago, while sitting with a few of my family members as they were drinking, smoking, laughing, and reminiscing about the past, my mother, Essie, shared a little about my sister, Amy and me. The story started with the day I was born.
The day was August 4, 1965 in Cleveland, Ohio. I had to stay in the hospital for a few weeks because I weighed five pounds and had yellow jaundice. When I turned one month Mama decided to move from her friend's home in Cleveland, Ohio, to Toronto and then to Steubenville with my Aunt Emma. While we lived there family members spoiled me.

My cousin Lena, who is close to my mother in age, described how tiny I was. My cousins were laughing, saying that I was so tiny that my bed was literally one of my mother's dresser drawers. She said that every time my mother would lay me down and come back to check on me, I wasn't there. When she would look for me, she would find me in one of my cousins' pants as they tried to sneak me out the house only to get caught when I would make noise.
I laughed. She said that would happen on different occasions, with different cousins, and the laughter continued. I didn't believe them. I told them I wish they would have taken a picture.

A question developed in my mind concerning my name. I was wondering why I was named after a man, after one of my male cousins. My mother said a few days after I was born, she hadn't named me yet. My cousin Ernest said he wanted me to be his namesake. Mama added stine at the end to make Ernestine.

I said, "I wish you would have given me another name." I hated my name. It's not only a man's name; it's also an old lady's name. I asked her if that's why my birth certificate has two parts to it. One part was incomplete. Everything about me was on it except my name. Attached to it was a small certificate that had my complete name on it.

Amy was born two years and two days from the day I was born in Steubenville, Ohio.
    "How did you plan that?" I asked Mama.
    " I don't know," she said. "It just happened."
Everyone continued laughing as she continued the story. She said not long after my sister was born, we moved from Ohio to Detroit. My mother said that everyone was upset because they didn't want us to move, that we moved to Detroit during the riots. At that point, a vision came to me.

I yelled out in excitement that I remembered that. They started laughing and said they didn't see how I remembered when I was only two going on three years old. I didn't know either, but I did. I told them I remembered sitting in the backseat of my daddy's car as he was driving. I could barely see the people as they walked past the car but I saw lots of them walking past my window. They were all wearing the same uniform. I heard them yelling that everyone must be in the house or off the street before dark. That's all the memory I have of the riot.

I asked my mother why we moved to Detroit. She said that my daddy, Sam, wanted to move to Detroit because of a job. Either his job was relocating him or he was hoping to get a job. Detroit is known as the Motor City, because of the automotive plants. She said we lived in an apartment on the west side, close to Daddy's job, Ford Automotive Factory.

She said my daddy didn't like living in our apartment building because all the tenants had to share one bathroom. I was being potty trained and would have to be taken to the bathroom all through the night, and my father didn't like that. When he came home one day from work, he had a big silver tub and a potty chair. It was big to me because I was only two. You can call me crazy, but I was fascinated with the big silver tub. I liked how it sounded when I hit on it and rubbed it with my hand. It was used for multiple purposes; we took our baths in it, I saw my mother wash clothes in it, and one day it was used to help stop my nose from bleeding after an accident at the grocery store. Let me explain.

My mother said I was a spoiled crybaby. She generally left us with her friend Carol who was my sister's godmother and lived next door. One time when she was leaving, I started crying and screaming so she had to take me with her.

Mama said as we entered the store, instead of getting in the cart, I wanted to walk and help her push it. As we walked down the aisle, I slipped and fell, and my face hit that bottom bar. After she picked me up and saw blood coming from my face, she panicked and ran out of the store, leaving everything she had behind, even her purse. She ran as fast as she could to the apartment. Once inside, she took off my clothes. She stood me up in my silver tub and was running back and forth to the sink, getting water to pour over my head to wash away the blood to see where it was coming from; it was coming from my nose.

She said she was trying everything that she could think of to stop the bleeding. To me, it seemed like I was in that cold water forever. My nose finally stopped bleeding, and the water was so red it looked like a tub full of blood. In spite of all the bleeding Mama did not take me to the hospital. Mama just cleaned me up and put me in bed.

From that incident, I continued to suffer with nosebleeds for no apparent reason. I also have trouble breathing. It was obvious that my nose was broken, but I was never taken to seek any medical attention.

It was different when my sister was involved in a little incident. Her godmother was watching her while our parents were out running errands. Amy was sitting in her walker and got too close to the radiator, and was burned on her arm. She was taken to the hospital when my parents returned home. When they got back from the hospital, my sister's arm was wrapped in a white bandage.

Contents

Chapter One	....	15
Chapter Two	....	29
Chapter Three	....	51
Chapter Four	....	77
Chapter Five	....	109
Chapter Six	....	163
Chapter seven	....	199
Chapter Eight	....	253

Chapter One

Memories of My Life Vary

One day, my sister and I were sitting in the backseat of the car, Daddy was driving. When he stopped in front of this large building, Mama got out and went inside. We waited in the car with Daddy.

"Why are we just sitting here?" I asked him.

"Picking up your little brother," he said.

"Daddy, go tell Mama to get us a sister," I said.

He laughed and replied that she couldn't, without any other explanation. I laugh now because at that age, I thought she ordered the baby. I didn't know where babies came from, nor did I know anything about pregnancy. And I know I hadn't noticed any changes in Mama's appearance or that she had been away from us for a long period of time. I learned later that the building we stopped at was a hospital, and that my brother had to stay in the hospital after birth because something was wrong with his blood, something about having blue blood. Mama didn't go into detail.

Commotion....

Amy my baby brother and I were in our room playing. My brother was inside his walker while Amy and I were sitting on the floor playing when Daddy came to the door and told us not to come out of the room. My sister and I looked at him as he closed the door. I was puzzled but we continued playing. All of a sudden I heard something hit the wall and then yelling and screaming, and Mama crying. It sounded like something was being thrown all over the floor.

I got scared and grabbed my sister's hand and my brother's walker. We hid in the corner, shielded by the baby bed. We had no idea what was happening. The bumping, yelling, and screaming continued. Suddenly, everything stopped. I could still hear Mama crying, but could tell she was trying to cry quietly. In fear of the unknown, I didn't dare go out of that room; we just sat in the corner.

Moments later, the door opened. I was still clutching my brother and sister. No one was at the door. Still holding on to them, we walked slowly out of the bedroom into the living room, not sure what to expect. I saw my mama on the floor, feeling around for something. I asked her what was wrong; she said nothing and continued crying. She told me to help her find her glasses. I helped search and found them under the couch. I was still curious about what had happened.

On my first day of school at Keating Elementary I didn't want to go. I was a cry-baby and had never been away from my family. We hadn't even left the house yet when I started crying, throwing a temper tantrum. I performed the same way when we left the house, as we walked down the street, and even when we reached the classroom.
As I was standing in the doorway kicking and screaming, a man walked over to me and introduced himself. He was my kindergarten teacher, Mr. Gus. He tried to calm me down, but I only got worse when my mother left me. I cried so long that I was making myself sick. My nose was runny and my eyes got puffy. I was coughing, gagging, and about to make myself throw up. Nothing Mr. Gus did to help worked.
I was happy when school was over and Mama came to pick me up. But the same thing happened the next day and the next and the next. My clothes would end up dirty because I would roll all over the floor. Other teachers tried calming me down with no success. Finally, Mr. Gus picked me up and sat me in a chair next to his desk. He told me that if I stopped crying, I could be his little helper. I stopped crying and started sniffing. He said my job was doing little things like cleaning the chalkboard, collecting paper from the students and running errands. He named everything for me to do, trying anything to keep me quiet. I began to feel like I was the teacher's favorite.

I liked the attention, but I was very sensitive and would cry easily. However, the more I went to school the less I cried.

One day after school, my mother told me to change my clothes and put on the clothes she laid out for me. I was always asking questions and I asked her why? She told me to just hurry up and put the dress on then she fixed my hair. Someone knocked on the door. A man I hadn't seen before came in the house. I was wondering what was going on as he and my mother stood there talking. He placed our coffee table in the middle of the room and sat us on it then he took our picture. He talked with my mother and he left, only to return a few days later with our first and only professional family portrait.

In class one day, Mr. Gus had us sit on the floor facing the chalkboard. He asked if any of us knew how to play any of the instruments he had displayed. I raised my hand and said I knew how to play the drums, knowing I never played anything before. He asked me to come up and show the class. I sat in front of the drums, grabbed the sticks, and started beating them. The kids started laughing.

Mr. Gus yelled, "Stop, Stop, Stop!"

He took the sticks from me, told me to take my seat, and said that I did well. I knew I did badly. He was just being kind trying to make me feel good, because the sound I was making beating those drums was horrible. I was so embarrassed and from that day on, I never raised my hand to say I knew how to play anything when I knew I didn't. Mr. Gus let the other kids try. I can't remember how they did; I just remembered how badly I did.

I was getting used to school, and I found myself clinging to Mr. Gus just like I did with my mother. The only other memory I have of kindergarten was of another teacher. I forgot her name, but I remember the perfume she wore. You could smell her before she reached you and after she left, it smelled so good. To this day I'm still trying to find that perfume.

It was winter and the snow was very deep and I loved

being outdoors. On this particular day there was no school. I wanted to go outside and play in the snow. My parents had company, which was all the time.

I asked, "Can I go outside and play in the snow?"

My sister asked if she could go with me. Mama got us dressed in our snowsuits. When we stepped outside, it was like a ghost town and the snow was real deep. I looked around to see what we could do, which wasn't much because we were the only ones outside. Unsupervised and with no one else to play with, I decided we should go to the playground. All we could do was swing. After being out there for a while, we started to get cold.

"Are you cold too? I asked Amy.

She answered yes and I told her we should go in the house. When we jumped off the swings, all I remember is being underwater. We had fallen through the ice. Somehow we came back to the surface and there was no time to panic. All kinds of thoughts were scrambling though my head about how we were going to get out. I knew we didn't know how to swim. I started kicking my legs, and my sister was kicking hers too. We were trying to keep from going back under. I kept kicking and trying to grab hold of the ice to pull myself out, but it was hard because my snowsuit was weighing me down. I fought hard and got out, then reached for Amy's hand.

"Grab my hand," I yelled at her, and she did. I pulled her out. I was shaking not just because I was cold but because I was scared about what had just happened and thinking we could have drowned. And we probably would have if I had panicked, but with God's help, we survived.

As I look back, I'm amazed at how calm I was at only six years old. We started walking home, and you should have seen us. It's funny now because we were walking like zombies. We were soaked from head to toe. We approached the house and knocked on the door; Daddy opened it.

"What happened to you?" he asked in a panicked voice.

"We fell through the ice," I said, my teeth chattering.

"Essie!" he yelled for my mama. She came running,

asking what happened when she saw us.

Daddy replied, "They fell through the ice."

We stood there shivering. Mama took us to the bathroom. She helped us take off all our clothes, and she ran water in the tub to warm us up, which turned out not to be a good idea. When we got in our bodies started stinging; the pain was very uncomfortable, and it didn't help that we were still cold. The more hot water was added, the more our bodies stung. We called our mother, asked her if we could get out; she wrapped us in a towel and took us to our room. Mama gave us our pajamas to put on and told us to get in the bed.

Daddy made hot chocolate for us and we sat up to drink it. When we were finished, we got under the covers, which really did no good. We were still cold, and shivering. I yelled for Mama and told her that we were still cold. She gave us an extra cover, and we fell asleep.

My parents would have company at our house a lot; if not at our house, they would be next door at our godmother, Claudine's. We would have to go to our room or next door to our godmother's house to stay with our god-sister, Cheryl and her brothers. Whenever we would go to my godmother's home, she would be sitting at the table playing cards and listening to music: Al Green or James Brown. I heard them so much that I hated their songs.

Occasionally she would play soul music by other artists but those two men were what we heard the most.

The parties stopped at our house when I got sick. I was taken to the hospital and was diagnosed and treated for Hepatitis. I got it because I touched the toilet while using it and didn't wash my hands afterward. I was never taught to wash my hands after each use.

There were so many people using the bathroom. That's when Daddy stopped the partying at our house. But then my mother started spending more time at my godmother's house, especially when Daddy was at work, and she started neglecting all of us. The commotion that I heard previously started happening again.

Once again, we would get locked in our bedroom. We could hear crying, yelling, screaming, and bumping; and when it was over, the door would open. I never saw what was happening, but it started happening more frequently. I was a "nosy" little girl. After we were let out of the room, I would look around just to see if I could figure out what had happened.

As I was coping with the continuing commotion at home, I had to deal with bad news from Mr. Gus. One day while sitting in class, he informed us that we would be moving on to the next grade; that he would no longer be our teacher when we returned from our summer vacation, and that we would have a new teacher. I couldn't accept the news emotionally; as he tried to explain the change, I started crying. I felt that someone I cared about was leaving me. I started saying that I wanted to stay with him. I had gotten attached to him.

As school ended for the summer he gave us a lot of educational supplies to take home for the summer. He gave each of us a hug and I started crying and I didn't want to let go of him.

School ended, and summer vacation began. Nothing exciting really happened until almost the end of the summer.

I was outside playing Cowboys and Indians with one of my god-brothers He was on one side of the porch, and I was on the other. We were using rocks and bottles as our weapons, throwing them back and forth at each other; we had been playing for a while.

For some reason I became distracted from the game and stopped paying attention and forgot to duck after I threw my rock. When he threw back, I was hit in the face with his pop bottle weapon. At first, I didn't have any reaction until I saw blood coming from my face; that's when I started screaming and crying. Everybody came running outside to see what happened. After I moved my hand from my face they saw the blood and they panicked.

As I was screaming, I could hear them repeatedly asking, "What happened, what happened?" I was crying and screaming so loudly and hysterically I couldn't tell them. My mother became hysterical. She wasn't listening to my god-brother as he tried to explain what happened. As I continued screaming, I could still hear him trying to explain. I took a quick glance at him and saw his face; he had this scared look on his face. Mama was making it seem like he did it on purpose. We were just playing and having fun. After all, we were just six years old.

My mother ran back into the house to get a rag for my face. With all the commotion continuing, my godmother yelled, "Get her in the car!" and she drove us to the hospital.
My mother held the rag to my face and she and my godmother were telling me to calm down. I was crying and screaming like I was dying. But to tell you the truth, with all the crying I was doing, I don't even remember the pain. I knew I was a big crybaby and liked the attention. As we arrived at the hospital, we entered the emergency entrance.

Questions were being asked as we were taken to an examination room to wait for the doctor. The room was silent as we waited. I had calmed down from the screaming but tears were rolling down my face. When the doctor entered the room, he examined me and said that I had to have stitches. I asked him what stitches were. Not sure if he answered, but I already had it in my mind that it was going to hurt. A nurse came in to set up and when I saw the equipment the doctor was going to use, I started crying hysterically, kicking, screaming, fighting, and trying to get loose. It took eight people to hold me down and I ended up kicking one of the nurses.

When I saw myself in the mirror, I started crying even more. I said, "Oh no! I look like a cat." I had whiskers on one side of my face. I looked horrible and I was so embarrassed. I covered my face as we left the hospital. There was silence on the way home.

When we arrived home, Mama still had an attitude. She refused to talk to my godmother about the incident. As we were walking up the stairs, she told us that we couldn't go over to my godmother's house again. She continued to blame my god-brother for what was an accident; it was no one's fault. I just forgot to duck. We had no idea about the danger of playing with rocks and pop bottles. The object of the game was not to get hit. When Daddy came home, I wasn't sure what his reaction was, but I knew he was a calm, peaceful person and would not over-react.

With no one to play with, Amy and I were sitting on the porch, feeling lonely watching everyone else play, and we just had each other to play with. I was sad and looking pitiful when I saw my god family going in and out their house, sneaking a wave "hi", wishing we were over there. As we sat there watching the kids playing, our front door closed. I jumped up and ran to open it and it was locked. I knew something was about to happen.

I started banging on the door shouting, "Let me in! Let me in!" Amy started banging with me. I could hear the commotion. My godmother came rushing out of her house when she heard us screaming. She nervously yelled for her kids to get us. My god-sister and one of my god-brothers grabbed us from the door and took us into their house. We were screaming and hollering. After being in my godmother's house for a while, we calmed down. We stayed until everything calmed down at home.

Our summer vacation was over, school was starting, and I didn't want to go. On the first day, just like in kindergarten, as my mother pulled me toward the school I performed exactly the same way, crying screaming and throwing a temper tantrum. I was embarrassed because I looked like a cat. I still had stitches in my face. I was afraid the kids would tease me, plus I didn't want to be away from my family. And I knew Mr. Gus wasn't going to be my teacher. When I approached my new classroom, I was still throwing a tantrum, especially after my mother left me. I tried hiding my face.

This time, my teacher was a lady, whose name I can't remember. She knew of me from Mr. Gus' class. She was nice, but I still didn't want to be in her class and would try and leave school numerous times, with no success. After talking with Mr. Gus, she made me her helper to calm me down. I do not remember much of my first grade experience other than when I ran errands and was able to go to Mr. Gus' class. When I would see him there or in the hallway, I would run and give him a hug.

We were very obedient kids, never getting into trouble until one day when Amy and I became a little curious. We were home alone. My parents were next door at my godmother's house. My sister and I saw a pack of cigarettes lying on the table. I can't remember whose idea it was to smoke, but we both decided to try acting grown-up. We went in the bathroom. I let my sister do the dirty work and made her take one of the cigarettes so we could share, thinking our parents wouldn't notice any missing. She lit it and took a puff; she did it like a pro. When it was my turn, as soon as I took a puff, I started coughing, choking, and gagging. I didn't know why, so I took another puff and the same thing happened, so I said I had enough. I stopped.

My sister continued until we heard somebody coming in the house. We panicked and started scrambling around the bathroom, trying to figure out where we were going to put out the cigarette. We didn't think to throw it in the toilet, so Amy threw it in the trash can. We were fanning trying to get rid of the smoke smell. We thought we had some of the smell out, but we didn't really do a good job. Then smoke started coming from the trash can where my sister had thrown the cigarette. It was not on fire, just smoldering.

I heard my father say he smelled smoke. "Uh oh. We're in trouble now," I said.

He had to pass the bathroom before he got to our room. He opened the bathroom door, and we were standing there, scared. We knew we were in trouble. He asked us what happened. I started crying, stuttering as I told him the truth about us trying to smoke. We were told to go to our room and wait for him to come in, and that's what we did. We sat on the bottom bunk bed. Daddy didn't come in the room right away. We sat waiting and waiting and waiting. Nervousness came over me because I didn't know why he hadn't come in the room yet. All of a sudden, he appeared at the door. He entered the room with a mean look on his face. My heart started beating fast, believing that whatever was about to happen was going to be bad.

As he stood there quietly, my heart began to beat even faster, I looked at Amy, and she looked at me. We didn't know what to expect. We sat there with our heads held down in shame and waiting for him to do or say something. As he continued to look at us he finally asked us why we did it. We had no reason so we didn't answer. I'm very sensitive and cry easily, so I started crying.

"Stop crying," Daddy said. "You weren't crying when you were smoking."

I couldn't stop crying; I didn't know what was about to happen to us. I was wondering if he was going to do to us what he was doing to my mother. Even though I never saw what he did to her, I just heard what was going on and it did not sound good. I don't know what Mama did to cause Daddy cause him to do whatever he does to her, but every time it happened I would hear her cry. I just hoped we hadn't done the same thing so that it wouldn't happen to us.

He sat down and started talking to us, telling us what we did was dangerous and something bad could have happened to us, or the house could have caught on fire. He went on and on and on. The anticipation was getting to me; I would rather he do what he was going to do to and get it over with. Instead he was prolonging it.

"Since you want to be grown-ups, I'm going to show you how to be grown-ups," he said. And he took the same pack of cigarettes, shook it around and said he was going to make us smoke the whole pack. He handed each one of us a cigarette and made us light it. I pretended that I couldn't light mine. He said for me not to act like I'm having trouble lighting it since I hadn't had trouble lighting it before.

Amy lit hers and started puffing. I was trying to be slick and take my time, but he caught on to what I was trying to do and told me to light it. I knew when I took a puff, I was going to start choking, and that's what happened.

He said, "Oh, don't start choking now." I started crying.

"What you crying for? You wanted to be grown-up," he said.

When I took another puff, I started coughing and choking again. Mama tried to rescue me.

"Sam, stop!" she said. "You know she has bronchitis."

He was angry, but he felt sorry for me and told me to stop but had my sister continue. On top of that, Daddy made her drink whiskey too until she got sick.

"That'll make you think twice before you try to act grown again. Now go back to your room to wait for your whipping" he said.

Daddy wasn't playing. On top of making us smoke and drink, he was about to whip us, and we didn't even know what whipping meant.

When he came in the room, we were sitting there nervously. He told us to hold out our hands. And to my surprise from not knowing what to expect, our whipping consisted of a couple of hits and another talking to. I made it seem like I was really hurting because this was our first whipping. After he finished, he went out of the room.

You could tell Daddy was hurt because he'd never hit us before. I was seven and Amy was five. I loved my daddy; it hurt me to see how hurt he was. We had never done anything bad before, and he'd never had to hit us before. What he did to us made me wonder if that's what he was doing to my mother, just worse.

Sometime had passed since we were locked in our room listening to the commotion between Mama and Daddy. But the next time it happened, we didn't show any emotion because I knew what was happening even though I didn't see it. When the commotion stopped, Daddy unlocked our door. I could see my mother trying to clean herself up so that we wouldn't know what had happened, but I knew. I was very observant and I asked lots of questions. Because of our whipping it made me put everything together and I realized that's what he was doing to Mama, but maybe a little different.

While my mother was in the living room, Daddy was in the bathroom, shaving. I stood at the bathroom door working up the nerve to say what I had to say.

Nervous as I was, I blurted out, "Daddy, can I ask you a question?"

"Yes," he said. "Do you love us?"

"Yes."

"Do you love my mother?"

"Yes."

"Could you please stop hitting my mother?"

He stopped shaving, and looked at me with a look of shock upon his face, maybe because I knew what was happening. He pushed me back, and closed the door in my face.

When he came out he never gave me an answer. But there was no more being locked out of the house or in our room, so I thought everything was going good until this one day my sister and I were playing outside with my brother. Daddy came home from work.

We said, "Hi, Daddy."

He replied as he went into the house. He wasn't in the house that long when he came back outside, which was unusual. What was more unusual was he had a bag with him. He told us to come and sit down next to him. We sat on the porch and the look on his face made me know something was wrong. He said that he wanted to talk to us.

"I won't be living with you any longer," was all he said.

My sister and I started crying but my brother didn't understand. Daddy didn't give us a reason why he was leaving.

Hearing this devastated me and I start crying hysterically, pleading, and begging him not to leave us.

I said, "Daddy, don't leave us!" I assumed it was my fault that he was leaving us because I knew what he was doing to my mother.

"I won't be bad anymore!" I told him. I pleaded with him thinking of anything to say. "Daddy, please don't go, don't leave us! Daddy, please don't go, don't leave us!"

But nothing I said convinced him to stay.

"I'm sorry, but I have to leave," Daddy said. Then he leaned over, gave each of us a kiss. He told us he loved us and that he would see us soon.

My mother was standing at the door saying nothing. I felt like she wanted him to leave. He turned to walk down the steps; I grabbed his legs and tried one last pleading, but I failed. I let his leg go and sat down on the porch, crying and watching my daddy walk down the street out of sight and out of our lives. I sat and blamed myself. I knew it was my fault. I loved my daddy so much that it was hard for me to handle his leaving. I was hurting so badly inside. I sat on the porch and stared down the street, hoping that this was all a dream, in which he would soon be coming home from work and I would wake up and he would still be living with us. This was devastating to me. Somebody else I loved and cared about left me, like Mr. Gus had. Daddy thought he was keeping us from being exposed to violence by hiding what he was doing to Mama and leaving.

Chapter Two

A Living Nightmare

Soon after Daddy left us, our lives changed. Mama stopped being a mother and started leaving us home alone. Most of her time was spent at my godmother's house. Sometimes she'd take us with her and we would have to spend the night because they were partying all through the night. When Mama wasn't at my godmother's house she was spending time with two of her new male friends, JB and Ronald, whom she met through my godmother.

Mama started making us do housework, things she used to do when Daddy was home. We had to do chores like cleaning the house, washing the dishes, making our beds, and looking after each other more often. She still did the cooking and washed our clothes, though.

My daddy had kind of shielded us from any direct violence, other than the time he had to whip us, but I know he did that for our own good. Now Mama began to whip us, with me getting the worst of it if I didn't do something right. I would get a whipping if I talked back to defend our actions when I knew we did nothing wrong. I believe she made up reasons to beat us. We were not disobedient kids. We didn't fight each other. I was close to my mother and always wanted to be under her. I couldn't understand why I was being treated so badly. Living with Mama became a living nightmare. I felt like we were slaves.

My godmother noticed the change in how I was being treated and would rescue me at times, finding ways to get me out of the house. She would take me places or have me stay at her house so I could spend less time at home.

Daddy didn't stay away forever. When he would come visit us, we would be so excited to see him. It was like a routine: he would never go inside the house; we would sit on the porch. He would play and talk to us, sometimes even taking us to the store just to spend quality time with us. Out of fear, neither my sister nor

I told him what was happening to us. Before it would get late, he would say he had to go, but we would try to convince him to stay longer. It would work for a little while, then he would say that he had to leave because it was getting too late. He said he had to go get ready for work. Before he would leave, he would give me money to give to my mother for our needs. He would give us a kiss, shake my brother's hand, and walk down the street to catch the bus. Once he was out of my sight, sadness would fill my heart because of how badly I missed him. Deep down in my soul, I knew it was my fault that Daddy left us.

    JB always seemed to be at our house more than Ronald, who was just there occasionally. To me it seemed like JB had moved in. He started trying to play the daddy role, as if he was substituting for my daddy. I remember once JB took us over this lady's house. I believe he said she was his sister. She was nice; she treated us like we were part of the family. But I was ready to go home because it had gotten late. We had been over there all day, and I was sleepy when we finally left. I couldn't wait to get home and get in my bed. That was just the start of him trying to portray the daddy role.

    We didn't care too much for JB, but we never disrespected him or anybody else. I felt he crossed the line when he started telling us what to do, but we did whatever we were told.
    Now, Ronald… we loved him. He really was like a second father to us. He was only around after Mama got into an argument with JB; and when she argued with him, he would leave, and we wouldn't see him for a long time.

    We moved! It was one block over, directly across the street from the school. So, instead of walking down the street to school, I walked right out our front door into the school door. Why we had to move I don't know. Of course, JB was right with us. When Daddy came to visit, Mama would have us tell her when we saw him coming so she could make JB hide.
    Before Daddy would leave, he would give Mama money

to take care of us. And before his next visit, Mama would have me call Daddy to tell him she needed more money for food.

Daddy would ask, "Why? I just gave her money. There should be plenty of food."

I said, "I don't know, but we don't have any food." He would bring more money and sit on the porch with us for a short visit.

Mama seemed to be running out of money fast, and she had me call Daddy again, asking for more money, and I did. And he would come. Once after he gave Mama the money, he sat on the porch with us, talking when he mentioned JB. I looked at him stunned, because I didn't know he knew about JB, but I felt relieved that he did. I whispered to Daddy so Mama wouldn't hear me, out of fear of getting a whipping.

"Daddy, JB is here all the time and we don't have a lot of food anymore." I continued, "I don't know what Mama is doing with the money you give her."

He said, "OK," but continued to give her money to support us. My mother rarely came out the house, never spending any time with us—only with JB—not checking on us when we were outside. We would see her when it was time for us to eat or when it was time to come in for the night. I felt she didn't care about what we were doing. I wasn't disobedient; I didn't take it upon myself to do

anything that I assumed I would get into trouble for. I always got permission if I wanted something or if I wanted to go over my godmother's house. She allowed me to walk by myself. My mother's friends had little girls and they lived near my godmother. I sometimes would stop and play with them until they moved.

Next door to our house was a four-family flat where white families lived. I befriended three of the boys; two were brothers, and one was just a friend. I forgot the brothers' names, but the other boy, I didn't forget his name—it was Tommy Bright. I remember his name because he was handsome. I had fun playing with them. We didn't have outdoor toys to play with, so they showed us how to play games. We would play games out of anything like Red Light/

Green Light, Frozen Tag using the tree as a safety point; Kick the Can, Jump-Rope, Jacks, and Dodge Ball.

There was this one game we played—I forgot the name, but we would sit on the stairs, then one person would stand in front. He or she had a small object in his or her hand, and would put it behind his or her back, scramble the object, then put it in front to see if one of us could guess which hand the object was in. If the answer was right you would scoot up a step, and when you reached the top you were the winner. Then the winner would stand to do the game. We had so much fun, we didn't need toys. And to tell you the truth, I don't remember having any toys. I loved being outside. Sometimes I would be outside alone or with my sister or waiting on my friends to come out.

Mr. Pauley was the father of the brothers. Sometimes when I was outside alone, I would see him in the backyard, and I would go stand at the fence, and talk to him. I'd ask lots of questions that he would answer. Then he would go back in the house, and I was outside alone again, waiting.

Once while sitting on the porch, waiting for someone to come outside and play, Mr. Pauley came outside and asked me if I wanted a puppy. I got excited and ran inside my house and asked Mama if I could have a puppy. She said she didn't care, but I had to take care of it. I ran back outside, full of excitement, and told Mr. Pauley I could have the puppy. He gave me a little black puppy. I named him Snoopy. After just receiving Snoopy, I was waiting on my friends to come outside to play with me, and I started running up and down the street with Snoopy on a chain.

When I started running back the other way, Snoopy ran around me, the chain wrapping around my legs. I started to fall. When I hit the ground, I slid, you know, just like the baseball players do when they slide in to a base. It took me a second to try and figure out what happened. I rolled over and started screaming; my legs were still tangled in the chain, and Snoopy was trying to free himself. The chain was wrapped around his neck. Mr. Pauley heard me and ran outside to help me. My mother didn't come out at all to see why I was screaming.

Mr. Pauley freed me from the chain, and looked at me. He hurried up and got me to my house. He explained to my mother what had happened. My face was hurting as the tears were rolling down; it was burning. I went to the bathroom and looked into the mirror and saw that all the skin on one side of my face was gone.. I wasn't taken to the hospital to seek any medical attention. Mama just treated me herself. As I started to heal, she sent me to the store to get cocoa butter to put on it.

It seemed like something was always happening to me. I was only seven, and that was the fourth incident that happened to me and was only taken to seek medical treatment once. By the time school started, I was healed, but my skin was a little two-toned.

Soon, Mr. Pauley and his family moved, and the other white family moved, too, including Tommy Bright. And once again my sister and I just had each other to play with.

When I began the second grade, Amy started kindergarten. I was shocked to hear how good she handled going to school and being away from home. I should have been ashamed of myself at how good my sister handled being in school; she did better than me. My crying faded, and I stopped having temper tantrums. What was the use? I was going to be made to stay in school if I cried or not. I only cried when I couldn't get my way or if someone yelled at me. I'm very sensitive and cried at anything.

I don't remember much about my second grade experience. Nothing traumatic happened to me, so I have nothing to say about it other than I got to take a school picture in an outfit that Daddy brought me, and you could barely notice that my face was two-toned. I did have to start wearing glasses because of the yellow jaundice I had at birth. The hospital didn't have the technology or equipment at that time to treat that kind of medical condition, and from that, my eyes were affected.

School wasn't my problem, but what was happening at home was. Mama began to beat us and swear at us more, calling us all kinds of bad names. The beatings were getting worse. My sister and I would get beatings with an electric cord with our clothes on or off. One time it happened while we were in the tub, I believe because we were laughing too loud, disturbing her phone call. Why else would she beat us while we were in the tub? The worst part was we didn't know why she was beating us so often. I was still getting the worst of the beatings and I questioned why. Like I said, we weren't bad kids, and we didn't fight with each other, so why were we getting beat?

We kept it a secret out of fear from what Daddy might do to her if we told him what she was doing to us.

School was out for summer vacation, but I didn't get to enjoy much of it. I was stricken with measles. I had to stay in the house, couldn't go outside to play. I was miserable and all alone. I had to lie on the couch and watch television. We only had one television, and we had to watch whatever Mama was watching, and most of what she watched, I didn't like. But I did love to watch the four o'clock movies. I used to run home from school, especially when it was Elvis or Godzilla or the muscle bikini weeks. Most of the time, I was just mad because I wanted to go outside and play with the other kids.

My sister was outside playing by herself. She was supposed to stay in front of the house. My mother went to the door and called her, but she didn't answer. Remind you, I was sick and wasn't supposed to be outside or in the sunlight. What Mama made me do was wrong. She wouldn't let me go outside and play, but she did

make me get up, put on my sweater and sunglasses and told me to look for my sister. I was mad, but I did what I was told.

It seemed like I hadn't been out in so long that as soon as I stepped out the door, the sunlight made my eyes hurt, even with the sunglasses on. As I was walking down the street, I yelled my sister's name, without any response. I had no idea where she might be or where to look. I went to my godmother's house; they hadn't seen her. Then I thought about my mother's friends who had the little girls we played with, not really sure she would be there because they moved a few blocks over. I didn't think she would walk off the block; she was just five, but I took a chance anyway. When I got to their house, to my surprise, she was there.

"Mama's looking for you," I said. "Why did you leave from in front of the house?"

"I wanted to play with someone, so I walked around to their house," she said.

"Well, you gotta come home." And we left.

I wasn't sure if she was going to be in trouble and when we got in the house, she wasn't in trouble. And after making me go look for my sister, I still wasn't allowed to go outside and play. I was furious. I didn't understand why Mama let me go out to look for Amy, but she wouldn't let me go out and play. Why didn't she go look for her herself?

One night we were lying on the floor, watching TV, when there was a knock on the door. I yelled to Mama saying someone was at the door. She told me to answer it. When I opened it, there was a lady and her son standing there. I'd never seen them before or should I say I didn't recognize them. I asked her who she was looking for, and she asked for my Mama by name.

"Is Essie here?" she asked.

I called for my Mama to come to the door. Mama asked me who it was, and I said I don't know.

"She asks for you. She said she is a cousin from Ohio."

Mama finally came to the door and let them in. After she settled in, I learned it was my cousin Lena, and the two of them sat on the couch to talk. My cousin said she came to Detroit to escape her abusive husband. She told Mama how bad he was beating her. I overheard her say how he made her lose three sets of twins before and after, the son that was with her, was born.

My mama knew how abusive Lena's husband was. She even shared a story about how he was when she was in Ohio. She said that she and Lena had gone out hanging, and he came looking for her and found them and started yelling at her, and they ran. He started shooting at them as they ran. She said he didn't care that she had brothers since they stayed out of it because she always went back to him.

Lena said she was tired of the abuse and she packed up what she had and headed to Detroit to start a new life. She had to stay with us. Mama introduced her to my godmother. She started hanging at her house, partying with them, leaving her son for Mama to watch. She would come in the house late or sometimes not at all. I saw her with different men when she would take me with her, even talking to a relative of my godmother.

We were getting a new neighbor, and we were excited when we saw that there were kids our age we could play with. This was a big family. One little girl's name was Angie. They weren't on the block long when Lena made friends with them. She made friends with anybody that partied, and often included me in visits to their house. My sister and I became friends with one of the girls around our age. She and one of her brothers would come to our house to play. The brother liked me, saying he wanted me to be his girlfriend. I told him I didn't like boys like that. I told him I especially didn't like him. He tried to persuade me to like him every time he saw me, saying I was going to be his girlfriend.

One day, Angie came to the house to play with us, and we were on the stairs, playing. Angie became angry, and for no apparent reason, she snatched my earring out my ear. My ear started bleeding a little, and before I got a chance to react, my sister grabbed Angie and started punching her. She had that girl's head down on a step, just stomping her head. I was shocked that my sister reacted that way. We never had been in a violent situation before.

Angie got up after Amy let her go and ran home, and then we saw the whole family coming toward us. When they got to our house, her Mama didn't ask what happened, but just started cussing at us, causing a big scene, and was ready to fight. My Mama came out and was arguing with them. While my mother was arguing with them, my cousin, Lena was trying to get everyone to calm down. I ran to my godmother's house and told my god-sister and god-brothers what was happening. One of my god-brothers said, "Let's go," and we started running back to the house.

We made it as far as the school playground when we saw everyone, in the street, arguing. As we approached, fists started flying, arms were swinging everywhere, hair was being pulled;

someone got hit with a two-by-four. One of my god-brothers tried to bite off one of Angie's sister's fingers off. Angie's sister tried to bite skin off his forehead, leaving blood running down his face. By the time it all ended, we looked like we had been in a war. People were cut and bleeding, with bruises everywhere and everyone was crying. When we all went home, our friendship with them ended. But my cousin Lena continued being friends with them, hanging at their house.

Mama started getting angry at Lena because she was leaving her son with her so often and staying out all night. Mama told her that she had to start staying home with him to stop her from hanging out so much. That worked temporarily. While she was home, Lena had to help take care of us, cooking, and helping around the house.

My brother and Lena's son were close in age. Those two together were always being mischievous, but weren't punished for the bad things they did. There was a near fatal incident when we were at the Laundromat with my mother and Lena. My sister and I had to help them while my brother and cousin ran around, playing. All of a sudden the boys got quiet; the overhead light started flickering then went dim. We stopped what we were doing to go see why; when we got to the front of the Laundromat, my brother and cousin were bending down, shaking. Lena ran and knocked them over. They had stuck a hairpin in the electrical socket and were being electrocuted. Their fingers turned black. And they did not get punished, even though it was a dangerous situation and they could have died..

Closed Box...

We were in bed, supposedly going to sleep. I got up to go use the bathroom, making a detour, when I heard Mama and Lena talking. I peeked into the front room and saw Lena give Mama a handful of pills. I didn't know why or what they were for, but I knew my mother wasn't sick. I saw her take some, and then I went back to bed.

The next morning, I saw her take some more. She would

drink something hot when she took them. I noticed that after she took those pills, she would nod her head down like she was asleep wherever she was sitting. I would go over to her and try to wake her up to make sure she was OK. I didn't know what was going on. She would tell me to move, leave her alone, and she would go right back to sleep. This happened every day. When she talked, we couldn't understand what she was saying. I didn't like to see her that way and her behavior started affecting me. I know my sister had to feel the same way even though we were too young to understand what was going on.

    Mama and Lena started going to the doctor and leaving us home with JB. Sometimes they were gone all day and would come home and take their pills and nod off to sleep. They were going to the doctor more often, but it didn't seem like anything was wrong with them.

    When they left, JB knew they would be out for a long time. He would tell my sister, brother, and little cousin to sit down and watch TV and not move. He made me go to my mother's room with him. He would close the door behind us and tell me to lie on the bed; then he would walk over to the bed and take off my shorts. Then he would pull down his pants and fondle himself as he was performing oral sex on me. He then would start rubbing his penis against my vagina until he ejaculated, leaving his semen. He never penetrated me. When he was done, he told me not to tell anybody about what he did. It was our little secret. That's when I became a closed box, not letting any of these secret things out.

    He did this every time Mama and Lena would go to the doctor; knowing they would be gone for a while. What he was doing to me… I thought it was normal; that I was supposed to let him. And it didn't hurt. To be honest, it felt good. I didn't know that what he was doing to me was wrong. We were never taught to tell an adult if someone touched us inappropriately. He had me thinking that it was OK and that I was supposed to let him do that to me, and at times, I kept hoping my mother had somewhere to go just for me to be with him. I felt special, loved. I felt like someone finally cared about me and because he was giving me the attention that I was looking for, I felt like I was his other girlfriend even though I was just seven years old.

My mother and Lena took us to Ohio to visit my grandmother and other family members while we were out of school for summer vacation. We traveled by Greyhound bus. The bus ride was long. I was restless, and the restroom was appealing to me after I went to use it when we first got on. It kind of reminded me of the silver tub Daddy had brought us. The sound fascinated me. I liked how the bathroom sounded while traveling on the road. There was something about the look of the stainless steel toilet and sink. It was fun to me. I made up excuses to go to the bathroom, but once when I got up to go to the bathroom again, Mama stopped me and made me sit back down.

We arrived in Ohio and went on to my grandmother's house. I was excited to see my grandmother. I didn't know what she looked like because we left when I was two. However, I was still excited. She was excited to see us and so were other family members. Everyone was hugging and kissing, saying how happy they were to see one another. I had gotten the most attention; my little cousin did too from his grandparents and uncles. They remembered him and me more than they did my sister, who was only a couple of months when we left. This was the first time everyone was seeing my brother. Spending all that time with the family, it seemed like time went by fast.

It was dark, and we had to take a bath and go to bed. I tried to convince my grandmother to let us stay up a little while longer, but it didn't work. She sent us to her room; we had to sleep in her bed. There was something about being in her bed and in her room, the way it smelled... it's hard to describe. But I liked being in there, and it was comfortable. She said to close the door behind us. We didn't go straight to sleep: we were lying there, talking to each other.

When the door opened, we thought they'd heard us talking and we were about to get a whipping; we closed our eyes fast, pretended we were sleep. As I peeked out one eye, I saw that it was my Uncle Lee, my auntie's husband. He came into the room and closed the door behind him. We all sat up; he asked us if we wanted him to tuck us in and read us a bedtime story. With excitement, we said yes because no one ever tucked us in or read to us. He sat on the bed beside me, his arm across me between my sister and me.

"Where's Lee?" I heard my grandmother ask from the other room. Her bedroom door opened, and she saw him sitting on the bed with us. "What you doing in my room with these kids?" she asked him.

"I was just about to tuck them in and read 'em a bedtime story," he said to her.

"You get outta my room," she said to him.

We pleaded with Granny to let us hear a bedtime story. But her answer was, "No, go to sleep."

My Granny stood there to make sure he left the room, and then she closed the door behind them. We didn't know why she didn't want him in the room with us. I know she was mad because he was.

The next morning we got up, ate, and got dressed when my Uncle Bill, my mother's brother, came back over to the house to see us. He asked my mother if he could take me with him. The other kids wanted to go; he said not this time and gave them some money. I was acting all bigheaded because I was getting all the attention. I kind of teased my siblings because they couldn't go. After we left, we arrived at our destination; the sign read Bar and Grill. My uncle took me, a seven-year-old, to a bar. Inside, he introduced me to his friends.

We went and sat at the bar. He ordered a hamburger for me. He didn't order himself anything; he sat and watched me eat, and we talked. After we were done, we talked for a little while longer; then we headed outside. There was a park with swings next to the parking lot. As we were walking towards the swings, I grabbed my uncle's hand, you know, like most little kids do. I was excited, skipping across the lot. I hopped on the swing; my uncle sat on the one next to me. Then I asked him to push me; I told him to push me higher and higher. I went so high that I got scared and told him to stop. That's when I knew I was scared of heights. I jumped off the swing, stood there for a minute, and then we walked toward the bench. He sat next to, me and we continued talking.

He put his arm around my waist, and then the next thing I know, he put his hand inside my shorts, touching my vagina. An eerie feeling came over me. I scooted away from him. I felt uncomfortable, nasty, and creepy. I felt that was wrong, what my uncle did to me. I was confused. Why did I think what my uncle did to me was wrong, but I didn't feel it was wrong for JB? I didn't get that eerie feeling when he did what he was doing to me, didn't feel uncomfortable being around him. I asked my uncle to take me back to my mother. My disposition changed toward him. I didn't tell anybody what happened, and I made sure that I wasn't alone with him again.

The next evening, Mama and Lena went out, leaving us with Grandma. I was excited because we were spending time with her. We didn't do much with her because she was old. We sat and talked with her, she showed us pictures.

When it was time for dinner I thought, this is Grandma. She know how to cook. I just knew Granny was going to make sure we ate some good food. Man, was I wrong. She gave us beans. I asked her what kind of beans they were and she said kidney. We never had them before but I kind of liked them. Mama and Lena had not arrived home, yet. The next morning they still weren't back. My Grandma fixed us beans again, for breakfast, then again for lunch. After we ate, we had nothing to do.

"Grandma, can we go outside?" I asked.

She told me yes, telling us to stay in the backyard. We weren't outside that long when my brother started acting bad, and at first I warned him to stop; when he didn't, I ran and told Granny. She came outside to see what he was doing, and then she hit him a few times and made him come into the house. We started laughing at him because this was the first time he had been punished. He just laughed when she hit him. She let us stay outside, and we continued playing when a lady that lived in the house behind my Granny's came out. She spoke to us and introduced herself. She said she was our aunt, my mother's sister. We said, "Hi," then she went back into her house, and we continued playing. We later learned that she has a mental illness and that's why she was acting strangely.

We really didn't have anything to do. There were no toys to play with so we started swinging on the clothesline. I started hearing this squeaky sound, but I didn't see where it was coming from, nor did I saw anything. We continued playing when I heard it again, and all of a sudden, the basement door came open. No one came out; we looked at each other and started running. We ran so fast and were laughing, and screaming, out of fear.

Granny stood at the top of the stairs and asked us what was wrong, and we told her that the basement door came open by itself and asked her to come and look. As she was walking down the stairs out the door into the backyard, we were right behind her, scared. She walked toward the basement.

I yelled, "Granny, don't go down there." She went anyway and said no one was down there. I said, "Are you sure?" She said yes and closed the door back and went back into the house. We didn't go back in the back yard again. I couldn't understand why that door, made of brick, came open by itself.

Dinnertime came, again. Guess what we were having? Beans! We had beans for breakfast, lunch and dinner. After we eaten, we sat and watched TV. Then it was time for bed and still no Mama and Lena. Our meal menu continued the next day. After dinner I decided to look through Granny's cabinet, looking at what food she had. I picked up one of the cans that I thought was cranberry sauce. Wanting something different after being saturated with kidney beans, I asked Granny if we could have some. She said yes and gave us some. I was excited because we were about to eat something different. I took a bite and spit it right back out. It was nasty.

I said, "What is this? This is not cranberry sauce," still spitting, trying to get that nasty taste out my mouth.

"Beets," she said.

"This stuff is horrible."

"It's good for you," she said.

"Not for me," I said and I didn't ask her for anything else that I saw that looked different.

The next day Mama and Lena came back from wherever

they'd been. It was a Thursday afternoon; they had been gone for four days, partying. We told them that we were hungry, and all Granny had been giving us to eat since they'd been gone was some kidney beans.

Lena said, "Granny, these kids don't eat beans like that. Lena and my mother went to the grocery store. They brought back chicken and cooked it for us. Oh, man, the aroma from that chicken smelled so good. We acted like we had not eaten in a long time. When it was done, we could hardly wait for Lena to set our plates down. We grabbed that chicken, tore it up, barely leaving the bone. You talk about something so good!

The next day, my mother and Lena were going to the store and they let me go with them. Instead of me walking, I wanted to ride a bike. It was a ten-speed; I could barely ride it. As I was riding the bike, it started going downhill too fast and I couldn't stop. I was almost at the corner, which was the main street, and cars were driving by. I started to panic, my heart started beating real fast. I used my feet, which slid along the pavement until I came to a stop, almost going into the street. I jumped off the bike, breathing fast. I walked with that bike the rest of the way. Questioning myself as to why did they have bikes when all the houses were on hills?

That night, another one of our family members came to my Granny's house and wanted us to visit him before we left. I think he had lost his mind to put us kids in the back of that truck. This man was driving so fast I felt that any one of us could have fallen out. He was driving on a gravel road, not pavement. Plus we were on a mountain or hill. I yelled for the kids to hold on tight and hold our heads down so that we could breathe.

After visiting all day, he took us back to our Granny's house. We rode back the same way we came. That morning, family members came over to see us off, saying their good-by before we left.

"Essie, let Ernestine stay with me. Give her to me, please?" my Uncle Bill asked my mother. As if I was a product to give away.

"I'll take care of her," he went on.

"No," Mama said.

He tried to persuade her. "I'll take good care of her. I'll buy her everything she need. And you can come visit her."

Again, she told him no. I was so glad she said no after what he had tried to do to me. That would have been a very traumatic situation. I am so glad she didn't leave me with him. The thought of how my life would have been if Mama gave him custody of me. After what he did, pregnant by him? Oh, man, that's nasty. My kids would be my uncle's kids. I am so glad she didn't leave me with him.

We were taken to the bus station, and we said our goodbyes again. As the bus was leaving the station, I was looking out the window. The bus was driving in a circular direction. Once we reached the top of the hill, I looked down and was amazed at what I saw. At the bottom, there was one little house, a few horses, and nothing else but pretty green grass. I said to myself, it looks so peaceful. I thought it was an underground city, and I wished that I could live there. I stared at that place until I couldn't see it anymore, then I had nothing else to see.

I wasn't that excited to be back home because I knew everything that was happening before we went to Ohio would start happening again. Being in Ohio made me safe from some of the abuse that I was enduring. Barely back home, it seemed like Mama and Lena couldn't wait to get to the doctor. The next morning, they got up early and we were left with JB. JB was back to molesting me again. I did not get that eerie feeling like I did with my Uncle Bill but I didn't understand… Why me?

School was about to start. Daddy came to visit and we told him about our trip. While he spent some time with us and before he left he gave Mama money for school shopping and for some food. The next day, we walked right up the street to the corner across the street, right into the second hand store door instead of going to where we usually shopped. I knew Mama didn't have to go to second hand store. Daddy provided her with enough money. We had no choice; we had to accept what she got us and wore the clothes anyway.

At school the teasing began because of what we wore, but

we didn't tell anyone. We kept it to ourselves and dealt with it. I observed people and could tell how they perceived us. I knew who I could talk to and who I couldn't. We were outcasts; no one wanted to be friends with us except one or two people; and when they started getting teased for hanging out with us, they stopped. I hated when we were forced to go play on the playground even when we didn't want to. My sister and I would either play with each other or we would stand by the door until the bell rang. Then Amy befriended this girl and would go play with her; I would stand at the door alone.

We were humiliated because of the way we dressed and looked. We weren't pretty nor did we have a light complexion plus we had short hair. It was sad how we were treated and judged because of our appearance. As the teasing continued, some tried to take it a little further and started making threats, wanting to fight us for no apparent reason. We didn't bother anybody. We ignored them as long as they didn't put their hands on us. We went about our business; it is funny now. There were these three girls that always tried to fight my sister. She had to run to where I was so I could protect her. This happened every day; they eventually let her alone when they saw that I was ready to fight them.

There was not much to say about the next school year because it was the same as the previous school year. It seemed like where ever I went I wasn't safe. We were beaten at school and we were beaten at home with no one to protect us. We were afraid to tell someone, so everything that I was going through, I had to go through in secret. I was suffering traumatically.

At first I hadn't noticed that we weren't getting beaten when Mama was high. It was only when she wasn't. Because we were getting beaten all the time, I hadn't paid any attention that there were pauses in our beatings. It was like when the high wore off we would get beaten again, and it was for no apparent reason. Then she would take more pills and nod back out, and we would be safe for at least fifteen to twenty minutes. My godmother would come get me, freeing me. I kind of felt bad because my sister was left at home. I didn't know what she had to endure. While I was gone, JB and Mama couldn't touch me.

I spent a lot of my time around people who were older than me. I got to observe a lot. I observed everything Lena did with her male friends, and my god-sister with two of her friends. I had developed a crush on one of my god-sister's friends. He looked so good to me. I was jealous of her because of the shape of her body and because of the attention she was getting from men. Unlike me, she was never alone. She had a few female friends who she hung around, and she would take me with her. I wanted to get attention, but I was ignored. I felt no one liked me. I knew I was only eight, and I wasn't into boys like that at that moment. I visualized being older and he was my boyfriend, because he looked good and I had a crush on him. I was mad at her when she broke up with him because that meant I couldn't see him anymore.

Lena started spending lots of her time with this one guy named Jo-Jo but still had a few other male friends on the side. They soon moved into the apartment next door to us, into one of the four family units along with three other families. I was excited about the other family moving in because we would have someone to play with. After they settled in, we started playing with this one girl. I was happy because we all got along; no one tried to fight one another. We spent a lot of our time outside playing or at her house. We barely saw Mama because she would be in the house, high. While Mama and JB were in the house, high all the time, we got to do whatever we wanted because no one checked on us. However, we never took advantage of that. I didn't go off the block without permission; the only place that I would go would be to my godmother's house. My sister and I would always be where we could hear Mama if she called us.

Nina was another friend who lived next door. She was a little older than me. We would sit outside and talk or walk to the corner of the block and back to the house. I never revealed my sexual secret or my abuse to her. At the corner of our block was an apartment building, and I noticed this man standing outside, checking his mail, we stopped to talk with him. He was nice and friendly; he took time to talk with us. I asked him if I saw him outside, would it be OK if I visited him. He said yes, and that's what I did.

I asked a lot of questions. He showed me his apartment; we sat on the wall and talked. The wall was like a bench. The relationship we had was like father and daughter, but I kind of developed a crush on him; and unlike JB who was around his age, he never approached me in a disrespectful or inappropriate way. I knew he was a police officer. I did not reveal to him either about my abuse. The next time I saw him, he informed me that he was moving, that as a Detroit police officer, he had to relocate. I was stricken with grief that someone else I cared about was leaving me. I seemed to get attached to people real quick. It was nice of him to let me spend time with him.

Mama had to go to the hospital to have an operation. I didn't know why or what kind of operation and I didn't want her to go. I felt it was serious and that she wasn't going to come back home, that she was going to abandon us, just like Daddy. The way she was treating us, especially me, didn't stop me from caring about her. I loved her, and I didn't want anything bad to happen to her. I hadn't had a tantrum in a long time until she had to leave me. My godmother tried her best to convince me that Mama was going to be OK and that she was coming back home. I didn't believe her.

She said, "Your Mama is getting one of her legs operated on."

I wouldn't accept what she was saying. I continued to cry; my godmother said, "Stop crying, let's go." She took me to the hospital, I guess to show me that Mama was OK.

The hospital wasn't that far from where we lived. As I entered her room, I lost control again. Seeing her lying in the bed made me cry harder. I was taken out of the room, and out of the hospital, so that I wouldn't disturb the other patients. Back at home, I stayed with my godmother. My sister and brother were with Lena. The next day, my godmother took me back to visit Mama. When I saw her I did exactly the same thing as the day before and was taken right back out. My daddy was called. My godmother informed Daddy that Mama was in the hospital. Even though he had just gotten home from work, he came right over. He talked with me and assured me that Mama was going to be OK. I don't know why, but after Daddy talked to me, I felt better.

Mama came home a couple of days later but had to go back to the hospital, suffering from complications from the operation to remove a tumor from her leg. We were left in Lena's care and not my godmother's; I don't know why. I was mad because I wanted to stay with my godmother. Lena called my daddy after he had gotten off work to let him know that Mama was back in the hospital and asked if he could bring some money for food. He came right over, gave her the money, visited with us for a while then left.

That night at dinnertime, Lena cooked liver, And I told her that we didn't eat liver, but she told me that we had to eat it or we could starve; remind you, she had called and asked my daddy for money to get us some food, but she didn't use the money he gave her for us. She took the money and got her and her man and her neighbor friends some Chinese food, marijuana, and some liquor. She forced us to eat liver, telling us that we were getting nothing else and not to come out of the kitchen until we finished.

As soon as she walked out the kitchen, we asked my cousin if he wanted our liver; he really didn't want it, but we gave him some anyway. We put some in the trash. We peeked in the living room to make sure no one was coming into the kitchen. After we were done, we went into the living room, pretending that we had eaten all our food, saying that it was good.

The next day, I called Daddy and told him that Lena took our money and spent it on her and her friends and what she spent it on. He came and confronted her, not in our presence, though. I don't know what was being said. Daddy came out, talked with us and left. When Daddy was out of our sight, Lena called me in the house and asked me why I called my daddy. I told her that that money was for her to get us some food not to spend it on them. I guess she didn't like my answer and she got a belt and whipped me.

The next day when I knew my daddy was off work, I called him and told him that Lena whipped me because I told what she did with his money. He said he couldn't come over right now to tell her he said not to hit me again. Out of fear, I didn't tell her right away.

I was contemplating on when I was going to tell her. Opportunity came when we had to walk with her and her boyfriend, Jo-Jo to the store. I was thinking of a way to say it when I just blurted it out. "My daddy told me to tell you not to hit me no more."

She said, "Oh yeah?" I don't know what she was about to do, but her man took off his belt, grabbed me by my arm, and started whipping me while we were on the sidewalk. I fell to the ground, kicking, screaming, and getting scars from rolling all over the ground.

When he was done, he said, "Call and tell your daddy about this." That's what I did the next day. I called Daddy, I told him that Lena let her man whip me and I was scarred up.

The next day, Daddy came over after work. He went inside of the house while we had to stay outside. I hated that I could not hear what he was saying to them. They weren't in the house that long before they were coming out the door. They were walking and talking all nice, cool and joking around as if what they said was funny. My daddy wasn't laughing. Daddy did what he always did, talk with us, and then he left. Whatever he said to them, they did not put their hands on me again.

When Mama came home from the hospital, I think my daddy had words with Mama about the incident and believe it or not, she got upset with Lena, they stopped talking for a while. But she didn't stay mad at her that long. When she got well, they were back to doing what they usually did, going to the doctor and sharing pills. I didn't understand why she was mad when what they did to me was no different from what she was doing to me. And nothing changed that year, or the next years.

It was spring, and the news I received was unexpected. My godmother informed me that they were moving, and hearing that took a toll on me. I already felt that everybody I cared about was abandoning me. I was miserable, angry, and depressed. I felt alone even though I had friends. Now who was going to rescue me from all the abuse?

A month had passed when my god-sister was sent to get me. Being away from home, even if it was just for a few days, had me feeling safe and secure. I was allowed to do things I wanted, I was free to be a kid and not have to worry about being beaten for no apparent reason. My god-sister let me hang out with her and her friend, someone she met who lived down the street. And across the street was a white family who allowed me and two of my god-brothers to play at their house, letting us get in their pool.

One day out of the blue my god-sister and god-brother told me to go beat up the neighbor boy we were playing with, no reason was given. Trying to impress, I walked over to his house and beat him up just because I was told to. My god-sister and brother bragged about what I did. Deep down, I felt bad but didn't let on how I felt. We weren't allowed back over their house, so now we had to play with each other. I didn't care. I was having fun. I was free. I didn't have to worry about being beaten and touched or go hungry. I felt bad being selfish because I thought about myself and not my sister, not knowing what was happening to her. My godmother came to get me because I was getting the worst of the treatment. When I knew it was time for me to go home, my happiness turned to sadness. My godmother continued to come get me occasionally, while every day the same thing continued happening to me at home and school.

Chapter Three

Moving... Again

I spent a lot of time next door, hanging with my friend Nina and her two brothers and sister. It gave me a great opportunity to see her brother, Chuck, whom I had a crush on since the first day I met them. They all knew it by how I was all google-eyed and smiling, flirting with him whenever I saw him. His complexion was light, and he looked good.

They soon moved about five or six blocks away into a nice big house. I got to help them move and spend the night. We were in the bedroom after we set up the rest of the rooms. Their parents were downstairs. The younger brother came up with the idea to play Strip Poker. I knew nothing about playing cards. I was trying to impress Chuck so I played anyway. They called themselves trying to teach me, but I couldn't get the hang of it and was losing. I had to take off my clothes, piece by piece each time I lost. I stopped when it was time for me to take off my pants and I was embarrassed because I hadn't developed breasts yet.

That night, we played other games, too, like Spin the Bottle. They made up different rules for that game because they couldn't kiss each other. After that, we played Double Dare. They dared me to go in the closet with Chuck and we kissed.

We all stayed up late. The boys in their room and us girls in Nina's room, talking, and then we fell asleep. Chuck came in Nina's room and woke me up. He had me sneak out to his room. His room was an addition like a sun-room. He had his door open because it was hot. He had me lay next to him and he started kissing me. He took off my pajamas. I didn't resist him because I wanted him to like me because I liked him.

He took off his pajama pants, rubbing his penis against my vagina, until he reach an erection. and we attempted to have sex but it hurt too much so I asked him to stop. I got up, put my pajamas back on, went back to Nina's room and went to sleep. We didn't try to have sex again.

He said we were going to keep what had happened our little secret. Each time I saw him, my crush became more of an infatuation. I knew I was too young for him, but he knew how I felt. Over time he started getting into trouble, and I didn't see him much. I was allowed to visit Nina only occasionally.

In the fifth grade, I endured the same things I did in the previous grades. I was a loner, wanting friends, but no one wanted to be my friend. I was being judged not for who I was but for what I didn't have. I wasn't popular and was being teased because of how I looked. I wasn't pretty. The kids made me feel like I was ugly. I didn't have nice clothes, so I was teased because my clothes came from the second hand store. I blamed my mother for us being bullied because my daddy made sure she had enough money to buy us nice clothes to wear.

My classmates and other kids at school always wanted to fight me, but no one ever approached me; they just made threats. If they had, I would have defended myself. In class and at home, I felt like an outcast. But I wasn't alone, because there was another classmate, Priscilla who was also being teased because of her looks. She was tall for her age. We became friends for the rest of our school year. We were just like that Bill Withers song, Just the Two of Us.

We were about to graduate, and I was excited. The next school

I was going to was a new junior high school being built right down the street. I called my daddy to inform him about the good news and asked him if he could buy me something nice to wear to my graduation. I liked when my daddy bought our clothes. That's the only time we had something nice to wear and didn't have to worry about it coming from the second hand store and get teased.

Daddy came over and gave Mama the money, saying she had to take me shopping for my outfit. My excitement turned to sadness. I begged Daddy to take me instead of Mama. I knew what she was going to do. He apologized for not being able to take me after giving Mama the money and told her what store to take me to. I thought that she would listen to him, but I was proven wrong.

The next morning she took me shopping, but not to the store Daddy told her to take me to. As we were looking though the clothes, I found a dress I liked. It was pretty, I yelled, "Look, Mama, I found one." And she came over, looked at the price, and put it back on the rack. I guess it cost too much. I knew she had enough, but she didn't want to spend all the money Daddy gave her on me, even though it was for me. This was for my big day and I wanted to look good and wear something nice so I wouldn't get teased.

"You can't get that one," she said and continued searching. She found one and it was ugly, the ugliest dress I ever had. It was powder blue with a coat to match. I was upset. I knew she had enough to get the dress I wanted, but I also knew she picked that blue dress because it was cheap and she could pocket the rest of the money.

On graduation day, before I got dressed, Mama pressed my hair. I wanted it one way, but she styled it in two pony-tails. I was so ugly that I didn't want to go to school. I dragged on. If there was a way that I could have skipped school, I would have done it. But I couldn't because the school was right in front of my house.

When I got to my class, all the kids looked so nice. The girls had on pretty dresses, and boys had on nice suits. And I had on this ugly powder blue dress. Even Priscilla had on a pretty dress. I was so embarrassed and upset, I wanted to go back home, but I knew I couldn't. I distanced myself and sat in the back of the class and tried not to communicate with anyone. But that day, my entire class was nice. Priscilla sat next to me. Talking with her kept my mind off how I looked.

At graduation time, the auditorium was packed. All the parents were there except mine. I knew Daddy had to work; I knew he couldn't have taken time off for me but there was no excuse for Mama not to be there to show me support. I was disappointed that she could not stop taking those pills long enough to come and see me graduate.

We were now on our summer vacation; all the families we were friends with were moving, and we were moving again too, four blocks over in the same neighborhood. The house we moved into was an upstairs flat. The situation hadn't changed; JB was right with us. When Mama and JB argued, Ronald would come live with us until they got into an argument. When Ronald was around, we had plenty of food. He did some of the cooking; he provided for us; he was like our second father. When he tried to make Mama straighten up her life, she would argue with him, and he would leave. Ronald came back a few times after that. Because Mama didn't want to change, he left her for good. I was hurt. JB, he didn't care about us or what she did as long as he was a part of it. He was just a user.

We hadn't been living at this house that long before I met a new friend, Deanna. She lived in the apartment building next door. One day I heard a man and a woman arguing and screaming. I went to look out the window to see where it was coming from when I saw a girl sitting at the window. I started talking to her. It was her mother arguing with her step daddy. She said they argued all the time and she would always come to the window. We became best friends. I'd found someone who could relate to me, because she was going through the same thing. She was older than me and was like another sister to me because I hadn't seen my god-sister or my friend Nina in a while.

One day, we were sitting in my room, talking and listening to the radio when this song came on. We stopped talking when we heard some of the words in that song. The song captured our hearts. It was called Toby by the Chi-Lites and we fell in love with it. We could relate to what it was saying, and it became our song.

We could listen to it and escape from all the madness:

> I remember when we were kids

We shared all the hurt and tears

No matter what the weather
We were always together

Then we grew up
And time went on
We became separated

When I went off to school
My sweet Toby waited
I went off to school
My sweet Toby waited

Was a sad day
When Toby went away
Was a sad day
When Toby went away
Toby by the Chi-Lites, ©1974

I wanted that record so badly.

Once, when JB was gone, my daddy came over to visit us while Deanna was over. I told him about the record and asked him if he could buy it for me. He answered yes and we all walked to the record store that was two blocks away. Once inside, I had the happiest feeling. Daddy asked for two copies of the record. When we left the store, he handed me one and one to Deanna. We both started jumping up and down we were so excited. We started hugging and kissing Daddy.

I said, "Thank you, Daddy. Thank you. I love you."

And my daddy answered, "You're welcome," and he had this smile on his face. Daddy didn't know how much that song meant to us, and how it helped us in our time of need.

Deanna had two brothers; one was always getting into trouble and was in and out of juvenile detention. He liked me, and I kind of liked him, but I was playing hard to get. I didn't want to get in trouble if anybody found out I liked boys. There was a time when he got into trouble and I did not see him again; they moved right before school started.

One day, Mama made me and Amy walk over Lena's house to pick up a package. We suspected it was pills. When we got there, we knocked on the door, but no one answered. I decided to turn the knob to see if the door was locked, it wasn't. As we entered, standing at the door, we could see Jo-Jo lying in the bed, naked and high. We asked him where Lena was; he was incoherent, mumbling as he was trying to tell us where she was; nothing he said made any sense. He made lewd comments and sexual requests "Y'all come on in," he said.

"Naw. We're all right," we said and were about to leave.

Jo-Jo said, "Come in and put this dick in your mouth."

My sister and I looked at each other—frowned up our faces. I closed the door, and we left, saying how disgusting that was. We didn't tell anybody about that incident.

The new school we were attending, Stark Elementary was quite a distance from our house. It was right off the riverfront; we had to walk by ourselves and really had no business doing that. Anything could have happened to us. Mama's friend had a daughter, Kim who also went to that school. We had to stop and pick her up because she lived near the school. One day on our way to school, we came upon an accident of a little girl who was hit and knocked under a parked car. People were panicking, trying to get the car off her. I looked under the car and saw she was bleeding from her head. They were waiting for the police and ambulance and trying to find who owned the car, to try and move it. They tried to lift the car off her but they couldn't. We had to leave so we wouldn't be late for school. That scene and the vision of that little girl under that car wouldn't leave my mind. Parents were too lazy to get up and walk their kids to school to make sure we got there safely.

It wasn't long before I started getting teased at this school, just like my previous school and for the same reason. So I did just like I did at the other school, stayed to myself.

During the winter months, we didn't like going outside because of the amount of snow that would blanket Michigan, and we really didn't have anything to do while we were in the house. We would just sit and watch TV. I was sitting in the front room, watching TV when Mama and JB began to argue, and it became violent. JB hit her, and I stood up in a rage and yelled at him to leave my mama alone!

"Don't hit her no more!" He didn't listen. As they continued arguing, I didn't know if he was going to hit her again. I ran to the kitchen, grabbed a butcher knife, and stood behind him still yelling, pleading for him not to hit my mama again. My mama pulled out this little gun. I was trembling scared because I had never seen this kind of violence before since my daddy shielded us from it. Mama yelled at him to stop, but he went on and hit her again. She shot over his head, and before I knew it, I stabbed him in the lower part of his back. I snatched the knife out of his back quickly when he yelled. I panicked. I ran to the doorway and threw the knife down the stairs, like a scene out of a movie, in fear I ran down the stairs, and out the door.

I hid behind the bushes that were beside the apartment building. JB came outside, screaming my name. I was frightened, shaking, thinking he was going to find me. He didn't come off the porch; he just continued calling my name. I was afraid that he was going to find me because I wasn't hidden well enough so that he couldn't see me, but he didn't. I was relieved. He went back in the house and closed the door. I waited for a few minutes just to make sure he wasn't coming back outside. I ran to Lena's apartment, which wasn't really that far. But some of the long blocks made Lena's apartment seem farther away. I wasn't wearing a coat or shoes and there was lots of snow on the ground. I was running on a main street, and not one person came to my aid. Out of breath, I made it to the apartment. I banged on the door and Lena opened the door.

"Oh my God! What happened?" she said. As I was trying to catch my breath, I told her.

"Calm down, breathe slowly," she consoled me. She got a blanket to warm me up.

Later that night, she took me back home. I was scared, not knowing how badly I'd hurt him and I wondered if the police would take me to jail. I was sitting in the living room, unaware of what harsh treatment I was about to endure after Lena left. JB was bandaged up; Mama stood between the living room and dining room. JB walked over to me, asked me why I stabbed him.

I said, "You were hitting my mother." He took off his belt. I looked at my mother to see if she was going to stop him from what he was about to do; she didn't. He started whipping me while she stood there watching.

I was trying to help her, and she was letting this man do this to me. After he finished, I was sent to my room. I said to myself that I would never defend her again, ever. Even after JB whipped me, I didn't say anything about our secret sexual encounters. I didn't tell Daddy anything about what was happening to me out of fear of the consequences.

Mama had a friend named Shirley. She and her baby Juan moved in with us. We had no choice but to accept the living arrangement. We had no idea when Mama met her or where Mama knew her from. When she moved in, it was my first time seeing her. My sister took to the baby right away. She treated him as if he was her baby.

I never saw Shirley high like my mother, so I don't know if she took pills like Mama and Lena. Me, Amy and my brother had been taking care of ourselves, but Shirley helped take care of us. She made sure we had enough food. She cooked, and helped us clean. She did a lot for us. She would take us over her mother's house.

One day while we were at her mother's, I was in

the backyard, playing. Being a tomboy, I decided to climb a tree. I got to the middle of the tree and got scared because I was afraid of heights. I decided to sit down to collect myself before I climbed down. I sat right down on a branch with limb sticking up; it went straight through my underwear. Penetrating my vagina. I lifted off that limb so fast, and I yelled so loud. I started crying a little because of the pain. Shirley and her mother ran outside to see what happened. I was taken to the bathroom. When I had to urinate, it hurt; and when I wiped myself, I saw blood, and I yelled for Shirley. I panicked because I didn't know what was wrong with me. I thought I cut myself. As I cleaned myself up, the bleeding stopped. I was taken home and was made to lie down.

There was another time Shirley and one of her male friends had taken us with her. This man is fine, I said to myself. How I wished I was older and had fine male friends like Shirley and my friend Cheryl. As we were returning home, all of a sudden, she told him she had to hurry up and get home. We had some distance to go. She told him that she couldn't make it, and asked him to stop at the first gas station we came to. He pulled up to one and she fumbled, trying to get the door open. I got out the car with her. We walked up to the bathroom door, pushed it open, and stopped quickly. I bumped into her because she stopped so abruptly, pushing me back; I guess she was trying to shield me from seeing what was going on inside that bathroom. It was too late. I had already seen it the second she opened the door. There were men and women in there at the same time, and they were naked and were washing up. She grabbed my hand, got back in the car as fast as we could, and she told her friend to drive.

When we arrived home, we got out the car. As she walked up the stairs, I was right behind her and noticed her white pants were red. I didn't know why, and I didn't ask. A few months after my tree-climbing incident, I started bleeding, and there was a lot of blood. I was having bad pain in my lower abdomen. I started screaming hysterically because I didn't know why I was bleeding or having pain. I thought the reason was because of when I sat on that tree limb. Shirley told me to calm down, that I was having my menstrual cycle. I blamed it on the tree. No one had told me about menstruation or any other things I needed to know. Everything that I was learning, I learned by experience and by asking questions and being observant. Menstruation was something I had no knowledge of. Now I knew why her white pants were red.

I hadn't seen my god-sister, Cheryl in months. When she came to visit me, she came with a surprise: a son around the same age as Shirley's son. She came to see if I wanted to go with her to take the baby to visit his daddy. Of course I wanted to go anywhere to get out the house. We walked down the street toward the area we'd moved from, right at the corner. The city had built a new apartment complex directly across from the junior high school that had recently been built. When we got to the house, she knocked on the door. The door opened and she asked for the baby's daddy. When he came to the door, my first impression of him was that he looked like a pimp from a movie I saw. His hair was long, straight, and he had those big pink hair rollers in the top. I was trying not to stare at him, wondering what attracted her to him. He wasn't as attractive as her other male friends, especially the one I'd had a crush on. We visited for a while and then she took me home.

Daddy came to visit, doing his same routine, spending quality time with us. We always asked him to take us with him or when was he going to find a house so we could live with him. Like all the other times, he said he was working on it. We held on to what he said. We held on to hope.

One time Shirley asked me if I wanted to go with her to take her baby to see his daddy. I said yes, and I walked with her. We walked toward the area we'd just moved from. I didn't think anything of it at first. We were headed in the same direction that my god-sister had taken me when we came to see her baby's daddy. As we got closer, we walked toward the same apartment complex. I said to myself, this looks familiar. When we went to the same apartment and the same man came to the door, I couldn't believe what I was seeing. He looked at me as if he knew me. I didn't say anything. Shirley's and my god-sister's babies had the same daddy. I kept it to myself. They found out on their own, and they were feuding with each other just like women do in the same situation. How ironic!

My life had been so traumatized by what had been happening to me I got up the courage and said to myself that I wasn't going to be a victim of any more bullying. When I went to school, one way or the other, I was going to let my classmates know I'd had enough and that I was fed up with all the threats and the teasing. The kids were throwing paper spitballs at me. I was kind of scared because I knew I couldn't fight a lot of people, but if I had to, I would. This one popular girl, Lisa had a wannabe follower. She was trying to bully everyone. Our teacher was called to the office and as soon as she stepped out the room, the popular girl saw an opportunity to get a fight started. I was sitting at my desk. Lisa walked over to Kim, who was supposed to be my friend, told her to walk up to me and hit me. I could tell Kim didn't want to hit me, but the girl threatened to beat her up if she didn't. I stood up; all the kids surrounded us, instigating the fight.

One girl took her hand and made her hit me. I told her that I didn't want to fight. The girl made Kim hit me again. At the time, I was thinking that Kim didn't want to fight, that it was them making her. They forced her to hit me again. This time, just like The Hulk, rage came over me, and I snapped, lost control, and I began to beat Kim down. Whatever anger I had inside me was being taken out on her. I took a folding chair and beat her with it. The teacher heard all the commotion and ran back into the classroom, when I was about to hit her with the chair again. She grabbed it, broke us up. Kim got up off the floor, and we were taken to the office. We explained what happened, and were sent back to the classroom. We weren't suspended. After that, no one challenged me again. But I was still being teased.

We experienced something that could have cost us our lives, if it hadn't been for me, and my bronchitis. It was some time in the winter, but there wasn't any snow on the ground, it was just real cold. I was asleep and began coughing and choking. I opened my eyes, and even though I couldn't see without my glasses on, I could see the room was clouded with smoke. It hadn't registered in my mind yet what was happening. I knew when Mama was high, she would start cooking and would burn her food, and sometimes the house would be smoky. This smell was different, though. I put on my glasses, still coughing, got up to check where the smoke was coming from. The bathroom was right next to our room. As I got to the door, I saw flames coming from the wall just above the tub and Mama leaning over the tub, letting water run into it. She was using a cup or something to try to put out the fire.

    I turned and walked back in the bedroom, feeling my way through all the smoke. I couldn't see. I woke up my brother and sister and told them to get up because the house was on fire. I told Amy to wake up Shirley and get out of the house. I stayed behind trying to get Mama out the bathroom where she was still trying to put out the fire. Of course she was high. When she was high, she was incoherent. She just pushed me away and turned to continue to put out the fire.

    Our neighbor downstairs, Mr. Edgar came up to rescue us. He came into the bathroom, grabbed hold of Mama; she was trying to fight to get away from him. She was determined that she was going to put that fire out. He got Mama out of the house. I went to the living room to make sure everyone was out the house when I saw Shirley and the baby still asleep. I was nudging her to get up, saying the house was on fire. She woke, grabbed the baby, and went down the stairs. I was coughing badly, but I didn't follow them. I went straight to the top porch. I had taken in too much smoke so I went to breathe in some fresh air. Everybody was out of the house except me. The neighbors were yelling at me to jump. I was scared of heights so there was no way I was jumping. I didn't want to break my legs.

    Mr. Edgar came back upstairs to where I was, trying to convince me to jump. He jumped to show me it was OK and nothing would happen. I looked down. I said I was not jumping.

I covered my face, walked back into the house, felt my way through the thick smoke to the stairs, and down I went, and that's how I got out. As I got to the sidewalk, the fire trucks were just pulling up. As they fought the fire, the ambulance took Mama to the hospital to seek medical treatment. Her hands were burned, and she had suffered second- and third-degree burns. Because she was high, it hadn't registered to her that she had been burned.

Amy and I stayed the night at Lena's house, and my brother stayed the night with my daddy. My sister and I were mad; we wanted to stay with Daddy, but no girls were allowed. Daddy stayed at the YMCA. Shirley and her baby went to her mother's house.

Mama came home the next morning. With no place to go, we had to go back to our burnt house. It wasn't burned that badly; the bathroom and the two bedrooms had the most damage while the other rooms had a lot of smoke damage. We lived in that house while Mr. Frank, the landlord was having it fixed. It was an unbelievably horrible experience. Most of the time it was dark; the only light came from two lamps and daylight. It was hard living in a situation like that because we had to eat, sleep, and stay in one room.

We hadn't been to school the first couple of days after the fire. When we returned, no one knew what happened, so I was teased because my clothes smelled like smoke. The whispers caught the attention of the teacher. She asked what was going on, and someone said that I smelled like smoke. I wasn't wearing any socks, and it was winter. She had me step into the hallway with her, and she questioned me. I told her that our house caught on fire and most of our things were damaged and that we were still living in the house. She sent me back in the classroom but she didn't follow me back in. When she came back to the classroom, she told me that she wanted to see me after school. When school ended and all the kids had left the classroom, she gave me a box with some clothes in it. She made me put on the socks. Some of the items I didn't like, but I accepted them because I had nothing else. I appreciated what she did for me. I wore the shoes, which were just like the shoes they wore on the television show Happy Days.

Just When I Thought Things Couldn't Get Any Worse our lives were slowly getting back to normal. As the house was being fixed, the worker from the welfare office gave my mother vouchers for beds, clothes, food, and furniture to replace what we lost. I don't know why we didn't get much help from my daddy. When the repairs were finished, no more than two days passed when we were sitting around the house, not really doing anything when all of a sudden, I heard a bang on the front door. Frightened, I went to the top of the stairs and asked who it was. No one answered. There was another bang and the door opened. Standing there was Mr. Frank and two big black men in, what looked to me, like police uniforms. They came upstairs, handed my mother a document and started removing our belongings from the house, setting them onto the sidewalk out in the snow. Emotions came over me; mostly anger. I started crying and cussing them out. The men were Sheriff's Bailiffs from the court. I didn't care who they were, we had just lived through a horrible experience, and now they came to traumatize us more. I was so angry, I was crying… couldn't believe this was happening. It didn't do any good; they continued to set our things out. I asked them how they could be so cruel to put us out like this, in the winter.

Mr. Frank was heartless, allowing us to live in the house while it was repaired, only to wait until the house was finished to evict us. He didn't give a reason why he was evicting us. What they did to us was cruel. I called Lena and Daddy to let them know that there were two men and the landlord at the house, and they were setting all our belongings out on the street. We had to sit out in the cold and snow to watch our things so nobody would take them. Daddy came over and sat with us while Mama and Lena left to go find us a place to stay. They hadn't been gone long when they came back saying they'd found us a place to live. I couldn't believe how fast they found one. It was five blocks east of where we just moved from, still in the same neighborhood. I believe that if my mother hadn't been under the influence of drugs, she would have been aware this was an illegal eviction and could have sued our landlord for her injuries. He added insult to injury when he let us live in the house while it was being repaired, then gave an illegal eviction when it was done. He was responsible for the maintenance; the fire started in the wall from old wiring. Mama's mind was so blank from those pills that she let him get away with what he owed her for her pain and suffering.

The house we moved to was another upstairs flat. The owner, Mrs. Carolyn and her grandson, Jessie, lived downstairs. We didn't live there that long, though and it was my fault.

After we settled in, Mama met a new man named Ray. I assumed she met him while she was going to the doctor because that's the only time she left the house. He moved in with us. It was like déjà vu. We didn't like him either; he was no different than JB. He thought he was our daddy or something; he was controlling us, and Mama knew nothing about this man. She had the nerve to leave us home alone with him when she went to the doctor. Being under the influence of those drugs made her make bad decisions such as feeling comfortable leaving us with a man she barely knew just so she could go get pills to get high. He knew how long she would be gone and started taking me into Mama's room to sexually molest me. I kept that a secret too. All I kept thinking was, Why me? What was wrong with these men? I am just a child, how can I possibly satisfy them?

The school we had to attend, Carston Elementary was really far, about four or five long blocks away. Mama had to enroll us and that was the only time she took us to school. The next day we had to walk by ourselves and we had to enter the building through separate doors. I knew my sister wasn't good with directions so I told her that when school was over, to wait for me at the door and not to move. After school, I walked to the door where she was supposed to be. I didn't see her there. I waited until everyone stopped coming out that door, walked around the building, and still my sister was not there. I went inside the office to see if she was there; but she wasn't, and I started to panic. I walked home thinking that she must be there, that maybe she found her way home.

When I got to the house, she wasn't there; I was already nervous and crying, not knowing where my sister was. Mama and Ray were at home, high, and I told her that I didn't know where Amy was. My mother didn't show any concern that her seven old daughter was missing. I thought she was going to get up and go look for her; she didn't. She told me that I had to go back to the school and find her. Those were some long blocks I had to walk. I walked around the school again; no sister, and no other people were in sight. I walked back home alone and scared because I couldn't find my sister.

It started to get dark, and my mother was going to make me go back out and look for her again. I didn't know where I was going to look for her. Before I left, the phone rang. When I answered it, a lady asked me if I knew a little girl named Amy. I said yes she's my sister. The lady said she found her wandering around, crying. She got the number from my sister's book bag. She asked if someone could come get her, saying she'd wait with her and told me where they would be. I thanked her and I told my mother, thinking again she would go get Amy because it was dark. Mama told me to do it. Her "high" was more important to her than we were.

I had to walk a little farther past the school. When I got to where Amy and the lady were, I thanked her for helping my sister, and we went on our way. I was so happy to see her. I asked Amy why she didn't wait where I told her to. She said she thought I had left her and she thought she knew the way home. She went in the wrong direction and could not find her way back. Imagine what was going on in my head as we walked back home in the dark. I told her to never do that again. As we entered the house, I woke Mama up to let her know we were in the house; she looked at us and dozed back off. This was the second school that was far from home, and we had to walk alone. I was filled with anger because of the way we were being neglected, because of a man and her drugs. But I couldn't express my feelings of being abused and being neglected.

Jessie came upstairs to visit. I told him what happened, and he offered to walk with us to school so we wouldn't have to walk alone. The next morning he was waiting to walk us to school. After lunch. Outside on the school playground, Jessie was telling the other kids that he liked me, and that I was his girlfriend. They start teasing me. I told him to stop telling them that. After school, he walked home with us. This boy was infatuated with me, and I let him know that I did not like him, nor was he my boyfriend. I asked him to please stop saying I was.

The next day at school, while on the playground, he did it again; and the kids teased and laughed at me. That angered me. I got tired of telling him to stop saying that he liked me and that I was his girlfriend. I told him I was going to beat his butt if he continued to tell them that lie. He didn't stop and I snapped, and I beat him up. I got him to the ground, and I sat on him, hitting him everywhere. Like a wild beast. I was out of control. A teacher broke up the fight and I was in trouble.

When I got home, I told my mother what happened at school. She didn't say anything. Then there was a knock at the door. When I answered it, Jessie's grandmother stood in the doorway. She was furious.

"Why did you beat up my grandson?" she yelled at me. "Because I told him to stop telling those kids at school that he

liked me and that I was his girlfriend, and he didn't, so I beat him up."

She started cussing at me and was all in my face. I had never disrespected anybody before. I became enraged. I started cussing back at her; even my mother came to the top of the stairs yelling at her. The lady threatened to beat me up. She raised her cane to get ready to hit me; my mother yelled at me to move out the way, and she shot at her. No one got hit, but that was another bad judgment call resulting from taking drugs. The next day, Jessie's grandmother informed my mother that we had to move.

I don't know how Mama found a house that fast again.

This next neighborhood we moved to was far, and all the houses were old, really old, in the area of Leland off Chene and Mack. The house was a two-family flat this time. We were downstairs. The house was small, didn't have a basement, and the furnace was in the kitchen. It had two small bedrooms that only one bed could fit in. My sister and I had to sleep in one bed, my brother slept with Mama.

The next day Mama took us all to enroll us in school. The school that I was to attend (Leland) was across the street on the corner. Amy and my brother's school (Campbell) was on the next block and they liked it. As for myself as soon as I enter the school, I knew I didn't like it, and refused to go. Summer vacation was about to start and I don't know why Mama didn't just let us stay home. On our first real day of school the next morning, I walked to the school, into the front door and right out the back door, and I sat outside until the school ended. I did that for the rest of the school term, which was soon ended for summer break. I don't know what the teacher looked like or the classroom; I didn't know anything about that school.

I didn't like our new house, or school, or the neighborhood, but what could I do? When Daddy came to visit, I begged him to hurry up and find a house so we could move with him. But like always, he said he was working on it.

It didn't take long for Mama to become friends with our upstairs neighbor, Mrs. Smith; didn't take long before she started asking her for pain pills, making up an ailment. I watched them exchange pills; Mama would buy or ask for drugs from everyone she met, even Lena, because of her addiction. We barely ate. It was Mrs. Smith who would give us something to eat.

Ever since Daddy left, our lives had been filled with humiliation after humiliation and for what? Because of Mama's addiction; because of the clothes we had to wear; because of how we looked. We did what we had to do to take care of ourselves.

The neighbors across the street from us were an older couple taking care of their granddaughter. Instantly you could tell they were alcoholics. I felt sorry for the granddaughter who was about five years old. It was too bad she had to experience being around people like that. She had to be the adult of that family and basically take care of herself and them. That was a familiar situation to us, the only difference was that she was alone; we had each other.

One morning we went to check on them. When we walked in that house, it looked like a hurricane hit it. Things were all over the floor, and the grandparents were sloppy drunk. We decided to clean up. As we started picking up things, underneath some of the trash were dead baby kittens. Some had been stepped on and the mama cat had eaten some of them.

Sometimes me and Amy and our brother tried to find some fun thing to do to take our minds off what was going on in our lives. We had met two brothers around our age; Terry's complexion was light; Eddie's complexion was dark. Eddie liked me, and Terry liked Amy, and I liked him. He thought he was a player because other little girls liked him. My sister really liked him. I didn't pay any attention to him or his brother.

The day after we met them, Amy and I were getting ready to go outside and play when they knocked on our back door. I answered the door and Amy was in the tub. The bathroom was right by the back door. I was playing around, trying to let Terry see my sister while she was taking a bath. She got up to close the door, and I was holding it so it wouldn't close and when I let go, the edge of the door cut him and put a long scar across his face. I started apologizing. It was my fault so I got a rag for his face, and we sat on the back porch. Amy came out after she got dressed. We joked around, talking, looking at one another, all google-eyed. The whole time all you could see were our teeth because, everyone was smiling so hard. After a few hours, they left.

The following day Daddy came to visit. He brought my brother a bike for his birthday, and he brought something for me and Amy, but I don't remember what it was. I really didn't care about the gift; I was just happy to see my daddy. I missed him so much; I wished that we could have seen more of him. What we were going through was hard; watching Mama, making sure she didn't burn up the house or harm herself. But one night I had to call 911.

Mama was high, and had fallen asleep on the toilet. I had to wipe her before I could get her up. Having no knowledge about the human anatomy, I thought something was wrong with her vagina. I was trying to wake her up so that she could get off the toilet and get into bed. Frantic, I called my sister to help. We couldn't lift her; she wouldn't respond to being lifted or to us calling her. All she did was moan. As we continued trying to lift her, the harder it got for us. We were young, and she was dead weight. We tried and tried, but we just couldn't move her. We were going to try and drag her, but I didn't want to make her fall, but we still weren't able to lift her. I called 911, tried to explain the whole situation to the operator as best I could. The operator started asking questions. She had me to check to see if Mama was breathing; she was. She had me do other things and everything checked out. Then she told me that everything would be fine, that she will be all right and to let her sleep it off and, if she stopped breathing, to call back. Then she hung up. I thought to myself, how could we just leave her like that, sitting on the toilet until her high wore off? We had no other choice.

Mama's drug addiction was hard on us. We had never seen her this high before. But I do have to say that since her addiction started, we never disrespected her or took advantage of her. We would go to the store and come right back home, and we would sit right on the porch watching her and looking out for each other. Like, the time when we told my brother not to ride his bike to the store, but he was hardheaded, and he rode it anyway.

When we got to the store he left the bike outside. After we entered the store, three boys came from out of nowhere and took off with his bike. We ran outside to try and stop them, but they were fast and got away. I told him that's what he gets for not listening. I was upset because he didn't listen, and I felt that we already didn't get nice things often and that we should cherish what we had. I tried to hurry up and get home so I could tell Daddy what happened. He told us not to worry about it and he came over with another one.

    The next time I went to the store, I saw some people setting up roadblocks on Chene from one corner to the other corner, blocking off two streets. I walked over to one of the guys and asked what they were doing. He said that they were setting up for a neighborhood block party. I became excited because I had never been to a street party. I hurried home and told my sister. She didn't want to go; she was shy. I was too, but this was a chance for me to have some fun. I told her if she needed me, that's where I will be and to tell Mama if she woke up. By the time I got back around the corner, they were playing music. Some people were playing games; others were eating food that was handed out. Even though I was shy, I started dancing, all by myself. Soon I forgot about being shy, and I let loose dancing to the music. My mind wandered off; I went into another state of mind. I was somebody else just for those few hours. I was free! I danced, danced, danced until the end. It had gotten dark when everybody started to leave. When it was all over; reality set back in and I was myself again so I went home.

    Mama hadn't seen Lena since we moved. She ran into her when she went to the doctor. Lena and Jo-Jo had moved on a street called Benson off Mt. Elliot. Mama had us walk with her to their house, even though it was quite a distance. While we were there, Lena told Mama about a soup kitchen, a church down the street from Lena that gave food to the unfortunate. They planned which day they were going to go.

    That day, Lena waited for us while Mama took her shopping cart. I didn't want to go; I didn't want to feel like we were begging. I felt like people were going to look down on us. I was ashamed, and I knew that we were not supposed to be there, begging for food, when my mother was getting enough money to take care of us. She chose to use the money on herself instead of her family's needs.

    Mama had us going to the church again a week later. We had to walk in a temperature that was almost one hundred degrees. It was so hot that we had to beg her to stop to get something to drink. We were a block away from Lena's house but she wasn't going to stop. We stopped at a store instead. Mama had a little change to get something to drink; she got one pop for all of us to share. She took a swallow then she had this strange look on her face. She said, "Oh my God! I can't see, I can't see." I started to panic; my heart started racing. I didn't know what to do. All kinds of thoughts came to my head: what were we going to do if Mama was going blind? How was this going to affect us? What if she stays like this? We would really have to take care of her more than we already did. We had her to sit down; we waited to see what was going to happen. Five minutes had passed before she started getting her sight back. We tried to figure out what made her temporarily go blind like that because the only thing she did was drink some pop. I assumed it was too hot to drink pop in heat like that.

    She got up and we went to the soup kitchen. After we ate and she got her food, we went straight home.

    Lena found out from a relative that my grandmother had a brother, Uncle Kidd, who lived nearby. Mama and Lena decided to pay him a visit and dragged us with them. We weren't in the man's house that long before they started asking him lots of questions, and then I heard them ask him for some money, using us as an excuse, saying they needed to buy us some food. While they were asking him for money they were rambling through his house, going through his belongings. Remember, they had just met him that day. I heard him say, "Don't you have a man? Ask him for some money."

    I knew they were lying but what if they weren't? He didn't know. We were his family members. His actions said to me that he was a selfish, uncaring, stingy old man. He didn't care if we starved. After I heard what he said, I didn't like him. When Mama and Lena saw that they weren't getting a dime from him, they were ready to leave.

Over the summer we moved again and I was happy about it. I hated that house and the neighborhood. We moved right back into our old hood, leaving our friends behind. A lot happened at our new house. So much so that I don't know where to begin.

The house was another two family flat and we lived upstairs. Mama seemed to already know the lady who lived downstairs, Mattie. She had lots of kids and we met most of them after we had settled in. She had two older ones that didn't live with her, and she was raising her grandson.

Once, Mama had left us home alone. We were straightening up our room when one of Mattie's sons sneaked into our house through the basement. He came into our bedroom and I got this eerie feeling. He fondled Amy while I was there. I didn't help her; I just kind of laughed, thinking it was OK for her to let him touch her. But, at the same time I was scared because of the bad vibes I was feeling about him being in our house and wanted him to leave. That wasn't like me to be scared but my sister handled it.

Afterwards she pushed him away and told his sister. She cussed him out and told him that she better not see him near us again. I believe he was a problem child. After that incident, he didn't come around anymore.

I was trying to live as normally as I could while suffering from all the problems I was going through. JB had manipulated my mind into thinking it was normal and OK for him to sexually molest me all those years. Even though he wasn't around to continue I was suffering from withdrawal, like I was addicted. The urges I felt were overwhelming. Because of what this predator had done to me, I needed to feed my addiction. I began acting out sexually toward a family member, but not in the same manner as JB had done to me. I even made my dog Blackie perform oral sex on me to relieve myself from my sexual urges and to feel a sense of sexual satisfaction.

One day there was a rainstorm that caused flooding in the neighborhood. When the storm was over I looked outside and saw my friends standing in the water with a bucket, trying to catch something. I asked them what they were doing; they said trying to catch some fish. I went outside to see what they were talking about. The water had little fish in it. I grabbed a bucket to see if I could catch some too. When we did, I said I was going to keep the ones I caught as pets. We sat on the porch, wondering how they got all the way to where we lived. We lived by the river. I guess they had been washed ashore when it flooded. The next day, every fish we caught died.

Our next-door neighbor was a lady named Miss Kalean with three sons, George, Eric and Christopher. They were friends with the kids downstairs from us. All of us girls had a pick of the boys we liked or thought was cute. The one I was attracted to liked a girl who was prettier than me. My attraction to him made me confused because I didn't really like boys. Maybe I was scared to like boys, thinking it was bad, and I was going to get into trouble. I was a tomboy and boys were easier to play with. I could be myself and didn't have to compete with them by asking who looked better.

The family soon moved and their house next door was torn down, but the debris was not removed right away. The roof was sitting on top of all the debris and I played on top of the roof along with George, Eric and Christopher who came back to play with us. I would play baseball with them or just sit on the porch talking.

I was real cool with one of Mattie's sons. He liked me but I didn't like him. My friends and his sister tried to get us together. I just wasn't attracted to him; we called him Ultra-man from that Saturday-morning cartoon because his head was shaped like a cone. He didn't get mad; he knew we were just playing. We were all cool and nobody wanted to fight. One of his sisters thought she was pettier because she had long hair and dressed nice; she got the most attention, and she knew that the boys were attracted to her. Amy and I were kind of looked over and we look passed her arrogance.

I loved it when my daddy cam to visit us. I loved him so much; he was sweet, and a kind and freehearted man. Oh, man! I loved him. I asked him if he could give us some money to go to the store, he told us to go with him. He didn't just take us, he told all those kids to come, and he brought all of us what we wanted. Now, when their daddy would visit, it was a different story. They acted like we were not friends; they ignored us for that day. But whenever our daddy came to visit us, all those kids were right there with us all excited just like we were. They knew how generous my daddy was; they knew he would not let them go without. Daddy was about to take us to the store, and he told them to come with us. I pulled him to the side.

"Daddy, don't take them with us
this time." "Why not?

"Because when their daddy visits them, they act like they don't even know us."

My daddy said, "You can't be like other people. Don't do what they do. We just be who we are and be the bigger person," he said.

His reasoning was very helpful. He showed us that we don't have to get even or be spiteful toward people; that what they deserve will come to them. That's why I loved my daddy. He was always teaching us right from wrong just by talking to us and we learned a lot from those talks. We called it preaching because when he talked, it was like we were in church. He would tell us about life, people, and what we should expect. I think he didn't think that it would ever happen to us. We enjoyed our time with him even though it was boring at times, just sitting and listening to him talk, but we didn't care as long as we were spending time with him. But... he never told us what to do if someone touched us inappropriately.

We would tell him about some of the things that were going on. He continued to tell us that he would get a place soon. Hearing that always gave us hope and helped us deal with the things we were enduring, believing that one day, our life would be better. We held on to that because it made us think that help would be coming soon. We didn't know when it was coming, but we still had hope.

I admired my daddy. He wasn't living with us, but he was being a man and handling his responsibilities. He did his best when it came to taking care of us. When we called and said we needed something, he was on his way.

One day, we were in the house when I heard music outside. I went to the back door to see where it was coming from and saw some guys on the top porch of the house directly across from my house. They were playing instruments, so I went outside; my friends came out too. I asked them who these guys and girls were. A friend started naming all of them. At that instant, I picked who I liked. They were practicing their music and we were all standing in the alley watching. Then I started dancing, and everybody else joined in when they played Brick House, by the Commodores. I let loose. I loved that song, as if I was shaped like a woman's measurements described in that song: 36-24-36. They played for a while and interacted with us like we were at a concert, and we were their audience. They were good! We were having fun; then they started taking in their instruments. We were trying to convince them to keep playing but they said they couldn't and assured us that they would come back out the next day, and they did.

We were very honest and didn't hide that we had a crush on them. They knew we were young; they thought it was cute. They didn't take it further. I was thinking how was I going to get to see them more. I walked to the store, took a detour to their block as if I was just taking a walk. I was going to cut through the lot that was next to their house. When I saw their sister I befriended her. She introduced me to the rest of them. One of the guys was the boyfriend of one of the sisters.

I became close to the older sister, Yvette. Even when she moved into her apartment over the store we stayed close. After she had a baby, I even babysat for her. If I wasn't at her house or her mother's house behind ours, I was outside, playing with my friends, trying to divide my time.

Chapter Four
Growing Up Too Fast

Just before the summer of 1978, we were on the move again, to a new neighborhood. And once again, I didn't know why. I was sad to go because we had really good friends and everybody seemed to care about one another in our old neighborhood. We were like family, and we were going to make sure we kept in touch. We didn't move that far. Ironically, we moved right across the street from the police station I went to after I was raped.

We moved downstairs, into another two-family flat. After we settled in, I took a walk though the neighborhood and saw that the whole neighborhood was a mixture of races, and I liked that. My outgoing personality allowed me to meet people instantly. The first people I met were two sisters who were white. I assumed that was their race. They lived across the street, directly in front of my house. One of the sisters was Linda, who had a little girl named Passion; I thought that was a pretty name. They seemed to be a nice family. Linda came and sat on the porch with me, and she secretly introduced the neighbors to me, telling me about them. Then she shared some personal information about herself and her ex-boyfriend, Johnny Hall. She said he was crazy.

While she was sitting on my porch, he drove up. He was a handsome man, but didn't appear to be white, so I asked her his race, and she said he was Hispanic. She said he would stalk her, do things to harm himself because he didn't want her to leave him. She said that frightened her. She knew what he was capable of doing, so she had to keep him away from their daughter.

I started questioning her about other neighbors, starting with the group of guys I saw leaving the house next door to her house. She pointed out the one that actually lived there, saying he lived with his father. She said the other guys were his friends; they were always over there to practice. They were in a rock band. She also said they were prejudiced. About two weeks later, they moved. Prejudiced or not, they were very handsome to me. There weren't that many kids on the block, so, other than Linda, we didn't have many friends yet. We did have things to do that occupied our time so we wouldn't be bored. We would sit on the porch listening to music and we made up a dance routine to the Village People's song YMCA that was fun.

Neglecting Her Responsibility....

Mama started leaving us alone to go to the doctor. After she would leave, my brother would be bad, not listening to us, running around the house, terrorizing us. The boy was out of control. We didn't know what to do, plus he was getting on our nerves. I told Amy we had to do something with him to get him to stop being bad.

I said, "Let's lock him out the house."

He didn't hear our plans. We surrounded him to grab him, and when we did, we pushed him outside and locked the door; all he had on was his underwear. He banged on the door for us to let him back in. We looked out the window, laughing at him. Then he ran to the window to see if he could get in that way; we locked all of them as he approached them. Then he decided he was going to get back in by breaking one of the windows. When Mama came home, we ran outside to tell her our version of how the window got broken; she got angry. We thought he would get in trouble; he didn't, but we did.

The next time Mama was about to go to the doctor, we begged her to take him with her. She told us she wasn't taking him and that we had to watch him. We knew as soon as she left what he was going to do. As soon as she was out his sight, he started acting bad, punching us cause he knew we couldn't hit him back, and running around the house, making us mad. He had us chasing him. I knew we couldn't lock him outside because we didn't want him to break another window. When we caught him, we tied him up and put him in the closet. He escaped, and we couldn't do nothing to him but let him terrorize us so we wouldn't get in trouble.

Road Trip...

My cousin Ernest, who I'm named after, and who said I was his favorite little cousin, came with his wife, Suzie to visit us for a few days. He asked my mother to let Amy and I go back to Ohio with them for the summer. He said he would buy all our summer clothes and school clothes. We were excited about going; we felt if we were gone for a while, we could rest from some of the abuse.

The next morning, we left for Columbus, Ohio. It was a long drive. It seemed like we were on that road forever. I kept asking them, "Are we almost there?"

"Not yet. Not that much longer," they'd reply.

A little while later, I'd ask, "Are we almost there?"

"Not yet," was the answer.

Then I finally saw the Columbus, Ohio sign and we were finally there. When we got out the car, their daughter, Christie came out to meet us. As we entered the house, we met the rest of his family. We weren't even in the house long when he had his daughters give us some of their old clothes, some of them still looked new. We didn't complain because it was better than having nothing or what we already had.

I guessed I was used to the city because where we were, we didn't really see anybody: no traffic, not even people walking... it was very quite. I got bored and didn't want to just sit in the house, but there was nothing to do. Corey, my cousin Ernest's son, had some friends who came to visit him. I liked hanging around boys; I just get along better with them. I went outside and my cousin introduced me to his friends. Instantly I became attracted to one of them. I hung around Corey just so I could flirt with his friend.

That night, we were all outside and I kept seeing something light up. I didn't say anything and no one else said anything. I thought I was imagining things, and then I saw it again. No one said anything.

When I saw it again, I asked, "What is that light I keep seeing?" "Lightning bugs," one of the boys said.

I was relieved. It was cool to me because I never saw bugs like that before. We stayed out late, we had nothing else to do, and it was too hot to go inside the house. It was like that the following nights too: hot, nothing to do, not wanting to go in the house. So Corey, and I and his friends walked around the neighborhood, talking, everyone telling a story. On the way back to the house, Corey and his friends were playing with firecrackers. Lighting them, then throwing them up in the air. I told them to stop, that somebody was going to get hurt. They thought it was funny and lit another one; this one went off by me. My left ear started ringing; I started screaming at them holding my ear.

I was mad and yelled at them. "I told y'all not to be playing with firecrackers; that somebody was going to get hurt." And that somebody was me. They got scared and begged me not to tell. I wasn't, but I still had ringing in my ear. After we got to the house, it turned out my ear was damaged, and I couldn't hear out of it. That didn't stop me from hanging around them, though.

The next day was very hot. Corey and his friends were going to the recreation center to hang out and swim. I knew I didn't know how to swim, but I was going to go with them even if I just had to play in the water. I had never been in a pool that size before, and I wanted to just get in. I wore a two-piece swimming suit that Christi gave me. I kept looking at myself in the mirror and thought I looked cute and sexy and I was excited. My shape was almost like the one described in that song Brick House. Corey's friends made comments about my swimsuit. Jesse, my cousin's friend, was paying a lot of attention to me; I had my eyes on him too.

Just like at home, I wasn't being watched. I was free to do what I wanted, but I knew how far to take it and what I wanted to act on. This was a new place for me. I knew nothing about this city, but I was allowed to walk back and forth to the center by myself, unsupervised. My sister never went with me; she just stayed in the house. I wasn't scared and wasn't worried about getting lost. I was very observant of my surroundings, a fast learner. If you show me something once, I don't need to see it again.

Jesse came up to me and suggested that I sneak away from everyone and meet him in the woods; he said that he would leave first and I should follow. He made up an excuse; five minutes later, I made up one, and we met up where he told me to meet him. We were deep in the woods. No one could see us; he told me to lie across a large tree that had fallen and we started kissing. He began caressing my body and soon took off my swimsuit bottom. He then pulled his swim trunks halfway down, exposing his well-endowed penis. (I'm in trouble) So we attempted to have sex but it was way too painful. I tried scooting back to ease the pain while he was thrusting and trying to enter the tip of his penis so we stopped. I sat up, put my swimsuit bottom back on, and he went one way, and I went the other. When we met back up with the others we acted like nothing happened. We continued to hang out and have fun. Then my fun turned into a nightmare.

Christie and her sister, Helen started bossing Amy and I around. They made us do house chores. All the things we had to do made me feel like we were slaves. We were doing all the work while they sat back and watched, but they helped a little. We were visitors and I was getting mad, and ready to go home because of all the work they had us doing. Actually, I really didn't want to leave because I wanted to be around Jesse, so I figured I'd rather do housework than go home. We didn't say anything; we did what we were told.

The next morning, we were cleaning up the downstairs bedroom, when we started smelling a strong smell of baby pee. I knew there wasn't a baby in the house.

I asked, "Why do I smell baby pee? There's no baby here?"

Christie told us that they have an older sister who used to live with them whose baby died, and the room we were standing in was her room. I figured the smell was because occasionally, some form of the baby's spirit manifested. After a few seconds, the smell went away, and we went back to our cleaning. When we finished doing our slave work, an older male cousin came to visit. I instantly developed a crush on him. He looked so good to me, but I had to get it out of my head; he was family. Later that day, my cousin Ernest had Christie take me to the mall to buy summer clothes for me; we caught the bus. He bought my sister clothes himself on a different day.

After we arrived at the mall, we went to a few stores, just looking around. The last store we came to Christie started picking out clothes for me. I liked them all. I was so excited because the only time we usually had something new was when my daddy bought them. I tried the clothes on and stared at myself in the dressing room mirror. I looked at myself in almost all the mirrors in the store and had a big smile on my face. Unfortunately, we didn't have the clothes that long.

When we got back to the house from shopping, Corey, his friends and I went to the recreation center to swim. We started playing in the pool, and they tried to teach me how to swim. I wasn't catching on, but I was having fun trying.

One of my cousin's friends said, "Look, do like this."

As he was in the water, he held his nose, closed his eyes and fell back into the water. The water splashed on everyone close by. He did it again. Then as he stood up in the water to do it again, I saw a lady who was about to swim behind him. I tried to tell him to stop and even tried to grab him, but he didn't hear me. I couldn't grab him fast enough, and he fell back right on top of her.

They stood up in the water at the same time. I told him that I had tried to warn him that she was there. But she wiped her eyes, pulled back her long hair, and didn't say anything to him; she came straight at me, saying that I pushed him onto her. I tried to explain to her that I hadn't pushed him, but tried to grab him. She didn't

believe me and continued to cuss at me. I snapped and started cussing back at her. I was so angry. I was about to beat that lady down. Corey and his friends held me back and wouldn't let go. I tried hard to get loose, but they managed to get me out of the center. I was very irate. I was still cussing and ready to fight. I just didn't understand why she wouldn't believe that I hadn't pushed that boy onto her.

By the time I got to the house I had calmed down. Later that night when my so-called "favorite" cousin came home from work, I told him everything that had happened at the center.

He said, "OK" and that was that. I went to do my chores, and then about ten minutes later, he called for me to come back to the living room. He asked me to tell him what happened again.

I said, "I told you."

"Tell me again."

So I told him exactly the same story I had the first time. Afterward he asked me again what happened, and by now I was trying to figure out why he was repeating himself.

Then he said, "Did you cuss out that lady?"

"Yes, I told you I did."

He said, "You didn't tell me that part."

I repeated, "Yes I did." We went back and forth with that.

Then he said, "Since you didn't tell me that you cussed out that lady, you can't go back to the center."

I knew that if I couldn't go to the center. I wouldn't be able to spend time alone with Jesse. He was the only reason why I stayed in Columbus that long. I felt Amy and I weren't being treated right, and we should have gone home. I got mad and I told him I wanted to go home. He asked my sister if she wanted to stay, and she said no.

He asked her if she was sure, and she said, "I am leaving with my sister." She wanted to leave anyway because she was being bullied by one of his daughters and hadn't said anything.

He said, "Fine. Y'all will be leaving in the morning."

The following morning when we got up to pack our clothes, we found out he had taken everything he had given us and bought us- even the clothes that I had stolen from my cousin when I first got there. All we left with was what we came with. He tried to get my sister to stay by offering her the clothes he had gotten me, but she said she was leaving with me.

I thought that he was going to drive us back home. He took us to the Greyhound bus station, got our tickets, and left us there; didn't tell us what to do nor did he wait until we got on the bus; he just left. This coming from the man who said I was his favorite cousin. He treated us like we were nothing, like we weren't even related. He took us girls, twelve and ten-years-old to a bus stop in a city we knew nothing about and left us by ourselves. We weren't scared, though. I paid attention to the signs and listened to the route announcements. When I saw people lining up for the same destination, we lined up too. I grabbed my sister's hand and we got on that bus.

We were on the bus for a long time. We had nothing to eat and no money to buy anything to eat. The only money he gave us was to catch the city bus when we got to Detroit. The bus was picking up and dropping off other people along the route. We arrived in this city that I thought was Detroit. It looked a lot like downtown Detroit. When I saw everyone getting up to get off the bus, I told my sister to come on, that we were home. Something told me to ask the bus driver if we were in Detroit. I had my sister's hand and I walked up to the bus driver and said, "Excuse me, can you tell me if we are in Detroit?" He replied no, that we were in Chicago. He asked me what city we were going to. I said we were going to Detroit. He told us to go back to our seats and he would tell us when we arrived in Detroit. I politely said thank you and we sat back down.

I thought about what might have happened if I hadn't asked the bus driver where we were and had gotten off the bus.. We couldn't call anybody. We didn't know at the time we had relatives in Chicago. All kinds of "what-ifs" went through my head, but I'm glad that I had the mind to ask. We finally reached the next destination after another long drive.

"Now this looks like Detroit," I said.

The driver turned and looked at us and said, "You're in Detroit now."

We got up, walked toward the front of the bus. Before I got off, I looked at the bus driver and told him thank you. After we got off the bus, we walked through the bus station and out the front door. We stood there for a minute looking around where we were. I knew the Greyhound bus station was along the route I took when I skipped school to walk over to my daddy's house. Going in the opposite direction, we walked until I came to the street where my mama and I caught the bus when we had to go to court. That was familiar to me.

We waited for that bus to come. When we got on, I sat by the window to watch for our street, paying attention to landmarks that I remembered so we wouldn't pass our stop. As we got closer to our stop, I pulled the cord so the bus would stop. After we got off the bus, I was kind of glad we were home. We walked down our street, got to the house, and knocked on the door. Lena opened it; Mama was inside. As usual, they were high. They had no idea that we were on our way home. In a sluggish voice, Mama asked me how we got home and why we were we home. I told them what happened. I don't even know if they understood what I said. We went in our room and put away the clothes that we took with us.

It was a shame that cousin Ernest didn't care enough to call and let my mother know we were on our way home so she could look out for us. He didn't call to see if we made it home, either. Anything could have happened to us and he wouldn't have known. He did nothing, and he called himself my favorite cousin. He was so scandalous toward us I said never wanted to talk to him again.

Back home now, I went outside to walk around, exploring the neighborhood and trying to meet new people. It wasn't that late and Mama and Lena were high, but I didn't stay away from the house too long; wasn't trying to disrespect my mother just because she was high. She didn't even know I'd left the house. I was gone just long enough to walk around a few blocks. I didn't meet anybody, so it became just a sight-seeing walk.

The next day I ventured out again, touring the neighborhood to see if I could make some friends. This time I went in a different direction. I was a block and a half from my street when I approached this house. There were two white girls lying on towels in their front yard. I asked them what they were doing; they told me that they were trying to get a tan.

"Can I lie in the sun with you?" I asked.

"Yes," they answered.

Right then and there, I had two new friends, Kit and Rosa. They introduced me to the rest of their family and I was invited to visit anytime I wanted. I stayed until it got dark, so I headed back home.

I visited them every day, lying in the sun with them, trying to get a tan like theirs. I liked the bronze color of their skin. I thought I would tan the same color they were, not knowing I was only making my skin darker.

Their house soon became my second home; I was over there so much. They treated me like part of the family. I enjoyed being there. I ate when they ate; drank coffee with their uncle Buck when I visited. I would sit around with them talking, watching TV; and when we wanted to have girl time; we would go in Kit and Rosa's bedroom to talk and listen to music.

At this time my mama was high all the time; she never knew where I was. She just knew I was at a friend's house. While I wasn't in Mama's presence, I behaved as if I was in her presence; I still had good manners and I would be home before it got dark.

I was treated with the same hospitality by my neighbor across the street from our house. Her name was Lady H. She was an older woman with kids. I befriended her daughter Tonia who was my age. I divided my time between my new friends, Kit and Rosa and Tonia, until Tonia started acting strangely. One day she would be talking with you laughing, joking, being your friend and the next day she would barely speak to you. Sometimes when I'd go to visit her, she would walk around her house as if no one was there and not say a word to anybody. Her whole demeanor turned different. She would hold her head up, daring you to say something to her so she could say something smart to you. Her facial expression was emotionless.

She just wasn't friendly. And then the next day she would be back to herself, all cheerful, happy, bouncing around the house as if nothing happened the day before. I asked Lady H what's wrong with Tonia, she claimed nothing; that she was like that all the time. I didn't agree with her. I knew something was wrong with that girl. She needed help, but her unexplainable behavior was ignored.

I started spending more time with Lady H sitting on the porch, talking. I was learning from her just by listening. She was like a mother to me; she would listen to my problems, and she was the only one with whom I shared what happened to me, about my abuse at home and when I was raped. I asked her to keep my secret, and she did. The more time I spent with her, the more I felt like part of her family. I could go over her house anytime I wanted, even when no one was home; I could stay there until they arrived. I'd cook if I wanted something to eat; she trusted me. I knew where she kept her money; knew the doors were never locked. I knew just about everything about her and her family. She even told me about the abuse in her past. I felt that there was a special bond between us.

Experiment...

Because of what been happening to me sexually over the years I began acting out, trying to experience sexual intimacy at a young age. Other than the rape, the only thing that prohibited sexual intercourse from happening the two times I tried was the pain. I wanted to take my sexual curiosity with older men a little further. I wanted to experience more than a crush, taking my flirting advances to the next level.

I saw a man who had just moved into the four-family flat at the corner of my block. I thought he was handsome, and I was instantly attracted to him and became infatuated. I flirted with him, smiling and conveying with my eyes letting him know I was interested. To my surprise, he acted on my advances. When he saw me walking past his house, he approached me. He told me his name was Chicken (his street name), the first thing he asked me was my age. Of course I lied, and told him I was seventeen years old. Physically and mentally I was mature, people didn't actually know how old I was unless I told them. As we talked, he suggested that we hook up. I agreed.

It's hard to describe what I was feeling. I stood there smiling, thinking about how we could do this when I remembered the fireworks were that day. Detroit has a big annual Fourth of July fireworks celebration downtown and people from all over Michigan come to watch. Most people in my neighborhood went to parks around the riverfront to watch, which isn't what I planned to do. I told him instead of me going to see the fireworks I could come over to his house and sneak in through the backdoor.

After a few hours went by. I waited until I saw most of the people from our street head toward the park. We had to keep it on the down low because of my age; I was just twelve. Even though I'd told him I was seventeen years old, he was still older than me. I walked through the alley to his house, went in through the backdoor just like we planned. As soon as I stepped through the door, he didn't waste any time; he started kissing me. He guided me to his bedroom and started taking off my clothes.

I knew I had no experience in sex, and I was nervous. I just let him be in control, let him guide me, not really rushing. He laid me down on his bed, still kissing me, he started taking off his clothes as he was caressing my body. Exposing his penis—wow! How huge and long he was. We attempted to have sex. It was hurting bad, but I wanted him. After a while I couldn't take the pain any longer, but just when I was about to tell him to stop, he stopped on his own. I was in so much pain and only the head of his penis was partway in.

He got up, and went to the bathroom to clean up. He walked back into the bedroom, asked me if I was on my period. I told him no, but he said there was blood on him. I said I didn't think I was on my period. He looked as if he was mad that I hadn't told him I was on my period. I tried explaining that I shouldn't have been on my period, and stood up to put my clothes on to leave when blood started running down my legs. I couldn't believe that I was bleeding. I was so embarrassed,

I wouldn't intentionally have tried to have sex with him if I'd known I was bleeding or on starting my period.

He didn't say anything else that made me think he was mad. I left, went home and cleaned up. I was bleeding like I had just started my period, but I didn't understand. I hadn't had any signs. After I cleaned myself up, I put on a pad and headed for the park to watch the fireworks. I got to the corner when a car pulled up beside me; it was Chicken. He said that it wasn't me who was bleeding, but the blood had come from him. He explained that in trying to have sex with me, a blood vessel had ruptured that caused him to bleed. I didn't know that could happen.

I walked back to my house and changed the pad I had on before I went to the park. It was clean. I left my house, walked to the park feeling relief from the embarrassment I'd felt after being with Chicken. When I got home after the fireworks, I checked to make sure I still wasn't bleeding. I didn't try to have sex with anyone else for a long time.

It was my thirteenth birthday. I felt like I was a little older even though it had only been a month since I'd tried to have sex with Chicken. We'd continued to be friends even though our first encounter hadn't gone right. I wanted to see if we could try it again. I knew he was home because I'd seen him in front of his house. That night I waited until I knew my mother and Lena were high and my brother and sister were asleep. I went down the basement and climbed out the window; that would be my way back in. Hoping that he hadn't left, because he didn't know I was coming over, I walked through the alley in the dark so no one would see me.

I went to the back door like I did the first time. I heard music playing inside the house and knocked on the door. When he let me in, I saw he had company, all men. I should have left, but I didn't because I knew everyone there. I had just enough time to tell everyone hi before Chicken grabbed my hand and took me into his bedroom; it was like he knew why I was there. He didn't completely undress me, just took off my shorts. I'd hope we were able to have sex this time. I don't know why I wanted to have sex with him so badly. He was a grown man, and I was this thirteen- year-old girl pretending to be older and I wasn't sexually experienced.

When he tried to penetrate, it was the same—lots of pain as he thrust. Then he stopped. I guess he didn't want to risk bleeding again, either. He put his pants back on and left the room. I stayed on the bed for a minute, displeased with myself because I was pretending to be older and sexually experience.

I had blocked my rape out of my head and wanted to consider this experience with Chicken to be my first sexual experience, because I liked him a whole lot. I sat up to put my shorts back on. As I stood up to fasten them, Larry, one of Chicken's friends came in. He was sloppy drunk. He walked over to me and started touching me, telling me to take my shorts back off. I didn't think he was serious, so I pulled away from him telling him to stop.

"I'm not taking my shorts back off. Don't touch me," I said.

I wasn't scared at the time because I thought that since he knew me, he would stop. I was wrong. I turned to walk away from him. My back was toward him, not seeing what he was doing; the next thing I felt was a blow to the side of my face.

"Take off your shorts," he said again in a drunken voice. When I didn't do what he said, he hit me in my face again, threw me on the bed and jumped on top of me. That's when I knew he was serious. I started crying. That didn't stop him. This was like déjà vu. The incident was almost the same as when Pookie raped me. Both times my face was the target to get me down, and he continued to beat me in my face to get me to do what he said. I could feel him unfastening his pants. He forced himself inside of me. My mind blocked out the pain and concentrated on the pain to my face.

While he continued to hit and rape me (ramming his penis inside of me) I screamed. The more I screamed, the harder he hit me. My screams went unheard because the music in the next room was too loud. When the music stopped somebody finally heard me screaming. Chicken busted in the door and ran over to us and tried to pull Larry off me. But Chicken wasn't able to get him off me. Even though the man was drunk, he was strong. While Chicken tried to get him off, he continued raping me. The more Chicken pulled on him the deeper Larry went inside of me. Chicken even tried hitting him; this man wasn't stopping. Chicken ran out of the room, and then ran back in with a bucket. He poured cold water over us and Larry jumped off me. Chicken pushed him out the room and left behind him.

I didn't know what happened when they left the room. I got up to put my shorts back on, leaning against the wall by the bedroom door. I was crying while I tried to pull myself together. It was difficult because of the excruciating pain I was in. Then the door opened and another one of Chicken's friends walked in. He stood in front of me, started touching me all over my body.

"It's my turn," he said. It was as if they all were going to take turns with me. I couldn't believe what I was hearing, what was happening. I just started crying harder. I started begging him.

"Please don't do this." I said, repeatedly. "I know you. Why are you doing this?"

He stopped touching my body and told me to look at him and I did.

"You better not tell anybody or I will kill you and your family," he said.

I believed him because he said he belonged to a gang in our hood. I hadn't seen any gang, but I believed him.

"OK. Just let me go," I said.

I left out the back door still in a lot of pain. I did not receive any help from Chicken because he'd disappeared. I stood outside, leaning against the house, trying to collect myself and looking around to make sure no one was outside. I could not believe that this had happened to me again, both rapes happened in the summer: 1977 when I was twelve and 1978 when I was thirteen. Both assaults were by someone I knew. What made this even more unbelievable is that both attackers had girlfriends. I didn't know Larry's girlfriend personally, but I would see her often at my neighbor's house, two houses from mine. She was friends with some girls I knew.

Concerned for the safety of me and family, I was not going to tell anybody, so Larry was going to get away with this crime. While outside trying to get myself together, I could not stop crying. It was very difficult because of the horrific amount of pain I was in. I wiped my face and walked back through the alley to the side of my house to climb back through the basement window. I pushed on it, and found it was locked.

I said, "Oh my God! Not this. Who locked the window?"

I knew whoever locked it knew I wasn't in the house and that I was in big trouble. I had forgotten that Lena didn't get as high as Mama did. I walked to the back door, got my nerves up, and knocked on the door. My heart was beating fast because I didn't know who was going to be on the other side of that door when it opened. When the door opened, to my surprise, it was Lena, and Mama was standing off to the side, still high, but not as high as she usually was. I wasn't even in the house yet when they started questioning me.

"Where have you been?"

"At a friend's house," I said.

I didn't want to tell them what happened. I was scared that Larry and his gang would kill us. Lena asked me the same question again, and I gave the same answer. We were standing in the kitchen between the back door and basement door.

"Were you out fucking?" Lena asked me out of nowhere.

"No," I said. But she didn't believe me. Lena told me to go in my room and take off my shorts. I looked at my mother for help, but she didn't do anything.

"Go take off those shorts," Lena said again.

I went in my room and took them off. I was feeling something indescribable. It was like my body and mind were being violated again. After I took them off, Lena made me lie on my bed, and she opened my legs.

"Oh my God!" they both yelled out.

I don't know what they saw, but it had to be evidence that I'd had sex. My mother gave Lena a belt, and she started beating me. My mother was standing there, letting my cousin beat me. I took the beating to protect my family. When it was over, I went to bed angry and holding on to a harsh reality: my family and a rapist had physically and mentally violated me. No one knew what had been happening to me; everything about me was kept a secret. Mama and Lena put me on punishment and I couldn't go outside.

I didn't see or hear from Chicken again. It was strange to me that he didn't even care enough to see if I was OK. Something was telling me that he was involved in gang activity because I didn't see him for a while. I felt like my life wasn't the same anymore and there was nothing about me to care about. I became something I didn't want to be. I was emotionally and physically destroyed inside and out, and I slowly started destroying and abusing myself, behaving badly. I didn't care. I started putting myself in dangerous situations after my punishment was over, and I healed physically from the rape.

I continued flirting with older guys in the neighborhood that I found attractive. I wouldn't talk or let anybody touch me unless I was attracted to him. The flirting turned to sex. None of the men I picked knew how old I was. The first guy I was with since my rape was a white guy named John. He worked at the furniture store four blocks from my street. I would flirt with him after I would come from the five-and-dime store that was next door to the furniture store. He stopped me and told me that we needed to get together and stop all the flirting and get down with some action. I agreed and he told me to come back up to the furniture store after it closed. I waited until my mother was high and Lena went back home (she only came around when Mama had some money to get high). I wasn't worried about getting into trouble.

I went to his job after it closed. A friend of his and a woman were with him, and we left. I didn't really know where we were going, but we ended up at a hotel close to downtown.

When we had sex, it was not painful. We continued to have sex through the night and fell asleep and overslept. When we woke up, it was morning; I was kind of scared because I had never stayed out without my mother knowing where I was. We hurried up and got our clothes on and left out the room only to find out that his friend left us. We had to catch a cab back to the neighborhood so he would not be late for work. I walked home. I just knew that I was going to be in trouble.

I told my mother a lie; that I'd spent the night at a friend's house. I didn't get into trouble. Later that day, I went to his job and asked him for some money, and he gave it to me. I knew when I needed money I could get it from him even if I hadn't had sex with him. He was not that attractive to me, but I had some sort of attraction toward him. I didn't want to be his girlfriend. I just wanted his money.

Not long after meeting John, I met Tony, a Latino. He was fine. I was very attracted to him. We met while I was walking home

from visiting Kit. Tony was very generous toward me. Whenever we would see each other, he always gave me money. There were times that we didn't have sex and he gave me money. At that time, Tony and John were the only men I had sex with. I was having sex with Tony for a couple of months until he moved.

Now that I was actually sexually active, Mama or Lena never examined me again.

The wrong kind of people...

My first day at a new school was off to a bad start. I was at Foch Middle School, in the seventh grade. "He didn't rape you," a girl yelled out.

I had just walked into the classroom and looked around. I didn't recognize anybody, and then I heard it again.

"He didn't rape you. Why he need to rape you when he has a girlfriend? I'm his girlfriend," she said. It was Pookie's girlfriend.

How ironic was it that I was in the same classroom

with my rapist's girlfriend? She had everyone looking at me as if I was guilty of a crime and that I had falsely accused her boyfriend of rape. I knew it was going to be hell, and I wasn't going to deal with that or have everyone stare at me like I committed the crime. The next day I didn't go to school. I started skipping school again. I would leave the house as if I was going to school. I would walk all the way to school; go in the front door, and out the back door until I got tired of doing that.

You wouldn't believe the places I'd hide out. I would hide out at the park, at friends' houses; in our basement, and in our garage. I even hid in bushes that were behind the gas station right off St. Jean and Jefferson. I was determined that I wasn't going to go to school. But I did stay close to home.

On the days I'd skip school, I started hanging out with the wrong kind of people. The first person I would hang out with was

Johnny Hall, Passion's father, the little girl who lived across the street from me. I had no business hanging with him. I knew he was crazy because of what Passion's mama told me, and I saw it for myself. He didn't harm anybody, but he was very suicidal, and he lived a dangerous lifestyle. He tried to kill himself so many times. He told me how he'd jumped off buildings, did self-mutilation, showing me his injuries and old scars. When driving, he was like a stunt-man, and I was crazy to get in the car with him; scared, but I didn't care. I knew what he did, and I hung out with him anyway.

One night, we were hanging out and he decided to get on the freeway driving 100 miles an hour. I didn't know where we were going, and I didn't ask. I just sat back, held on, and went along for the ride. I had no idea where we were. I saw signs that read 94

East; New Baltimore, then Algonac. I thought we were out of town. When we arrived at our destination, we entered a house full of people. Johnny Hall told me these people were some of his friends. I looked around and start laughing.

I was the only black person there. I wasn't worried about my safety, though. Everybody was nice and very respectful. They where drinking, getting high. I was offered something to drink. I had a beer, which I thought was so nasty.

I told Johnny that I had to get home before curfew. He let his friends know we were leaving and we got back on the freeway, again, going a 100 miles an hour again. That was just a little of his dangerous activity, and my crazy butt was right there, alone with him. But I was never with him when he tried to harm himself. Sometimes when I saw him, he had new injury. I never understood why he was trying to kill himself and why it was over a female. He was not ugly, it shouldn't been that hard to find another woman.

To add to my list of the wrong people to hang out with, Johnny Hall introduced me to a lady named Nancy. She had an older boyfriend named Jim. Jim was goofy. His head would move in this goofy way when he laughed. It was funny and Nancy was crazy just like Johnny. They were a lot alike. She practiced self-mutilation, too and had cuts all over her skin. She always had this weird spaced– out look on her face. Their lives were filled with destruction. I didn't judge them for who they were or what they chose to do to themselves, nor did I let it influence me to do what they did or stop being friends with them.

I did notice that each of my friends had a different lifestyle; some led destructive lives, while others had somewhat normal lives. And my personality interacted according to their lifestyle, but I knew how far to let their lifestyle influence me. I did the drinking, but I would never do drugs. I didn't take what I did at one friend's house and impose it on other friends. Like with Kit, Rosa, and the rest of the family; when I was at their house, all we did was talk, listen to music—pop, rock and roll, easy listening— drink coffee, go to rummage sales, lay my crazy butt in the sun, which only made me darker. I even went to the bingo hall with them. And Nancy and Jim drank. At Lady H's house, we sat and talked and did other things I considered normal.

Lady H treated me like a surrogate daughter, giving me the maternal and some financial support I was looking for; in return, I showed my gratitude. I helped with housework, yard work. Sometimes I helped her prepare food. Other times I would sit and watch. Her own kids barely helped her do anything. Most of the time we'd sit on the porch, discussing things. She gave me advice me, or we'd just gossip about the neighbors and friends. I rarely disrespected anybody. I tried to maintain a respectful personality.

The more I hung around Nancy, parts of her lifestyle began to influence me. I went to her house and I started drinking with her, but not often. I sometimes helped collect bottles with them to buy more beer and liquor. They would buy beer before they would food and this was their everyday ritual. On one occasion, I was sitting at the table, talking with Jim, laughing at him because of his goofy laugh. Even when he walked, it made me laugh. Laughing is something I didn't do that often.

Nancy's brother came into the house and sat on the couch. He was all hyper, jittery and asking for a brown paper bag. He squirted glue into it, held it up to his face and sniffed. Then he passed it on to Nancy then to Jim.

"What are y'all doing?" I asked.

"Sniffing glue," they said.

"Why?"

"To get high," they answered.

"Can I try?" was my next question.

They handed me the bag; I sniffed and I sat there waiting on what I didn't know. I didn't feel anything. I thought I wasn't doing it right so I sniffed again, and still didn't feel anything. The glue dried up, they scraped up some change to buy more. I gave them what I had. When they'd bought more, I tried it one more time, but still I didn't feel anything. I didn't try again. I didn't know what or how I was supposed to feel.

The next day, I went to visit, they were drinking, as usual. I started drinking too; it was early in the day, and I knew I wasn't going to go home intoxicated. Things kind of got out of hand. I was drinking heavily all day without eating. I was trying to be like the pros. I drank until I got sloppy drunk. And before I knew it, it was dark outside. I wasn't ready to go home; wasn't even in the right condition to go home. I wasn't stupid enough to let my mother see me drunk. I would be asking for another beating. I was the only one who was sloppy drunk because I wasn't a drinker, plus I hadn't eaten. I started crying, vomiting, and could barely walk. I appeared not to be in my right frame of mind, but I knew everything that was going on, but no one knew how aware I was.

Nancy's brother Robbie thought he could take advantage of me because I was intoxicated. I wasn't in control of my actions, but I was aware of my surroundings and what was going on. Not really sure how, but I left the house with Nancy's brother, who was leading me toward the park. As I was walking, or should I say as I staggered, I was doing the emotional crying. It was dark and quiet, and I was disturbing the peace, making all sorts of noise, yelling, calling for my mother, saying the craziest things that I barely understood. I was behaving badly. I acted like the same people I despise: drunks, who don't know how to handle their liquor.

In my head I thought this boy must think I was stupid, thinking I was not aware of what was going on. We got to the park, and stopped; he laid me down on the grass. I felt lifeless, without enough strength, like I couldn't make him stop even if I wanted him to. He pulled off my underwear and started having sex with me, with me crying and screaming the whole time. I was acting like I was being forced, but I wasn't. As he continued having sex with me, this guy I know named Mark walked up to us. Had the nerve to ask us what we were doing. He could easily see what we were doing.

Nancy's brother was scared. He got up, pulled up his pants, said we weren't doing anything, and ran, leaving me there alone. The coward. As I tried to fix myself up, Mark stood over me, looking down at me.

"Why in the fuck are you out here making all this noise?" He yelled at me.

"I was in my house, and I could hear you all the way from there! It's late, and you're out here screwing some white boy who obviously doesn't care about you since he just ran off like a punk and left you."

"Don't worry about what I was doing," I said to him. Before I could say anything else, he slapped me.

"Get up and take your butt home," he yelled.

I got up staggering and crying and quietly walking out of the park. I knew I couldn't go home in my condition so I fumbled my way back to Nancy's house. Her brother wasn't even there. I got in the door and passed out.

I realize that I put myself in dangerous situations as the result of trying to escape tragic trauma at home and because I was excited to have a lot of friends and didn't have to feel lonely. I had something to do to occupy my mind and time that kept me from being at home, watching my mother getting high every day or being abused in between. My sister stayed at home, and Mama just sat on the couch all the time "incoherent". Amy was a homebody, always wanted to stay at home, learning how to cook, and handle the house and business affairs.

I was the outdoors, adventuress type, acting wild, spiraling out of control, and being rebellious. I was trying to spend less time at home, away from the physical and verbal abuse. Eventually I convince Amy to get out the house, taken her with me to visit my friend Kit and Eden, secluded her from the friends who were bad influences, though. She soon found her own set of friends, and occasionally got out of the house to visit them. As for me, I was running around trying to divide my time between friends.

I had missed a few days of going by Nancy's house, when I started back, nothing had change. The same people were there drinking, which was no surprise. I stayed all day. I didn't go home to eat or check in or to check on my sister to see if she needed my help watching Mama. I hadn't even let anybody know where I was. Usually when I was away from home, I'd walk back home to see what was going on or see if I was needed for anything. If I was needed, I would do what I had to do, and if no one needed me for anything else when finished, I would go back to wherever I was. But not this particular day.

I got to drinking, nothing like the last time, but just enough to get drunk. I was having too much fun and I let my curfew pass. I was supposed to be home before it got dark, and got scared, not knowing how badly I would be beaten. I didn't go home that night. The next day, I was still frightened and worried and still didn't go home. I had not eaten or taken a bath. I washed up but had to dress in same clothes I'd been wearing for two days. The thought of me being beaten was more on my mind.

By the third day, I'd barely eaten. We scraped up beer bottles to get something to eat that day. I was sad that I endured all that because I was scared to go home. I took my chances going outside or to the store with them to cash in bottles to get something to eat or something to drink for that day. I even sat on the porch; I wasn't hiding. I knew Mama wasn't coming to look for me because she never took interest in knowing who my friends were or where I was.

I was sitting on Nancy's front porch. Her next-door neighbors, a bunch of kids were outside playing. What drew my attention to them was the cussing; they were kids under my age. I walked over to the fence and asked if their mother knew they cussed like that. They said yeah, they cussed in front of her all the time. I asked where their mother was and they said she was sitting on the couch. They even did it when she came and sat on the porch. I said to them, if I cuss in front of my mother, I would have my mouth busted in. They laughed, and then we introduced ourselves. I walked back into Nancy's house amazed at how they got away with all that cussing in front of their mother and how young they were. They were being disrespectful and if I behaved like that, I would have gotten beatings.

The fourth day was the end of my freedom. I had walked to the corner just a few steps away from the house to go to the store when a man who knew Lena approached me as I stood outside the store. He knew who I was because everyone knew me. He grabbed me and would not let go. I was trying my best to get him to let me go by prying his hands off my arm all while I was saying, "Let me go."

He was holding onto me tight. Man, was I struggling with him. Out of breath, he told a guy who was with him to go to my house and get my mama. He told me that my mother had been looking for me. I wasn't trying to hear that, I was trying to get loose. I was crying and begging him to let me go, looking in the direction of my house, hoping not to see my mother coming. That's when Mama and Lena turned the corner walking toward us. He didn't let me go until they walked up on us. I wanted to call that man all kinds of cuss words. I normally don't disrespect older people like that other than when Jessie's grandmother tried to attack me.

My mama didn't say anything because she was under the influence. Lena was being her mouthpiece, asking where I'd been. I didn't answer, and that man who caught me didn't know where had been. He let me go, and he and his friend walked off. Lena told me to come on, and we walked home. I was scared because I knew when I got to the house it was over for me; I was going to be beaten. We were across the street from the Fifth Precinct police station.

"Come on. We have to go tell the police we found you so they can take you off the runaway list," Lena said.

I said to myself, I didn't runaway I was just scared to go home. When we went inside, the officer at the front desk asked, "May I help you?" Lena told him who I was and that they'd found me. She told him they could take me off the runaway list.

"Let's go," Lena said, and she grabbed my arm.

A voice in my head told me not go home with them; that I should tell someone what had been going on. I pulled away from her and I told the officer that I didn't want to go home that she was going to beat me. Lena grabbed me trying to pull me out the station and I just snapped. I started fighting with her at the same time screaming for the police officers to help me.

"I can't go home with them," I yelled. The policemen were standing there, watching her hit me.

I said, "Please don't make me go with them. All she's going to do is beat me, please. I want to live with somebody else."

As Lena was pulling me, I fell to the floor so she couldn't pull me out the door. Then she sat on top of me hitting me.

"Oh no, get your fat ass off of me!" I yelled at her. I became angrier. I started hitting her and kicking, trying to get her off me when I felt my mother hit me, telling me to stop in this sluggish voice. I continued kicking, squirming, trying to get Lena off me when, by mistake, I kicked my mother in the stomach. She looked up at the policeman and told him to take me, that I'd kicked her and I couldn't go back home with them. I wasn't trying to kick her; I just wanted my cousin to get off me.

"That's enough," one of the officers said.

By then I had gotten Lena off me.

"Take her," my mother said.

"Yes, take me. I'm not about to live with you anymore," I said.

Mama and Lena left and I was taken to the back and placed in a holding cell. When I'd told them not to let me go home, I didn't think I would be treated like I was a criminal. I had to sit on this bed that was made out of cement, and they kept me in there for what seemed like forever. I just wanted them to find me someplace else to stay: a foster home, maybe.

I wondered why they were taking so long. A different officer finally came and got me. The shift had changed. I was taken out the back door and put in the back of a squad car, not knowing where I was going. It was getting dark. I was in that cell almost the whole day. We pulled up to this building. I thought that I was being taken to another family home, but instead the sign read Juvenile Detention. I didn't really know anything about that place except that was where they took kids who have been in trouble. I knew I hadn't committed any crime. I thought it was going to be a good place to be; that anything was better than being at home. I knew I was wrong the second I stepped in the door.

The atmosphere wasn't pleasant. I was being treated like

a criminal. I couldn't believe that I was being treated this way when all I was guilty of, was not wanting to live at my mother's house. I was made to strip, and my body was sprayed with some kind of chemical. Almost immediately, I had an infection that produced a bad smell. I didn't ask to go see a doctor because I didn't know what it was at that time. But I knew after I was sprayed. I was told to put on a uniform and was taken to a little room or cell that was smaller than the holding cell at the police station. This was so confusing to me. I couldn't understand why they would put me in a place like that. I was surrounded by criminals and treated like a criminal.

Then I was made to sit and watch television with the other girls in the lobby. The intimidation started right away. They started teasing me and wanting to fight me for no apparent reason. It got worse when we had to go to school. Yes, I was made to go to school. It was on the third floor with the boys. That was the only time that the girls and boys were together. Just like being at any other school I went to, I was the outcast and had to distance myself from the rest of the kids.

I couldn't understand what it was about me that made people not like me. Why was I the one who was picked on and what made girls want to fight me? I had to watch my back. Being there was no different than being at home. I was being treated the same, except no one had touched me sexually. I was talked to in a rude way, so I was afraid to ask for anything. When class was over, which wasn't that long, we had to eat and had to go to bed at 8:00 p.m. That was hard to do because it was still daylight, and I wasn't sleepy. After lying there, thinking of all the things I was enduring, I suddenly panicked because I was locked in a room. It was small, and it made me feel like I was in a dog cage.

The next day, they woke us up earlier to get in the shower so we could get ready for school. I had to take a shower with one of the girls and I didn't want to because I still smelled bad from the infection I had. I tried to be the last one in their two-by-two system. I was so embarrassed. I washed and washed, and that smell wouldn't go away. And of course, the teasing started. We were on the elevator going to school. I could hear them making fun of me, saying someone stinks, looking in my direction. I didn't say anything. I just lowered my head, not trying to make eye contact.

After class I headed back to our floor when to my surprise, my mother and cousin had come to visit me. I didn't think I would say this, but at that moment I was happy to see them. My mother brought me some hygiene products. I didn't care about that stuff. I wanted to get out of that place and go home. I hated it, but I begged my mother to take me home. I told her that I would be good even though I wasn't bad. I just was saying anything for her to agree to get me out of there. She left and came right back, and told me I was going home. Oh my God! I was so happy. I hurried and got dressed. All Mama had to do was go downstairs and sign me out, and I was free to go. Unlike the other kids, I was there voluntarily, even though I really hadn't volunteered to be there. I was free. Those two days of hell seemed like a year to me. The experience of being locked up and treated like a criminal only added more trauma to my already-troubled life.

When I walked out that door, I took a deep breath to take in the fresh air. We got downtown to catch the next bus. My mother took me into Kresge, Woodward, and brought us something to eat. We sat and ate; she brought me some cream for my infection. I told her I got it when they sprayed me with that chemical. We left the store and walked to the bus stop and headed home.

I kept my promise for a while, staying close to home, only hanging out with friends on my block. I was still being abused at home, so I did anything to stay away because that was the only time I didn't have to endure any abuse. Can you imagine being beaten over the head with a broom, being hit with an electric cord, having welts across your body? Knowing I was the only one getting beaten was why I tried to stay away from home. I gradually started visiting my other friends who lived in a different block. I felt safe at my friends' homes because I didn't have to worry about being beaten for no apparent reason. I wasn't gone all day like before. When I would come back onto my block I wouldn't go in my house. I just visited people I knew, going from house to.

At one point, my godmother sent my god sister to get me for the week. When I was with them, I always had something to do. They would do things to keep my mind off the things that had been happening to me. My godmother belonged to a lodge for women, almost like the men's lodge, the Masons.. They had a hall where different events were held. Because this was my week to visit and was the same week of a cabaret, I was allowed to go with them. My godmother made sure I knew the rules and I followed them. I had fun; mostly dancing and talking to the people I knew that were family members. When my godmother saw that I behaved well, she took me with her all the time. I was excited. I was only thirteen and had gone to my first cabaret.

I met a boy who was the son of my godmother's best friend. His name was Ronnie. He was pursuing me. I kind of liked him. He came to visit me at my godmother's house. We sat in his car talking until it was dark. He leaned over and started kissing me. At that moment, I felt excitement. We kissed so long that when we came up for air, all the windows were fogged up. And when he left, I couldn't stop thinking about him.

I loved my godmother. To me, she was my mother; she rescued me when she could. I hated when I had to go back home. But when I was gone, I worried about my sister, wondering what was happening to her. I was concerned about her safety even though she wasn't being abused like I was. Being at my godmother's house caused me to miss my daddy when he came to visit. We didn't get to see him that much, so I tried to be home when he came. Whenever he visited he always gave me money. If I missed him, he would leave it with my sister.

Shirley came to visit. I just happened to be home when she came with surprises: she had two more kids. I was happy to see her, and when she left, she kept in touch with us. I didn't see her that much because I was gone so often. Amy would baby-sit for her.

Ronnie came to visit me. He took me to the park; we continued where we left off: kissing. He tried to take it further. For some reason, I couldn't bring myself to have sex with him. I told him the next time he visited, I would. I didn't see him until that weekend because he worked. He tried to hold me to my word. He wanted me to ride with him. I didn't know where we were going, and he didn't tell me. We drove to an area that I'd never seen before, a house at the corner of Seymour and Queen; it was his house.

Inside, we went upstairs to his room, and immediately started kissing, taking off all our clothes. I didn't feel any excitement toward him. I pulled away from him, and started getting dressed, and told him to take me home. I couldn't understand what was wrong. I liked him, but just couldn't have sex with him. He was mad as he was getting dressed. He took me home, and I didn't see him for a while.

I slowly found my way to Nancy's only to find out she'd moved. I found out she'd moved just three blocks from my street. Their lifestyle was still the same even after the state had taken her baby away due to neglect. I had changed. I didn't have that desire to do what they were doing anymore, just to fit in. I had stopped drinking and trying to be like them, which I only did when I was around them occasionally. I just sat and watched them. Jim's son, Steven came to visit. I found myself attracted to him. He kind of flirted back with me, and he became my reason to go over there more. I wanted to see if I could persuade him to be my boyfriend. I did, and he became my first boyfriend or should I say my sexual partner, but it only lasted a week.

I hadn't had sex in a long time; I only wanted to have sex when I wanted to. My sexual experience with Steven was different, something that I had never experienced before. It wasn't necessarily the sex act itself that made it different, it was what happened after it was over and what I made him do to me afterward that was different. I stayed the night with him; my mother thought I was at my other friend's house so I didn't have to worry about getting into trouble.

Steven and I were lying on the floor in the living room

having sex. When it was over, he turned his back to me and was going to sleep, and for some reason that made me furious. In my mind, it was like he was satisfied and got what he wanted and forgot about me. I felt like he needed to give me some kind of attention. And I like attention. I felt used and alone even though he was right next to me. I wanted some kind of affection. When he didn't, I got really mad, and I started pulling his hair, hitting him with anything I could think of just so he wouldn't go to sleep. I was provoking him to hit me. Why, I can't explain. I wanted him to hit me—that should have been the last thing I wanted anybody to do to me.

When he did hit me, I got scared and excited, and I achieved what I was striving for. He turned to lie back down, and I hit him again. By then he was so mad that he started hitting me more.

"What's wrong with you?" he yelled once.

"I don't know" I said, and started crying.

He started kissing me, telling me he was sorry. I continued crying when he got on top of me, and we started having sex again He started kissing me, telling me he was sorry. I continued crying when he got on top of me, and we started having sex again. The way he was thrusting his penis inside me because he was angry and the harder he was doing it was exciting. I felt like it was the best sex I'd had; it was amazing. When we were done, I felt I was satisfied enough, not completely, but just enough to make me tired and go to sleep.

The next morning, I went home. When I went back over there, he was gone. He'd gone back home. A family emergency came up. I was upset and disappointed and felt abandoned. I really liked him. He was the type of man I was seeking; he was a domineering man, one that could control me to be forceful, aggressive, wouldn't take nothing from me; who could make me scared of him just so I could have better sex and to feel like I was loved.

Since Steven, I didn't have sexual contact with any other guy for months.

I learned over the years why I seek out men like Steven in order to have better sex and feel some sort of satisfaction in a sexual relationship—because I was raped at a young age, and that was all I knew. That's how I felt I was cared about. It was hard to find anyone that fit that description. Basically now when I have sex, it is just to please the man.

Chapter Five
Path of Destruction

I went to dramatic measures to destroy myself because of all the physical and mental abuse. Deep down in my soul I was suffering.

Lena was living with us again, separated from Jo-Jo. I wasn't too thrilled about the situation because of the violent history between us. I also didn't understand why she continually whipped her older son with an electric extension cord for inexcusable reasons; she beat him for wetting the bed instead of seeking medical treatment. It was obvious he had a problem, and I thought it was hypocritical for her to whip him when she had the same problem growing up, even through her marriage. The abuse she inflicted upon him was very cruel. She'd taken an electric extension cord, wrapped it around his neck three times, and started choking him all because his little brother said he hit him. And he had no one to rescue him. She was not concerned with who she hurt.

My Little cousin slept in the room with my brother, and Lena slept in the living room. One night while I was asleep in the dining room on the floor, I was awakened to whispering. I heard a female voice; it was Lena. Then I heard a man whispering. I didn't recognize his voice because he was whispering really low. I lay there quietly listening. He then said something, and I recognized the voice. My heart sank. I was outraged. The man was Chicken. Then they started moaning. I instantly started crying; she was having sex with the man that I was infatuated with. I was so angry, hurting inside, and wanted to hurt them. But I couldn't because we had a secret, a forbidden affair because of our age difference.

Promiscuity with preference....

I was angry, mentally destroyed. I started using and abusing my body. I don't know who I was trying to hurt, but I was only hurting myself at the time. I didn't care anymore. No one cared about me, and mentally and physically, I was damaged. I was not able to be satisfied sexually or mentally because of the rapes. I was promiscuous, having sex with men for fun. The guys I was with were very generous, and I was compensated with money after having sex, but I never asked. I didn't always have sex to get money. I never had sex with a lot of guys, just the ones named in this story, and it was never back-to-back. It could be a week or two or months before I had sex. I really didn't like sex. Like I said, it was only to hurt myself.

I'd met this old man name Joe-bob in my neighborhood, and whenever I needed money, I met him in the alley behind his house or at the corner store. People were spreading rumors that I was having sex with him but I wasn't. He was an old man that liked me and would give me money when I asked.

Joe-bob introduced me to a guy named Williams but everyone called him Bill. He had just separated from his wife. Bill wasn't appealing to the eyes, but I didn't care. All I wanted was his money. He was also giving me money without having sex me, but I planned to reward him with sex. He invited me to his house. Once inside, he took me to the living room sat me on the couch. I wanted to see his bedroom, but he wouldn't let me. I didn't care anyway.

My first sexual encounter with Bill was not that good. He performed oral sex. I don't know why, but it felt nasty; I didn't enjoy it. The only other time oral sex was performed on me was by my mother's boyfriends, JB and Ray. I believe that was the reason why I didn't like oral sex.

Bill was one of three guys I had sex with within a two-month span. Dennis was another; he lived upstairs from us. He also was the brother of one of my mother's friends. With Dennis, it started out with us just flirting, over time it lead to sex. We would give a signal and meet in the basement to have sex.

Our basement was divided, and had two small rooms. We met down there three or four times and no one knew we would.

Tommy Bright was the other man I had sex with. He was a childhood friend who lived next door to me when I was seven. I ran into him once while I was on my way to Nancy's house. He was visiting friends in my neighborhood. We talked for a few minutes, and then he asked me for my address so he could stop by some time.

A day or two later he did. After we talked about what was going on in each others lives, we made plans to be alone. I had him meet me in my garage and we had sex. A week later, we had sex again. That was the last time I saw Tommy Bright. I had sex with Bill on two more occasions.

The following month, March, I was late. I hadn't started my menstrual cycle yet. I was feeling sick, nauseated, and started to wonder if I was pregnant. I kept my suspicion a secret out of fear. I knew for sure the next month. I was really scared, I was fourteen, and I was pregnant. I didn't want to tell my mother because I didn't want her to make me have an abortion.

The first person I told was Williams because he was the last man I'd had sex with, so I assumed he was the father. He told me that he would help me take care of the baby. All I could do was take him at his word. Now that I knew that I was pregnant, I really wasn't going to go to school. I didn't want to take a risk of being injured just in a fight. I would leave the house as usual; make a detour to sneak back into my favorite place to hide, my basement.

When I was in the basement I could hear everything Mama was doing. I would wait and watch her leave to go to the doctor, then I would sneak upstairs, fix something to eat and sit at the window to watch for when she got back home. Sometimes I would almost get caught because she would come from a different direction. I had to run, turn off the TV, and run real fast to the basement. When I skipped school I would have to wait until I got home to eat because I didn't have any money. Now that I was pregnant, I had to eat.

Amy told me that she didn't want to go to school. I hadn't let anyone know about my skipping school. I trusted her, so I let her in on my little secret. In the morning, we left for school, made a quick detour, walked down the alley and through the unlocked window to our basement. We hid in the small room in the back. We listened out for Mama to leave. I was showing her everything I did just in case she wanted to skip again. When Mama left, we went upstairs. I told her I would sneak some food, watch TV, and sit by the window, watching out for Mama. When we saw her coming, we ran back to the basement. And when we knew school was about to let out, we climbed out the window, walked halfway to school, turned around, and walked back home.

My sister and her friends got my hiding place discovered, which I was unaware of until later. Early one morning before I left home to go to a friend's house, Amy told me that she and her friend decided that they didn't want to go to school. She repeated the routine I'd showed her, listening out to hear Mama and Lena leave. We never knew how long they would be gone and had to watch out.

While hiding in the basement, they decided to smoke. When they were finished, instead of throwing the cigarette butt in the drain or sink, my sister threw it out the window. It landed right in front of Mama and Lena. Amy and her friend were caught. From that day on, Mama or Lena would check to see if the basement window was locked before they left, but that didn't stop me.

I came up with another way to get in and hide. They never knew. Before I would leave the house, I would go in the basement, go to the neighbor's side of the basement and unlock their window or unlock their back door and hide on our side. And when I heard Mama or Lena walk into the kitchen to come down the basement to make sure the window was locked, I would run back on the neighbor's side and hide in the back room. I'd make sure I was real quiet, my heart beating real fast, thinking I was going to get caught when they were in the basement a long time.

When I heard them going back up the stairs and out the

door, I waited a minute just to make sure they didn't come back in the house. Then I'd sneak upstairs, get something to eat, and not taking any risks, I went back in the basement to wait until it was time to leave. I laugh now when I think about what I had to do to not be caught. I had to stop when it became hard for me to fit through the window.

It was hot outside, and school was about to let out for summer vacation. I just went and hid out at the park, not eating until I came home from the school I wasn't attending. I was getting bigger and had to change my appearance so I started wearing big clothes to cover up.

Summer arrived, and I didn't want to draw attention to myself. It was hot outside and I was supposed to be wearing summer clothes, but instead I wore a big tee shirt. I knew eventually I would have to tell somebody, and the only person I trusted was Lady H. I went to her house and told her. She asked me what I was going to do. I said I wanted my baby. I was already four months. She asked if I was going to tell my mother. I told her not yet. She asked if I wanted her to tell my mother. I said no, not yet. I knew I had to soon, so I waited until I was five months.

I figured I was safe, that my mother couldn't make me have an abortion at five months. When I was at Lady H's house, she asked me again, if I wanted her to tell my mother. This time, I said yes. I knew I hadn't seen a doctor, and I hadn't been taking care of myself right. As we walked to my house, I saw Mama wasn't as high as she usually was. I was nervous and scared.

Lady H sat down next to mama on the couch in our dinning room. I stood up, nervous as she started to tell her. At first, my mother didn't say anything, and didn't have any reaction to the

news. She waited until Lady H left. My mother walked up to me, didn't say anything, and just went wild. Without any regard to my condition, she started beating me. I looked at her in disbelief. She pushed me down on the bed and just started hitting and punching me all my face, and chest. Then she sat on my stomach and continued to beat me. She started calling me every cuss word she could think of. I felt she was trying to kill my baby; she was hitting me like she was a wild animal just like all the other times.

I felt I had to defend myself. I snapped, and I started fighting back. My mother was trying to kill me or my baby, and I had to stop her. I somehow freed myself. I got up and ran out the house, she ran right behind me, telling me to come back here. I was running and screaming, crying. Our neighbor, Diana came running out her door to see what was going on. When I saw her, I was started running toward her for safety. Before I got to the steps, I felt pain in my back. My mother had thrown a brick at me, and it hit me in middle of my back. With Diana's help, I got up the stairs to her porch, and into her house, with Mama trying to get in. Diana stopped her and told her she wasn't getting in to hit me, and I wasn't coming out until she calmed down. Mama left off her porch, cussing, saying what she going to do to me when I come out.

Diana walked over to me. I was crying, in pain, and disbelief that Mama did this to me while I was pregnant. Diana asked me what was going on. I told her that Mama just found out I was pregnant and that she just started beating me. Diana made me stay at her house overnight. We talked, I cried, I let loose some of my feelings to her. I let her know some of the things that were going on at my house.

In the morning, she called my mother down to her house so we could all talk. The question was asked: what did I want to do with the baby. Abortion was not option; I was five months. Diana suggested options. She asked me to give her the baby. I knew that the baby would have been taken care of, but I wanted my baby. Diana told my mother there was nothing she could do about it now; that the baby will be here whether she liked it or not.

Mama didn't say too much. She asked me who the father was. I told her it was Williams, a man who lived on the next street. She said that she wanted to meet him. Diana wanted to talk to Mama alone to make sure I was going to be safe after I left her house. When they came back to the living room and everything was OK, we left and walked home. Later that day, when I knew Bill was home from work, I walked around to his house. I told him my mother wanted to see him. We had sex before I left his house to go back home. He gave me some money and told me that he would be around when he got dressed.

When I saw him walking toward my house, Mama and I met him halfway. When Bill walked up to us, I introduced him to my mother. She had an attitude toward him and started questioning him about what he was going to do about helping me with the baby. He told her he was going to help take care of me and the baby. After a few more questions, he left, and we walked back to the house. That was the last I saw of him.

I found out from his friends that after we'd had our discussion on the street, his wife somehow found out I was pregnant. She came and got her husband. They reconciled and moved out of town, and I have not seen that man again. I don't know if he is alive or dead or if he knew anything about my baby. People asked me if I was mad or angry because he left me to take care of a baby by myself, I told them no. People have been walking in and out of my life all the time. With all the abuse and what I have endured, I developed an 'I-don't-a-fuck' attitude.

My feelings toward men was the same. Basically, all I wanted from a man was sex and money, and sex wasn't really satisfying me. I really didn't like having sex. I just wanted to have a man around to fill the void of loneliness and to get some attention. What I was worried about was that I had to depend on my mother to help me take care of my baby.

When she started accepting the idea that I was pregnant, that there was a baby coming, her attitude changed. She got me to a clinic and I started receiving prenatal care. My mother started giving me money to buy things for the baby. I couldn't believe it because all my mother's money was for her pills. Everyone knew about me being pregnant, except Daddy. I knew he would be coming to visit soon. How was I going to break the news to him? Hearing this was going to be devastating to him.

Out of the blue, my daddy came to visit. I saw him getting out the car and walking toward the house. I ran to my room, got a sheet and sat on the couch and covered my body up. It was ninety degrees outside, and I was sitting there on the couch with a sheet covering me. When Daddy came into the house, I was all covered up.

I didn't get up to give him a kiss and a hug like usual. Amy and my brother did; he looked at me waiting for me to get up. I made up an excuse as to why I wasn't getting up. I told him that I had stomach pain. I just held my head down in shame and just continued to sit. I wasn't acting like I normally did when he come around. I didn't say too much to him either. He knew something was wrong because I was acting strangely. As he was kidding around with my brother and sister, he reached down in his sock, pulled out his wallet, and gave us some money. He then focused his attention on me, trying to figure out why I was sitting down with a sad look and not really responding to him.

Daddy always liked playing with us, trying to do something to make us laugh. He tried to get us to smile, but it was hard because of our living with Mama; it was hard to show any happiness. This time my long face had nothing to do with our living situation. I was scared to let him know I was pregnant. Daddy started tickling me. I wanted to tell him to stop, but I just kind of moved to the side so he could stop, and so he wouldn't feel my stomach.

He tried it again, and I did the same thing again and didn't smile. He saw that nothing he did was making me smile, so he gave up. He looked disappointed, and I was too. I loved my daddy; I knew he was going to be hurt when I told him, I just didn't know how. He said good-bye and that he'd see us later.

After he walked out the door, Lena asked me if I wanted her to tell him. I answered yes. I didn't want to prolong this any longer but I didn't have the courage to tell him. She ran outside and stopped. They were standing there for a minute, and then they started walking back toward the house. She was still talking to him. I braced myself as they came back into the house. I started crying when I saw the look on my daddy's face.

"No need of crying now. What's done is done," he said.

He said he understood why I was acting so strangely. He sat down beside me, and talked to me. He didn't ask the how and why or who questions. He just told me that he wanted me to stay in school and that he would help me. He didn't know that I was still skipping school. Daddy said he wasn't mad, but he was disappointed. He wanted me to do better. What Daddy said to me touched my heart. I didn't want my daddy to be disappointed in me. I didn't tell Daddy how my mother beat me when she found out I was pregnant.

I felt a big sense of relief that Daddy knew. I enrolled in a TAPEC school for pregnant teens two blocks from my street on the east side, but was transferred to their other school on the west side not far from where my daddy lived. The first couple of days, I enjoyed going. I stayed to myself and I sat back and observed my surroundings and saw it wasn't any different from regular school. I tried to stick it out until things started happening between the other students; talking about one another, teasing about looks and all. I'd been through that all my life and I couldn't take it any more.

I made a decision after two pregnant girls were about to fight over a boy and their friends joined in. They were about to fight endangering their baby's life over a boy. I couldn't believe it. I stopped going. I was excited that I was having a baby. I wanted this baby so I could love him or her, and to be loved back.

I started getting attention from friends in the neighborhood. I was eating right. They made sure I had everything I needed to have a healthy baby. I appreciated everything everybody did for me. My friends made me feel special, something that I also was missing. I didn't stay home that much because I didn't know what would happen to me. I didn't want to be beaten, plus I didn't like seeing Mama high like she was all the time. That took affected me mentally.

We were tired of having to stay home to watch her so she wouldn't hurt herself. She would cook, nod out, burn her food, wake back up, and fix her plate. When we'd go check on her, she would be sleeping, her head in her food. When we tried to take her plate, food was on her face. We would try and take it from her, telling her she couldn't eat that, that she'd burned it. She'd snatch it back and get mad and try to hit us. Then we would just leave her alone, go about our business.

I was tired of looking after Mama even though I wasn't home that much. That's why I would go to from one friend's house to another just to stay away from home. I even started going to church. It was just like the church in our neighborhood, a mixture of nationalities. I found myself going for the wrong reasons, not to seek God, but just to get away from home. I had a crush on John, the deacon who also was our church bus driver. I enjoyed being at church. I was learning, but the more I continued to go, the more infatuated I was with Deacon John.

That summer, Lena moved back with Jo-Jo, and was living at his mother's house in the North End. While visiting, the radio was playing, and at first I wasn't paying attention to what I was listening to. I knew I was rocking to it. It had a beat that you can dance to. I asked them what they were listening to, and Jo-Jo said it was Rap. I said I like this; I had been missing my own culture of music because I had been listening to pop music, which I still like. In August, for my fifteenth birthday, I went to my first Rap concert. Lady H's younger daughter, Kyle went with me. We didn't get to see the concert, though because I had to be rushed to the hospital.

The concert was at Cobo Hall downtown. There weren't any seats in the concert so it was standing room only. Everyone stood around, all bunched together. The crowd of people was pushing everybody, including me. I asked a police officer if I could sit down somewhere, but he said no. As I was continuously getting pushed, I started having pains and was taken to the back. I got to see some of the rappers but missed the concert. I was taken in an ambulance to Receiving Hospital for false labor pains. Kyle rode in the ambulance with me.

After a few hours, the pain stopped, and I was released. We had to catch the bus back home at three in the morning. As we were waiting on the bus, this old man was harassing Kyle. She was ignoring him because he was drunk. That angered him, and he threw a bottle at her. In my condition, I couldn't confront him, but I wanted to. The bus finally came and we went home. I was angry because I'd missed my first concert.

I was almost injured again when I went to the grocery store to buy some chicken broth. I found that it helped with my morning sickness and dizziness. As I was walked down the aisle I felt myself fading to black. The next thing I knew I was coming to on the floor and a store employee ran over to me.

"What happened?" he asked. "Did you fall? Did you hurt yourself? You didn't fall on your stomach did you?" He was kind of worried.

"I'm OK," I said, and he helped me up as I brushed myself off. Other people gathered around. The store owner came running to see what was going on, telling someone to get me something to drink. I believe he thought I was going to sue him but that wasn't on my mind.

"I just fainted. I'm OK," I said.

I left after I didn't find what I was looking for.

Two months later, I experienced something that scared me. Kit's brother James, who I liked, had a girlfriend who just had his baby. The baby died a week or two after he was born. That news saddened me. They didn't know what caused the baby's death. I was scared because I thought that would happen to me because I hadn't had prenatal care until I was five months. I told Kit I would go to the funeral. I wanted to show my support.

I'd mentioned to someone that I was going to the funeral, and I was told I shouldn't go while pregnant because grieving causes mental trauma to the unborn baby or could make me lose my baby. That information scared me even more, but I told Kit I was going anyway. I liked to keep my word. I went anyway and just prayed that my baby would be OK. It was a closed casket family hour and funeral. The baby's body was deteriorating because the medical examiner had the body so long, trying to find the cause of his death. The smell was so bad; I couldn't stand close to the casket.

After the funeral, I kind of stayed close to home, craving milk like. I would beg people to buy me milk or give me money to buy milk. Every day I would drink two gallons and a half of milk: white and chocolate. If I didn't get any milk, I would go through withdrawal. I had to have my milk! That was the only craving I had with this baby.

At my doctor's appointment, days after the funeral, I found out the baby was doing fine. I was excited about that since my prenatal care didn't start at the beginning of my pregnancy, and because of what I was told might happen if I went to that funeral. On November 16, 1980 I began having intense pains, but we waited to call 911 until we were sure I was in labor. About an hour later, we made the call and I was transported to the hospital. But not the hospital where I had prenatal care because there was a big fire downtown, so I was taken to St. John Hospital.

I was taken to the labor and delivery room on the fifth floor. I was told that I was in the early stage of labor and I had to wait. I waited alone without any family members to give me the love and moral support that I needed. While lying in bed, waiting for my new arrival, I was in so much pain I was going crazy. I just couldn't lie in the bed. I had to walk around, trying to ease my pain. I took a shower. As the water ran over my stomach, it felt like a massage. The pain was so unbearable; I wanted to pull my hair out. I was crying, telling God to please stop this pain. I was begging God to help me. I was even calling my mother to help me.

Seventeen hours later, I was about to deliver my baby. But before I went to the delivery room, the nurse told me I had to be prepped. I didn't know what that meant. When another nurse came in, I asked her what prepped meant. She said that I had to be shaved and given an enema before I delivered the baby. I didn't know why that had to be done, but I really didn't care. I just wanted the pain to stop. After I was prepped, I was taken to the delivery room and transferred to the delivery table. After a few seconds, I was told to push. As I was pushing, the doctor told me that I had to be cut a little so the baby could come out.

After a few pushes, my baby was born. The doctor told me it was a boy. I had a beautiful son, born November 17, 1980, at 12:02 a.m. He weighed eight pounds and twelve ounces. The nurse asked if I want to hold him, I said yes. I looked at him. It was so amazing. I checked him out; he had all his body parts. He was wrinkled, pale, and had a head full of hair, and he was mine.

Feelings of joy, and happiness filled my heart while I held my baby, looking at him.

I was going to try to be the best mother I could be to him and give him so much love. I was in pain but was happy; I had me a son! They took him from me so that they could clean him up while the other doctor stitched and cleaned me up. I was then taken to the recovery room. I asked the nurse if she could call my mother to tell her that I'd had the baby. After I was taken to my room from the recovery room, I called home and Amy told me that my mama and Lena were on their way to see the baby. She didn't say they were coming to see the baby and me. I pretended that that part didn't affect me, but deep down inside it did.

Before they arrived, I told the nurse I was having visitors. She told me that the baby had to be taken to the nursery. Babies weren't allowed in the rooms with visitors because of health reasons. When they arrived, barely entering my room, the first thing mama asked was where was the baby? I told them he's in the nursery. I gave them directions to the nursery and they were only gone for five or six minutes. They came back to my room saying that the baby wasn't in the nursery. I told them he was, that the nurse had just taken him there. For a minute they had me worried because I knew the nurse just left my room with him. So, in pain, I got myself out of bed and walked to the nursery to show them the baby. I had to walk real slowly because of the stitches. I was holding the bottom of my stomach, thinking that would help ease the pain. I was talking to them the whole time, telling them my baby was in there.

When I got to the window, my baby was the first baby I saw. "There he is, that's my baby," I said.

"He's so white, he need to get a tan to add some color to him, and we have to put some grease on his hair," were the first words out my mother's mouth.

We stood at that window for about ten minutes. I had to go back to the room and lie down. They came back to my room, my mother talking about what she was going to do for him when he gets home. Over the intercom a woman's voice announced that visiting hours were now over. Later that night, I called home and my mother told me they had to walk home from the hospital because Lena claimed she'd lost their bus fare.

"Oh my goodness!" I said, because the hospital was about twenty or more miles away from our house, and it was the middle of November. That was a long walk. Luckily, it wasn't snowing. I believed Lena did something else with the money, but if Mama was high, she wouldn't know.

Two days later we were released from the hospital. Before we left, he was circumcised. The nurse asked me what was I naming him because I hadn't given him a name yet. His name needed to go on his birth certificate. My mother was on the telephone when the nurse asked me about his name. I said Christopher. My mother said no, that his name was Emmanuel. She said that name came from the Bible, and she wanted his name to be similar to his grandfather and uncle. I was mad because I wanted his name to be Christopher after Lady H's son. I'd become obsessive with him while I was pregnant after meeting and talking with him, finding out our past was kind of similar. I felt like he'd shown me compassion and the attention that I was looking for.

I couldn't think of another name because I had Christopher already pick out. Because I was only fifteen, my mother was legally the baby's guardian. She made all the decisions concerning my baby. She made me name him Emmanuel, and I made Christopher his middle name. My son's full name is Emmanuel Christopher Moore. Lady H drove me and Emmanuel home from the hospital. We weren't even through the door yet when my mother took over.

"Give me my baby," she said, and she didn't want anybody to touch him. I mean she was so protective of him. But remember, this was the same woman who beat me and tried to kill us four months ago. She began taking care of him like he was her baby. He received more things from her than we ever did. A lot of visitors came to see him, and my mother had him, barely letting anybody else hold him. And no one came to see me, so there wasn't anything for me to do but lie down and go sleep.

That same week, Dennis came over, using an excuse to see me. He asked me if my mother had seen his sister but secretly asked me to see the baby to see if he was the father. He wanted to be the father so badly. I told him he wasn't. He didn't believe me, and he left.

Two weeks later, Diana wanted the baby to spend the night at her house. I let him since she was his godmother. Early the next morning before anybody had a chance to wake up, Mama made me go get him. I wish I could get you to understand how evil and cruel this woman was. She acted like she couldn't wait until Diana's household woke up.

I walked down the street, knocked on Diana's door, and told her that Mama was making me come get the baby. She understood. She knew how my mother was. When I took him home, my mother undressed him, getting mad when she saw he had a rash all over his body. This woman went crazy. She instantly started blaming Diana for the rash, saying that she used the wrong soap on him or she had him lying next to the dog. She just wanted an excuse for him not to go back to her house.

She made me go ask Diana what she'd used on him and she said she used his baby soap; that the dog was not around the baby. The rash didn't go away. I took him to the doctor and was told he was allergic to the brand of diaper we used. Mama wouldn't allow me to take Emmanuel with me when I went to visit my friends. She said she didn't want him around different people because of germs, and it was too cold for him to be out. She was being overprotective of my son, but he was well taken care of, better then we had been.

Because I was only fifteen, my mama had control over me and my baby, and I did what she said out of fear of being beaten. I blamed myself for not being more responsible at that time. I say this because sometimes I left my baby with her when she was high. I felt as long as my sister was home, he would be OK, and I wouldn't be gone that long.

I did get to take him to church with me. I remember they gave me a gift for Christmas, and I gave it to the baby. On our way home, Deacon John informed everyone on the church bus that he was leaving our church. He was getting married and moving out of town. I was saddened by the news and after he left, I stopped going to church. I was just going to see him, anyway. God was still with me to guide me.

Going to that church was the second time I'd ever had been to a church. I had gotten baptized when I visited my cousin in Columbus, Ohio for summer vacation. I was young, and the purpose of baptism was never explained to me.

One morning, Amy and my brother had left to go to school. I don't remember where Lena was. I was lying on the floor in the dining next to the vent to feel the heat and the baby was in his bassinet. Mama was in her room going back to sleep. I started hearing a male voice. I knew Mama and me were the only people home, and Emmanuel, who was the only male, but he was only one month old. I cut the TV down so I could hear clearly. I heard it again. I got up to look around the house but didn't see anybody, so I laid back down and continued to watch TV. When I heard it again it was coming from Mama's room, and it was getting louder. I jumped up to see what was going on. I peeked in Mama's room and heard her talking in a language that wasn't English and fighting; she was hallucinating. I ran to call 911. When they arrived, she still wasn't talking English and still fighting. She was even fighting the technician. They had to strap her down to take her away. I asked them where they were taking her. They said the new Receiving Hospital's Trauma Center.

I was running around, going crazy because I didn't know what was wrong with her. At first I thought it had something to do with her taking those pills. Amy had gotten out of school early and when she got home I told her what happened. My sister and I caught the bus to the hospital. To tell you the truth, I don't remember who was watching my baby, but I think it was Diana.

When we arrived at the hospital, we were taken to the ICU. As we stepped into the room, all we saw were tubes and needles in Mama's body. We started crying; seeing her like that made us so emotional. The doctor who examined her came and told us that she had pneumonia, and that she had a fifty-fifty chance of surviving. That news was so devastating. We just broke down.

We stood there by her bedside, staring at her, holding her hand. I prayed to God to let her live. I know some people might look at my reaction and say, "How could you care about her after all she'd done to you?" I know how she treated me was wrong, but God gave me a forgiving heart, allowing me to look past everything I had endured from her. She was my mother, and I didn't want her to die.

Then Amy got sick from the smell of all the medicine that was flowing through the room. We had to leave, and caught the bus back home. I called Daddy, and he came over and gave us some support. He encouraged us to be strong; said that she would be all right. He said that she would pull through. Every time my daddy gave us advice or words of encouragement, it gave us hope.

We would catch the bus to the hospital. It was hard for us to see her that way with tubes coming out her nose. We asked the doctor what the tubes were for. He said they were pumping black fluid from her lungs. The smell of the medication was making us feel drowsy. It was so bad that we had to leave before our twenty-minute time limit.

Lena was staying at our house while Mama was in the hospital. We knew how she was, and had to hide anything that was valuable so she wouldn't take our things or our money, like she did when she took our baby doll clothes and gave it to her friend. My brother thought it was a good idea to hide his money in the new pants my daddy had just bought him. That turned out to be the wrong idea.

When he went to sleep and woke up the next morning, his pants and his seven hundred dollars were gone. Man, was he mad. We looked for them all over the house. Lena even helped look. We knew she had something to do with them disappearing. We searched everywhere and did not find the pants or the money. We couldn't prove she did it, but there wasn't anybody else in our house. My brother called our daddy and told him what happened. Daddy came over and replaced what he could and told him not to leave his money where anybody could find it, and then he left. The reason my brother had so much money was because he saved his money.

Two days later, before my sister and I were going to go visit Mama at the hospital, I had to wash some clothes for the baby. I went in the basement, and Lena was standing there with a lady and a man I'd never seen before. They were standing next to the washing machine. The man was holding his arm out with a band wrapped around it, and on top of the washing machine were drugs and needles. Lena tried to make up an excuse to make it seem like I didn't see what I saw. When she told them to hurry up and put it away, it was too late. I already saw what they were doing. She claimed she didn't have money; that was part of our proof right there.

Day by day, Mama was slowly getting better; Daddy was right. On one of our visits, they had taken the tube out her nose and mouth. The first thing she asked was how was her baby and were we feeding him. We assured her he was OK and that he was being fed. Amy handled all Mamas' financial business. She would take Mama's money up to her after cashing her check. We were surprised when Mama gave us some money without being asked, and she gave me money and told me to get her baby some baby food. She told us that her thinking of the baby is what helps her recover. The next day we visited, I stopped at the gift shop and bought Mama a brown fluffy teddy bear. When she was released about a week later, she put the bear in her bed, and she cherished my son and that bear. Twenty-six years later, she still had that bear.

After she was well, she started back to her usual habit. I went back to visiting my friends for short visits. Then there would be times I wouldn't go visit anybody. Over the months, various situations occurred. New neighbors moved in upstairs, a big family with ten or more kids of different ages. They all went to church. And we had no problems with them. Some of the kids did not live with them, but we met them all. We did what neighbors do: visit each others home; borrow this or that.

Everyday Something Else Happened...

Spring was here; we had a surprise visit from our family members from Ohio; my Auntie Emma and my Granny and Lena's brother Perry and his wife Martha. I was always happy to see them especially since we hadn't seen them in years. That first day, I sat around listening to them reminisce about the past and trying to catch up on their lives, like they did in past visits. I didn't go visiting friends that day so that I could spend time with my family.

My relatives were outspoken. They didn't care what they said, even if it hurt your feelings. Lena's brother Perry and his wife Martha thought they were better than us. They criticized everything, from our house, to the furniture, to the roaches and the mice. My mother and Lena didn't let what they said bother them, but it bothered me. I said to myself, why am I sitting here listening to them criticize us? So I left. Mama had the baby. I knew she wasn't going to let me take him. I came back later that evening before it got dark.

Perry complained about something he knew nothing about. He confronted me, asking why I wasn't home with my baby or why he wasn't with me; that I was his mother. That confrontation led to such a big argument between my mother and cousins that they decided to leave. As they were packing, they didn't say anything to us. We said our good-byes to my auntie and grandma, and they left. I was mad that my auntie and Granny had to leave because of Perry and his wife's actions. To have family members treat or talk to us like we were beneath them, it was better for us that they left.

I asked Mama and Lena why they acted like that. I was told that they had a problem with my baby because of his race, because my son was biracial, and they didn't like white people. They were prejudiced because of what they experienced growing up. She told me about the time they fought the police when they tried to beat them. I asked my mother why she didn't tell me that they were prejudiced; I would never have left my son around them. She said she didn't know they were still like that. I was stunned to know they were prejudiced.

I left and went back to visit Kit, leaving my baby with Mama. I really shouldn't have been leaving my son with her because of her drug addiction. But I knew that no matter how high she was, he would never be in any kind of danger. Before I left him with her, I observed how she handled him while she was high. She took good care of him. When it came to him, she was alert to his every movement. She took care of him better than she did us. And I wouldn't be gone for a long time. Anyway, she was never completely alone with him. My sister was always there. If she felt my mother was too high to care for Emmanuel, she would get him until I got back home. I felt the less I was at home, the less abuse I had to endure.

I believe that having to grow up early, at the age of five, I didn't get to experience my childhood. And because of that, I was acting irresponsible when it came to my son and me.

I was always walking through my neighborhood. I met a lot of people, especially men, and almost instantly I knew what their intention was. I met this man named Bill. He was an older black man who worked at the Chrysler plant. Clearly I knew what his intention was because of what he would say. He made a lot of sexual comments toward me. Because of how he approached me I didn't find his advances flattering. It turned me off. I would laugh and walk away, but I developed a friendship with him. When he would go to the store on his lunch break, he would stop by the house to see me, and he would give me money without me asking. I would tell him every time I saw him that I was never going to have sex with him. His friend would laugh and stare at me lustfully. I ignored him, and when he saw that he wasn't getting anywhere, he played it off by asking me if I had any friends he could talk to. I told him no.

Bill was very outspoken, blunt with what he said, always saying how and what he would do to me sexually if he got a chance.

"That's why you will never have sex with me," I would say to him.

That didn't stop him from giving me money, though. I never asked him for the money. He would ask me if I needed anything. If I said yes, he'd reach in his pocket and pull out money for me.

I was walking over Kit's house, not wearing any shoes. I always walked barefoot through the neighborhood. Bill pulled alongside me.

"Where you going and why don't you have on any shoes?" he asked.

"I don't have any," I answered.

He looked at me and said, "I'll be over your house after work." I said, "OK," and he drove off.

I went on to Kit's house and was back home by the time Bill got off work. When he came over, he and his friends, wanted to go in my house. I really didn't want him to come in because Mama was high. He insisted. Once inside, he gave me some money and told me to make sure I went to buy some shoes. I assured him that I would. He sat down and had me stand in front of him, while he held on to my legs. He was asking me, in front of his friend when I was going to let him get some. I laughed.

"Girl, if I get a hold of that, pus-pus, I will fill you full of babies," he said.

"That's why you will never get some of this pus-pus from me," I said.

He laughed. After being there for a while, they left. He visited me a few more times, giving me money. All of a sudden, I stopped seeing him. I really don't know why. The next time I saw him, he said that he was a father, that his wife just had a baby, a son. He was so excited. That was his only baby, and that was the last time I saw Bill.

I kind of missed him because he was blunt with what he said, he made me laugh, and I never had sex with him. I think because of the way he approached me. He was very handsome for his age; he looked like he could have been Billy Dee's father. Their facial features and good hair were the same. I think his bluntness about explicit sexual comment was unattractive to me because I was sexually involved with this other older man who was a city bus driver. He generously gave me money and would let me ride the bus for free. When I didn't really have anything to do during the day I would just ride his bus route with him. That affair lasted less than one year, so maybe it was just Bill and his mouth that stopped me from having sex with him.

My brother graduated from the fifth grade, and our daddy proudly attended his graduation. Daddy's attending my brother's graduation made me remember that he hadn't attended mine. But the thoughts quickly left my mind, because like always, I was happy to see him. After the ceremony, Daddy took us home. Before we got in the car, I snapped a picture of him because I knew he didn't like taking pictures. Once we got in front of our house, I had somebody take a picture of me holding my brother's graduation hat on my baby's head. I was smiling, pretending to be happy when, I knew deep inside my soul, I wasn't happy. I was hurt, but this was my brother's day.

While we were standing outside in front of the house, Daddy came to me, saying that he wanted me to go back to school, and if I did, he would help me with my baby. I wanted my daddy to be proud of me, and I promised him I would.

After Daddy left, I took Emmanuel with me to visit Kit just for a little while. As I was walking to the corner, a group of about five suddenly stopped and a girl around my age approached me, asking me if that was my baby. I said yes. As we stood there talking, I remembered she lived next door to Nancy. She was part of that family. I called them "the cussing family". As we stood there talking, our personalities clicked instantly. Her name was Eden and we found out we had a lot in common, including our birthdays, which were a week apart and her birthday was two days from Kit's. And there were other things we had in common, except abuse. We talked for a while, and time passed by. We had been there for a while, talking. The baby was getting restless.

The next day, I took Eden up on her offer to visit. At her house she introduced me to her whole family, even some of the grandkids, and was more shocked to hear them cuss too. I was so amazed. I asked Eden's mother about the kids cussing in front of her. "Hell, I don't care," she said. " It don't bother me," she laughed.

"If I cussed like that in front of my mother, I wouldn't have any teeth," I said.

Eden said, "Let's go to my room."

As I entered her room, the first thing I saw was Prince pictures and posters on her wall. We were talking and listening to Prince's music. I found they were more like the black people I did get to meet her other two siblings; they didn't seem to be prejudiced. Talking with Eden, I found it in my heart that I could share my secret with her. I didn't want anybody to feel sorry for me; I just wanted somebody that I could talk to. Eden and I bonded so fast that it was hard for me to believe it because of my past with other females. I never opened up to anybody about my life as fast as I had with her. We really hit it off. I was glad I had someone to share my secret with, and we became best friends even though I was Kit's best friend, too. I knew who I could trust with my secrets. We became inseparable.

One particular night, it was hot, and I didn't want to go in the house. I decided to walk to Eden's house to visit. We had just entered the house when we heard screams coming from across the street. We turned and saw that the house was engulfed in flames. Eden's two brothers ran to the house to rescue an elderly woman who lived there alone and was trapped in the house. After Eden's brothers ran across the street into the burning house, they brought the older lady out and carried her into their house, wrapped a white sheet around her, and someone called 911.

Two other brothers ran back to the house, grabbed the water hose trying to put out the fire before the fire trucks arrived. They couldn't because the lady had so much junk inside and outside of her house that the fire spread quickly. Seeing her like that made me so sad, even though I didn't know her. I would just see her when I would visit Eden. She was crying because of the pain, and I was crying with her. Seeing all this was traumatic for me. It made me remember when our house caught fire, and when my mother's hair caught on fire. The EMS arrived and took her to the hospital; part of her flesh and body part was left behind. I've never seen anybody burnt so badly before. We were all saddened when we received a phone call that she didn't survive. We learned that Nancy's brother and another boy who lived in the hood had something to do with that fire. I was told they didn't like her because she was black, and she was a bag lady, a garbage collector, and her house was an eyesore. They weren't charged with the crime because nobody told on them.

I had to divide my time between my two best friends because they didn't like one another. I had just left Kit's house and was on my way to visit Eden when I stopped at the corner store, but never made it inside. I was approached and hemmed up against the wall by this guy name Black Bill. He was just one of a group of dirty, perverted old men that hung out in the neighborhood and drank and preyed on teenage girls for sex in exchange for money. I was polite when I would see them, and I carried on a casual conversation because I knew them. But I didn't like them because they were a bunch of drunken old men who used vulgar language and because of their actions I had a bad opinion of them. And I was not and never have been attracted to guys who drink, especially the ones who can't handle their liquor.

A few of my friends were impressed by the attention they were receiving from that group of old men. I wasn't impressed, nor did I let their money influence me to have sex with any of them. I made my own choices as to who I wanted to have sex with. They hung around him and his friends, secretly engaging in sexual activities in exchange for money. One friend even had a baby with one man who was married.

Bill grabbed my arms. As I tried to get away from him, he pulled out a gun and held it to my head. He started questioning me as to why I didn't want to be with him, accusing me of not liking black men. I looked at him with a crazy look. He asked me again. I didn't respond. He accused me of being prejudiced.

I said, "What are you talking about?"

"You don't like your own race," he said. He implied that I didn't like black men because every time he saw me, I was with somebody white, and I wouldn't give a brother the time of day. As he was holding that gun to my head, thoughts of what he said went threw my head. I had not paid that any attention before, but he was right. I had endured a lot of pain from the black men I knew. They raped me, molested me or tried to molest me. Unintentionally, I'd isolated myself from my own race and unconsciously was drawn to white men and white families because of the violent history I had with my own race. I was not concerned for my safety around families of other races.

Uncertain of what this man might do because of his irrational anger and the gun at my head, and his drunken behavior, I didn't try to escape. I didn't want to be shot. I tried to convince him that I wasn't prejudiced and that I couldn't like him because he was too old for me; that I was only fifteen, knowing that wasn't the truth because I had been with men his age before. I was trying to explain to him in a positive way because I wasn't sure how he would react to hearing that I wasn't attracted to him. He just wasn't my type. He was ugly. He looked like a broke-down pimp and his complexion was too dark.

"I don't believe you," he said. "You ain't fifteen and you gonna be with me," he yelled in my face.

"How you gonna to tell me how old I am and make me be with you?" I said to him.

After I said that, I saw my friend Chase who lived upstairs from me come out the store. I told him to run go get my mother, tell her that Black Bill had a gun on me. I kept trying to convince this man that I was only fifteen and that he was too old for me. He wasn't listening, waving his gun around my face, asking me to just give him a chance. I felt some relief when I saw my cousin and mother running toward me.

"Bill, man, what you doing? Man, that's my little cousin. Let her go, put the gun away," Lena said, as her and Mama came toward us.

For a moment, Bill wasn't listening. As she continued talking to him, she finally convinced him to let me go. There was no confrontation. He went his way, and we went ours. All while this man had that gun on me, I had not heard my mother say a word.

As we walked back home, we talked and joked about the whole ordeal. But my knees were trembling, and my hands were shaking. The best way to calm me down was to joke about the whole thing. I could not believe he went to that extreme measure to get me to like him. After the shock wore off, I sat down and I really thought about what he said. I had black friends, but at that time, there was no black man I was being sexual with. I just wasn't attracted to black men then, and I didn't find anyone in my hood that I was attracted to.

The traumatic incident with Black Bill had me concerned for my safety, so I only went over Kit and Eden's houses occasionally. I visited other friends who lived on my block. My nonjudgmental personality allowed me to be interactive with everybody. There was Jack; he was about three- or four-hundred-pounds. His wife Linda was not as heavy, and they had a little girl. They lived in the front apartment of the four family flat at the corner of Hilliger across the street from Diana. Their neighbors were Eddie and Marianne, who lived in the back apartment. Marianne's parents and siblings lived at the opposite corner, close to Jefferson Street; next door to Miss Ann. Miss Ann was an elderly white lady who was very nosy. She knew everything but barely came out the house. If she saw it, she'd tell it all.

Marianne's family was mentally challenged. Her sister Lisa would have sex or perform oral sex with anybody for a quarter. The brothers always begged for a quarter. Marianne had a baby who was born with a heart defect because all she did every day was drink coffee and smoke while she was pregnant. I went to visit them one day, and there was this fine white young teenager at their house. I found myself attracted to him. He was Eddie's son, Eddie Jr.

It didn't take long before we planned to meet to have sex. Not having any place to go that night, we went and sat on the back porch, and that's where we had sex. Not just that night, the next night too. Then he was gone; he was only there for a couple of days. When I was attracted to someone, I made myself obvious by visiting that person's house or whoever house more than usual.

Two weeks after Eddie Jr. left, I started my cycle. It wasn't normal, very light, and mostly spotting. It just suddenly stopped, so I assumed I was pregnant. I didn't know for sure and I knew I wasn't going to tell anyone what I suspected. I stayed around my house, sitting outside on the porch or sitting with Lady H on her porch. Lady H's daughter, Tonia had a friend named Brice who worked at the deli across Jefferson, next door to the Fifth Police Precinct. He was attracted to me. I didn't have any attraction toward him. I knew instantly he wasn't the type of guy I wanted to be involved with. He was a wimp. I knew I could make him do anything I wanted; I made plans to use him. I used him for food, money, and sex. I became very vindictive, from all that I endured.

I didn't have an emotional attachment toward any man. I just used them for my personal needs whether for sex or money. When I was done with them, I moved on to the next guy. I told Brice to bring me something to eat. When he got off work that night, Lady H and I sat on the porch, waiting for the store to close at 2:00 am. We could watch their every movement, and then the light went off. I laughed when Brice hopped on his bike and pedaled his way toward the house. He gave me what he'd gotten for me; he also had some food for Lady H. After he gave Lady H her food, she went inside the house.

I suggested we go to my house. We sat on my porch, and talked for a while. We did the same thing the next night. Lady H received her food and went in the house, and we went and sat on my porch. I went in my house to check to see if everyone was still asleep. When I saw that they were, I had him sneak in the back door. We had sex and again two days later, and after that sexual encounter, I said that this was going to be my last time because in my mind, I felt no sexual connection with him. Having sex with him made me feel disgusting. Brice was the first black boy I had sex with since the second rape, when Black Bill pointed out that I was prejudiced against my own race.

Some time in that same month, Ronnie came to visit. I had not seen him close to two years; he came to see if I'd changed my mind about being his girlfriend. I rejected his offer again. I was attracted to him but not in the way he wanted. Something inside of me wouldn't let me bring myself to have sex with him. That angered him, and he left.

My son was six months. I wanted him to have his picture taken by a professional photographer. My sister and I took him to Kresge, the five-and-dime store on Jefferson. Other people were ahead of us. While we were waiting in line, he started crying, wanting his bottle. I gave it to him, but it wasn't enough. He started crying again. I'd only brought one bottle for him, thinking we wouldn't be that long. I had to buy him juice because the store didn't sell milk. Immediately after he finished drinking the juice, he started vomiting, and ruined his outfit.

I hadn't brought an extra outfit, nor did I have extra money to buy him a new outfit. I couldn't let him take a picture with his clothes like that. Not knowing what to do, something popped in my head to go to the baby aisle. I picked up a superman outfit, I took off his clothes, put them in his diaper bag and put on the superman outfit. After I did all that, he threw up again. I said I wasn't going to steal another outfit. I saw a pack of bibs, I opened it and put one on him he and he threw up on that. It was his turn. I said forget it and I wiped it off. I tried to fix his hair; he'd lost most of it. His picture was taken, and home we went.

I felt bad, because I hadn't stolen anything since I'd taken the baby clothes for my dolls from the thrift store. But when I saw how easy stealing the clothes for Emmanuel was, I realized I needed some shoes. My thievery continue. I used what money I had, to catch the bus to K-mart. I wore house slippers so that I could switch them for a pair of shoes.

My heart was beating fast. I didn't put the shoes on right away. I walked around to make sure I wasn't being watched, and then I hurried up and put them on when I thought no one was watching me. I walked around the store just to make sure that I wasn't being followed. When I was sure I wasn't, I left the store. But I was so scared I told myself I wasn't doing that again; I couldn't be sure when my luck would run out. What I did wasn't part of my character anymore.

I tried to keep my promise to my daddy. I enrolled in Job Corp, which was a school for teens that had dropped out of regular school. You got paid for going, and you could learn the basics and a trade. It was about seven blocks walking distance from my home. On the morning of my first day of Job Corp, my father came to see me. He brought the baby some shoes and gave me some money for him. Daddy said he just wanted me to stay in school, and he would help me. At the moment, Daddy had such a joyful look on his face just from knowing that I was back in school. My father was proud of me, and I was happy to see a smile on his face. But, that joy turned to disappointment again.

I stayed in school for only a few weeks. Just like all the other schools I attended, I started having problems. Instead of facing them, I gave up. Mentally, I tolerated things in the last fifteen years of my life and I couldn't handle any more. It seemed like wherever I went, girls always wanted to fight me and I didn't know why. I didn't interact with any of the boys; they teased me, saying I wasn't pretty enough for them. I didn't understand why these girls felt that I was a threat.

I didn't interact with others, and was withdrawn, quiet and a loner. I didn't understand what was wrong with me that people wanted to harm me. There was one guy that I secretly had my eye on but he had a girlfriend and I never made it known that I was eying him. I liked him so much that I told myself if I had another baby and it's a boy I would name him, Von, after him. Because I wasn't sure if I was pregnant and I wasn't going to risk being harmed or harming someone, I dropped out school.

My daddy didn't say anything to me about dropping out. I knew he was hurt over it. Having me in school was all he wanted. But I couldn't do it. And I couldn't tell him why.

That following month I start getting sick, vomiting. Then I knew for sure that I was pregnant. Emmanuel was eight months and I was pregnant again. Just like with my first baby, I kept it a secret. I was going to wait until I was further along in my pregnancy. Tony, Lady H's son moved down the street into the basement of an apartment she manages. This gave me more of an advantage to really pursue him. I would sit and watch him come and go and if he had company, I watched his every move.

I gathered information about him, while talking to his mama. I found out he had a girlfriend and he was the father of her baby. I did get upset when I saw them together wishing I was with him. The first day I met him something inside of me told me that he was going to be my husband. I decided I was going to do anything to make that a reality.

I was told that his baby had died shortly after I had seen him and that he found out he wasn't the baby's father. I knew hearing that news devastated him and I wanted to try to comfort him anyway I could. My comfort wasn't a shoulder to cry on; I did it physically and materially. I waited until I saw him leave for work and I sneaked into his apartment to see what I could do for him. I saw his place was a mess, so I cleaned it up. I grew concerned when I saw he didn't have any food. There were a bunch of open jars of baby food and I know no baby had been to his apartment recently.

I told Lady H my concern; that I suspected her son was eating baby food. She didn't seem to be concerned and she didn't question how I knew, nor did she say she would assist him. So I took what little money I had, and bought him whatever I thought he needed. I bought him food and clothes. And I didn't even have those things for myself.

I did what I could to try and convince this man that I would be a good woman for him. I wanted to try and win his heart. I'd already let it be known how I felt about him. One night I saw Tony come home. I waited until I didn't see anyone outside or looking out their window before I sneaked out to his apartment. I was sneaking because of our age difference; he was twenty-six and I was fifteen. Our families wouldn't have approved of it. He let me in and I start kissing him. He didn't resist. I thought that if I performed oral sex on him that would be the start of me winning his heart. I knew that I didn't have any experience in performing oral sex, but I figured I'd try it anyway so I could please him. He stopped me saying I wasn't doing it right. I was disappointed and embarrassed because I didn't know how to do it I got mad and snapped at him and told him show me how. He told me to lie down and he opened my legs and he start licking on me. As I was lying there I started having flash backs seeing JB's face instead of Tony's. It didn't feel good to me so I told him to stop and we just had sex.

Afterward, I left and sneaked back into my house. We were intimate a few more times. I was in love with Tony but we were forbidden lovers because of our age difference. Around our families we just acted like friends. Then we discontinued our secret affair.

I like to secretly test people to see just what they would do for me; to see if they cared about me. I wanted to see if Tony cared about me because nobody else did. Amy and I and our friends were sitting on the front porch and I knew Tony was at his mother's house. I was still on that path of destruction.

I told them that I was going to the store. I headed toward the store but cut through the alley and went into my backyard. I stood at the garage thinking, and decided to set the garage on fire to see if that would get his attention. Before I did I thought about all the things we used to do in this garage. I was hesitant about doing it, but I wanted to see if Tony cared about me. I decide to do it anyway.

I walked inside and piled up whatever I could find onto a chair and I set it on fire. Then I ran to the store. My plan was to walk back home so by the time I got there, the fire should be a blaze, but it wasn't. I had time to sit on the porch when someone said they smelled smoke, then you know how people do; they started looking around to see where the smell was coming from. I went into the house to check. I did that because we all knew that when my Mama was high, she would cook and burn her food.

I came back out and said nothing was burning in the house. Then I walked to the backyard and went into action. I put on my best performance.

"It's back here! Call 911," I yelled. I started screaming and being all dramatic. "It's going to catch my house on fire and my baby is inside! Help us!"

Tony and Lady H ran across the street into the alley. He grabbed hold of me trying to calm me down. I was putting on a good performance, if I had to say so myself. To get the attention of someone and wanting to be loved, I had to resort to doing something dangerous. I stood there watching all our memories go up in flame. I did get some attention from Tony but it only lasted for the time of the fire. When it was out he left along with everyone else.

No one knew that I had started that fire and it was never talked about. I stop pursuing Tony for a while because I was pregnant. It didn't bother me that we didn't go further with our relationship. I was just at the pursuing stage, anyway.

I started showing and I had to tell somebody because I hadn't had prenatal care yet. By that time, I was close to five months along, When the time came, just like when I was pregnant with Emmanuel, I sat on the porch with Lady H and I told her that I was pregnant again.

"What are you going to do?" she asked.

"I'm going to keep my baby," I said.

"You want me to tell your mother, again?" she asked.

"Yeah, but not yet. Let's wait until it's safe, when I know Mama can't make me have an abortion."

So like last time, when I turned five months I asked Lady H to tell my mother. Nervously, we walked to my house, went inside and Lady H told Mama. Then she left. And, the whole scene played out exactly the same way it did when I was pregnant with Emmanuel. Mama walked up and started beating me all over my head and face; sitting on top of me, beating me; trying to kill the baby, just like she did with my first baby "wild animal."

Amy was screaming trying to get her off of me. I had to fight her back to get her off. This time I didn't run, I just went to my room and cried wondering why I was brutally attacked. She had no concern for the safety of my unborn baby or for me. After everything calmed down, Mama took me to the doctor. When I got back from the doctor's office, I walked to Eddie's house to tell him to tell Eddie, Jr. I was pregnant.

Unfortunately I never saw or heard from Eddie Jr. again. I really didn't care. Then Brice came to see me. When he found out I was pregnant, he said he was the baby's father, and that he wanted to be in a relationship with me. He wanted to provide for the baby and me. I told him that he wasn't the father, and that I believed I was already pregnant when we had our sexual encounter. I couldn't convince him otherwise so I let him keep assuming.

My brother and I weren't getting along; he would do things to get on my nerves. I would call him all kinds of bad names. The worse was when I would call him "black this" or "black that." It seemed like he purposely did things just to aggravate me. This one night when I was asleep, something told me to wake up and when I opened my eyes, I saw my brother crawling toward me on his knees. He was almost in my face when he started hissing at me like he was a spider or snake. I screamed and sat up yelling at him telling him to get back. Then he crawled toward my cousin who was lying at the foot of my bed. She folded up newspaper and hit at him telling him to get back. He turned around and went back to his room. After the shock wore off, we lay there laughing. It was kind of funny.

That morning when everyone woke up we told him what he did, but he didn't believe us. We'd found out that earlier that day he and Lady H's younger son, Stan had been outside playing with spiders. That affected his sleep, because he was sleep walking, or should I say sleep "crawling," imitating a spider. I was his first target.

In the last month of my pregnancy, Lena took me places with her, introducing me to her lifestyle, which I'd already known about. I was very observant. I would go anywhere just to get out the house, but I didn't participate in any of her activities. We walked around the corner to her friend, Darlene's apartment across the street from Kit. There were a lot of little kids there, and they were partying around them. As I was sitting there, I was looking around, observing the scenery.

"When are you due?" Darlene asked

"Any day."

"Do you know if you're having a boy or a girl?" she asked.

"I'm having a girl."

I think we were there for twenty minutes or so when I start having pains. I didn't say anything because I didn't want to leave yet. I was having fun, plus I wanted to make sure that the pain continued, and it did. I told Lena that I was in labor and the pain was getting stronger fast. The way the pain was hitting me I didn't think I was going to make it home.

Before I left, Darlene asked, "Would you name your baby Montoya?

"Yes," I said. I didn't have a name picked out yet and I like that name.

"If I had another baby, I was going to pick that name. I want you to have it," she said.

I had to be helped back home and the ambulance was called. I was taken to the St. Joseph Mercy Hospital downtown because that's where my health insurance was accepted. When I saw that hospital, I didn't like it because it looked so old and run down. I was alone, again. I did not receive any family support, but I didn't expect to have any. I was in pain, praying the same thing I did when I was in labor with Emmanuel: God, Lord help me with these pains. I promise I won't have another baby. I was calling out for my mama; for my daddy. I was in labor for twelve hours.

When it was time for me to deliver, I thought that I had to be prepped like I was at St. John's Hospital; had to get shaved and given an enema before giving birth. I was surprised when that didn't happen. I didn't like this hospital. The staff seemed unprofessional. I was taken to the delivery room, transferred to the delivery table, and was told to start pushing. I pushed a few times and my baby girl was born May 20, 1982, at 5:28 pm. She weighed seven pounds and one ounce.

The doctor had to put a few stitches in me like the last time. While I was being cleaned up the nurse asked me if I wanted to hold her. As I held her, I was surprised because she wasn't light like my son was. But I insisted that she was Eddie Jr.'s daughter and that she was biracial. She was just a little darker than my son. I blamed her being dark on me because I had been calling my brother "black this" and "black that." That was why I felt my baby girl was born so dark.

I called home to tell everybody that I had the baby, but they already knew.

"How did y'all know? I asked Lena.

"Jerry (my little cousin) got sick, vomiting and having stomach pains and it stopped all of a sudden. We had a feeling that you had the baby. We were sure of it when you called," Lena said.

We stayed in the hospital a few days and did not receive a single visitor. Before we left I had to sign forms for my baby's birth certificate. Her full name was Montoya Lashanda Renee Moore. When we got home, she didn't receive the welcome home reception like my son had. Everyone acted like, oh well, another baby and that's it.

She didn't get as many gifts as Emmanuel. She barely received anything. Family and friends came to see her. Others just wanted to see if she was biracial. They really couldn't tell because she was darker than my son, but her complexion was still a little light. After everyone left I laid her in her bed and she started crying; crying like she was hurt. I laid her in my bed next to me, and she stopped. She did this every time I laid her in her bed. My mother assumed that I'd been holding her a lot while we were in the hospital. I told her that I didn't hold her that much; if anybody spoiled her it had to have been the nurse.

Lady H tried to help me out. She had a baby swing that she had from her grandson who was born two months earlier. We tried everything to stop Montoya from crying. I put baby food in her bottle; gave her toys that made noise. Lady H gave me a baby bouncer, but nothing seemed to work. This baby would not stop crying unless she was lying next to me. I wasn't getting any sleep, and started feeling stressful. I felt like I was going to shake her and did a little but caught myself.

I needed a break to get away from all that crying, but my mother wouldn't watch her. She told me this baby was a crybaby and I had to take her with me; that she wasn't going to help me with her. I took her to visit my friends and my son stayed home with my mother. I took her to see Eddie Sr. The family didn't say it to my face but I found out they said that she wasn't his granddaughter. I insisted she was because of how my cycle was at that time.

I started staying home because I didn't want to take her anywhere with me, doing all that crying. Day by day Toya (that's what I called her for short) was getting darker, which really made people doubt her race. They said she can't be a biracial baby, but I wasn't backing down. I believed that Eddie Jr. was my baby's father and I didn't care what anybody said. I did get angry and defended her race. I said just because she was dark doesn't mean she can't be biracial, she could just have more of my gene. I wasn't letting anybody tell me otherwise.

Two weeks after giving birth I was still bleeding and having bad pain. I knew that the pain should have stopped by that point. I took all the pain medicine they gave me but nothing seemed to stop the pain. I went to use the bathroom and after I was done, I wiped myself when I pulled something. I wiped again and this time I pulled out something long. I started screaming and I put it on some tissue. It smelled like rotten meat. I took it and showed it to my mother and she didn't know what it was either. I flushed it down the toilet, and called the clinic. I was told to come in right away.

The doctor examined me, and he said that I have to go to the hospital for out patient surgery. I had to have a D&C, because the doctor who delivered my baby hadn't removed all the afterbirth. I believed something happened when he put his arm all the way inside of me. If I had been thinking, we could have sued that doctor or the hospital for endangering my health, but I was scared. I felt better when I got home, but was a little overwhelmed by everything that I had endured.

Toya wasn't crying as much as she used to until she turned five months. She began crying uncontrollably. She was a crybaby like I was and her crying was driving me crazy. Somebody suggested that she might be teething. One of my mama's pill buddies, Vera who often come by to sell her some pills came over. Once Vera came over and my son was sitting in his walker rubbing on her legs. She won the lottery that day. She saw that I was having trouble getting Toya to stop crying.

"What have you tried to stop her from crying?" Vera asked.

"Everything I can think of," I said. "I been using Ora-jel and that didn't work. I been rubbing her gums. Nothing works."

She said she knew an old folk remedy that would guarantee she'd stop crying and it would help with her teething, too.

"Take a sock that she just wore and put a egg inside and hang it over the entrance way of the room she is in the most."

I did that and the next day she stopped crying and she stopped teething. But her teeth stopped growing, too. Her teeth didn't come in until she was eleven months.

The pain...

I was mentally overwhelmed and depressed with all the abuse that was intrusive upon my life. I became unstable and I began to take my anger out on the one person I protected: my sister and she should never have had to endure what I was doing to her. I was her protector; she came running to me when she needed protection. But who was she going to run to when she needed protection from me? But I wasn't thinking about that.

I was overpowered with emotion and anger. I took my frustration out on myself and on my sister. She didn't deserve what I did to her. It was like every time she said something to me that I didn't like or looked at me the wrong way, I would go after her and beat her up. I saw my sister as an enemy and not my sister, whom I loved. She was the one closest to me. When I would hit on her, the thought of killing her was on my mind. When I finished beating my sister, I would get in trouble and my mother would beat me with a broom. She'd beat me all over my body, but my head got the worst of the blows.

I couldn't take it any more. I went in the bathroom and

I took a razor blade. I stood there contemplating if I was going to end my life. I had two babies; who would take care of them? What I was enduring overpowered the thought of them. I took the razor and cut my left wrist. I felt that no one cared about me so why should I live and I did it to get some attention; I needed to know that someone loved me. I had been reaching out for help only to be ignored. I walked out the bathroom bleeding, but I didn't get the attention or the concern I was looking for.

The police came after 911 was called. I was taken to the hospital to the mental ward where I was handcuffed to the bed. All kinds of crazy people were walking around. My wrist was stitched up and I had to stay to talk to a doctor about why I tried to kill myself. While I was waiting for the doctor and still handcuffed to the bed, a crazy man stood at the bathroom door trying to get my attention. When I looked up at him he motioned for me to come in the bathroom with him while he was holding his penis in his hand. I quickly told the male nurse and he made him go back to his bed.

I was mad because I was handcuffed to my bed. I was the only female in the room with a lot of crazy men. They were walking around freely and I felt that anyone of them could have attacked me at any time.

While I was waiting on the psychiatrist, they rushed this guy into the room. They tried to put an IV in his arm, but they didn't find a vein to put it in; every vein they checked was useless because he had shot them all out with his excessive drugs usage. I heard the doctor say to put it in his penis, and I felt squeamish at the thought of having a needle put there. I'd never heard anything like that before.

Finally the doctor came to talk with me. I didn't tell him the real reason why I tried to kill myself. I made up a lie. He asked me if I was I going to do it again, and I told him no. He released me and I went home. Nothing really changed over the next few months.

Someone to Love Me...

I started back pursuing Tony. I was determined to make this man mine, and I was going to make him love me. I didn't care what I had to do. In my heart, I knew that I loved this man, and I didn't know why I was that obsessed over him. But I felt I had to have him. While I was pursuing Tony, Ronnie came to visit me. I was going to try and see if he was still interested in me; to see if we could be in a relationship even though I still felt the same way about him. I was going to try putting how I felt aside just so I could have a boyfriend, since I couldn't get Tony.

Ronnie took me to the park and we started talking. I told him that I wanted to be in a relationship with him.

"But I have to tell you something," I said.

"What?" he asked.

"I have another baby, a little girl." That didn't sit well with him and he started cussing me out.

"Do you think I'm a fool? You been playing games with me ever since we met," he said.

'You think that you can have sex with other guys and not with me? And when I came back around you before you had a baby and now you have another one."

After cussing me out he wouldn't let me explain and he took me home. I didn't see or hear from him again. I moved on to the next one.

I met this guy named Maurice who lived off Woodward. I would catch the bus to see him for sexual encounters. After one of our many sexual encounters I started having bad pain in my vaginal area. When I urinated the pressure was unbearable. I called Maurice and cussed him out, saying he gave me a disease. I didn't know why I was in that much pain. I went to the emergency room but left when they questioned me about my insurance. We had two different kinds of insurance and I didn't know how to answer their questions.

I called my daddy because he had us on his insurance too. He came and took me back to the hospital. I was examined and the doctor told me I had a bladder infection. I called Maurice and told him what was wrong with me and I stopped seeing him. He wanted to continue being with me, but I was heartless toward his feelings.

Lena was living in the North End area down the street from Jo-Jo's mother. Amy and I caught the bus to visit and while visiting I met this guy named Mike. We hit it off pretty well and he asked me if he could visit me some time. I said sure. I'd visit him only at Lena's house, and never had sex with him.

One night I called him and his roommate answered the phone. I asked for Mike but he wasn't home. I said to myself, this guy on the phone sounds good, and we struck up a good conversation. I kept him on the phone because his voice turned me on. I told him that I was getting excited by his voice and it was doing something to me.

"Let's do something about that," he said, and we made plans to meet the next day.

I caught the bus to where they lived, all excited to meet him. His voice had me hot and when I got to the house, this guy opened the door. I recognized the voice but the man that it belonged to was ugly! I should have turned around and left but I didn't. I was being destructive plus I wanted to see if he could do what he bragged about; I wanted to see if he was the one who could satisfy me.

I got undressed and let him do what he said he could do. I closed my eyes so I wouldn't have to look at him. My excitement was gone. I didn't feel a thing. I think I was thinking more about how he looked and it turned me off. When he was done, I got up put, my clothes back on and made up and excuse and left. I said to myself, that's what you get. I had a guy who was nice looking and I stopped talking to him because I heard a voice that sounded good.

The next day Mike came over mad and hurt, asking me how I could do what I did to him.

"I really liked you," he said. I'd wanted someone to say

that to me for a long time but because of what other people did to me I took it out on him. I hurt him because I was hurting. I didn't like a man who was attracted to me, who was pursuing me. I had to be the pursuer. I didn't explain why I had sex with his roommate. Mike cussed me out, but I had no remorse.

"What's done is done," I said to him. He left and I didn't see him again.

I stopped having sex and communication with any other men. I barely went off the block, occasionally spending time with my friends. My attention was on Tony; it was all about him again. I thought because I loved him that I would stop destroying myself and he would fill my emptiness in every way. I was searching to be filled. I was determined to achieve what I set out to do and that was to make Tony my husband.

When I felt something was meant to be I don't give up. Tony saw that I wasn't giving up on pursuing him, and he gave in. My persistence and persuasion worked, we became a couple. I was happy and things between us were so nice. We sat and talked and did family things together. When he got off work he'd be at my house, sitting on the porch with me or watching television. I'd watch him playing the father role to my son.

He brought my son his first power wheel bike and did things for me that no one ever had. We acted like two people who were really in love. Day after day we would sit on the porch and talk. We were discussing our abuse. He was the only man I'd told about some of my abuse and he told me about his. I don't know if he was telling me the truth about one of his abusive incidents, though. It troubled me.

He said he was younger, and had done something wrong. For his punishment, he was placed on top of a stove and his bottom was burnt. I don't know if that happened for sure. I took him at his word. I didn't ask his mother nor did I tell her about his allegation. Every night when he came home from work we would sit on the porch, sometimes in the cold and talk about life and what we wanted. I say in the cold because this was a summer that was hot in the day and cold at night and you had to go in the house earlier or sit outside with a coat on and or wrap a blanket around you. That's what we did because he didn't disrespect my mother and lay up in her house with me.

Our relationship was wonderful and my love for him was growing stronger every day. I desperately wanted to move out and live with Tony, but I expected Mama to say no, but I figured I'd give it a chance anyway. I got the nerve up to ask and she said no. I got mad. I didn't know why she wanted me to continue to live with her when I knew she didn't love or care about me. I figured if we moved she would lose part of her income and she wouldn't be able to afford to buy her pills. She wanted me to stay at home so that she could continue to abuse me and still receive money from ADC.

There was nothing that either of us could do. I had less than a year to go before I was eighteen. We were getting along good and we were getting closer until out of the blue he come to the house and said he had something to tell me. He looked sad.

"We can't be together any more," he said.

"Why? I asked him. "What's wrong?" I thought it was something I did.

He left with no explanation and I just stood there in shock, heart-broken watching the man I love walk out my door, across the street and out my life. I lost it. I started crying and depression came over me. As I laid in bed crying, thinking about why this was happening to me, I got frustrated. Why was I losing someone else I loved again? It seemed like losing people I loved was becoming a pattern.

My sister continue to be the target of my rage. She had said something to me that I felt was disrespectful and because of my rage the anger inside of me was boiling. My mind was scrambled with all kinds of thoughts of my past and of all my abuse and I couldn't stop thinking about it. I was hurting and she was standing their doing nothing. As I was standing there looking at her, the more it felt like she was taunting me and the more the rage was boiling. I let it explode, and I went after my sister like I was a wild beast, hitting her all over her body like she was an animal. Then she got away and ran into the bathroom. I wasn't done with her.

I chased right behind her on her heels as she tried to close and hold the bathroom door. In a rage, I pushed on it as hard as I could. I wasn't going to let her get away. The rage I was feeling was horrible and I wanted to hurt her bad. The thought of killing her was going through my head again. When I got into that bathroom I was beating her so badly that we broke the bathroom sink. It fell on the floor and I didn't care. I was having flash backs of all the beatings I had taken. But something came over me, and instantly I stopped. I started thinking that my sister didn't deserve what I had done to her; she hadn't done anything to me. I was her protector.

Mentally I hadn't been myself for years I didn't know who I was. When my mother came home she saw what I'd done and she took the broom and beat me, always aiming for my head. When she was done, I knew that I didn't want to live. I was tired of the abuse, tired of everything. I felt abandonment my whole life so why should I live?

When my mother wasn't paying attention, I took all her pills out this bag we call her pill bag and went in the bathroom. I looked at myself in the mirror, and saw emptiness; someone that no one loved. I saw someone in that mirror who shouldn't be alive, but I was there being abused. I'd had enough and I poured a handful of those pills into my hand and I took them; all of them.

I walked into the dining room, and sat down.

"I took all your pills," I said to Mama. Amy called 911and I was rushed to the hospital. I was made to drink this nasty liquid that tasted like chalk. Then they pumped my stomach to make me vomit. After they were done they let me lay there. I had to see the psychiatrist, again before I was allowed to leave. When the doctor saw me, he realized that I had tried to commit suicide before.

"Why are you trying to kill yourself?" he asked me.

"I don't know." I kept my secret.

"Do you have kids?"

"Yes."

"You know, trying to kill yourself isn't good for them. You're unstable and if I see you back in this hospital for trying to commit suicide, I will have your babies taken away from you."

I knew he was trying to scare me straight. After he released me I had to take the bus home, unlike the last time when I was sent home in a cab. I barely made it inside the house good when I saw my mother sitting on the couch.

"Did you take all my pills?' she asked.

I answered, "Yes."

"If you going to take my pills you should have taken the over the counter ones." She was more concerned about her pills than me. She laughed about it and I went into my room with my babies.

I thought about what the doctor said to me. I knew how my life had been filled with nothing but trauma and I did not want my babies to ever experience what I was experiencing. If I wasn't alive they would. My babies were all I had and I was all they had and I loved them so much. I thought about what would happen to them if I wasn't around. Their lives would be like mine.

Instead of thinking about suicide I thought of other ways to deal with my problem. But I continued on my path of destruction, abusing myself by having sex because sex was the only way I could hurt myself. I was destroying my life because I was dead inside. I went back to my promiscuous ways, but I never turned to prostitution, though. I would never degrade myself to do what they do for any amount of money and I could never stand on any street corner to sell anything, including my body.

I wouldn't let anybody touch me unless I felt some kind of attraction toward him. In fear of being attacked, I let my intuition or my spirits guide me to take some precaution in deciding who I would have sex with, who I would be acquainted with. And like I said before, money wasn't always involved. I was seeking attention; someone to belong to or just to hear someone say they loved me.

I was also looking to have some sort of mental

stability. I didn't want to be alone, but I knew the only thing I was good for was sex. I used bad judgment regarding where I had sex and with whom. While I was using sex to hurt myself, I had sex with the man that worked at the corner store in the back room on the floor lying on a cardboard box. I would get money from him, but didn't always have sex with him. I even lowered my standards and had sex with the younger brother of my friend who lived upstairs from us. He was barely a teenager, but he made sexual advances toward me and like I said, I didn't care. I was out to hurt myself.

I wasn't in my right frame of mind, so in a whisper, I told him how we were going to meet. I made up a signal just like I did with Dennis. We met in the basement. After he took down his pants, I said to myself, wow, how am I going to handle this? He wasn't mature in age but his penis was. He was the third teenager that I was about to have a sexual encounter with that was well endowed. When we had sex, it was painful. We had about three or four more sexual encounters with no one ever knowing, at least not on my end. I had to stop, though because I wasn't getting anything out of it. but a sore vagina.

On my crusade I ran into Brice. Nothing sexual happened, he was just around to occupy my time, and take away the feelings of loneliness. He asked me to get a picture of my daughter and walk with him.

"Where are we going?" I asked.

He didn't tell me until we walked up to this house. He had taken me to meet his mother. He took the picture from me and showed it to his mother.

"Yes, yes! That's my granddaughter," she said.

I looked at her and said to myself, why do she think this is her granddaughter? Wondering what had he had told her.

"Why do you have your mother thinking Toya is her granddaughter?" I asked after we left.

"Because she is my daughter," he said.

"You are not her father," I said and I kept insisting that her father was white. Then I told him that I didn't want to see him again. He wasn't aggressive and did whatever I told him. I didn't want to be around a wimp. He let me control him. I wanted to be controlled, but when I was around him I felt like I was the man.

I really didn't want to be with any male in my neighborhood. None of them were really my type and weren't attractive to my eyes. Especially not the drunken, dirty old men. That's why I would approach the ones who would visit the neighborhood who were attractive to me, which wasn't that often.

At that time Tony was the only attractive man to me. And because of my preference, I was alone. Sitting around knowing how bad I missed Tony, I would sit at the window and wait for him to come home just so I could get a glance at him. That satisfied me for the moment. I was stalking him from my window. I felt that we weren't ever going to get back together but I wasn't giving up hope. I gave up chasing him and when I did, it was like things had taken an about face.

One night I was asleep in my bed. I was awakened by a knock on the door. I didn't get up right away to answer it. But then I heard the knock again, and got up. The knock was coming from the back door and when I opened it, I was shocked to see who was standing there: it was Tony. He walked up to me and started kissing me, telling me how much he missed me and the kids and how he loved me.

"I want us to get back together," he said.

I was at a loss for words. All I could do was hold on to him. I thought that I was dreaming. The whole scene was like a fairytale.

"I'll see you tomorrow and I'll explain everything," he said when I let him go.

The next day he came to my house, we sat on the porch. He told me that his mother and Robert, her friend had paid him to stay away from me. They threatened to stop helping him financially. I was hurt, I felt betrayed because I thought Lady H would be the last person to betray me or judge me for what I'd been through and for my rebellious behavior. She used what I shared with her in confidence against me. I never thought she would judge me because of my past, especially when she had been in a similar situation in her past; rescued from an abusive relationship.

But I was wrong. Observing her over the years, I saw how she put her kids on a pedestal when they wouldn't do anything for her. They were all spoiled and I felt she thought she and her kids were better than my family and me. They were just as dysfunctional as we were. I was hurt. Who gave her the right to judge me? To say I was not good enough for her son, when I was the one who helped him when he needed help. He'd betrayed me too, by giving into their demands.

What also made me mad was she felt it was OK that he was treated badly by another woman. She didn't interfere then, but she interfered in our relationship and tried to say who was best for this grown man and all I wanted to do was love this man. He went against them and let them know he wanted to be with me and that we were back together. Knowing how I was perceived, ridiculed, mistreated and downgraded by everyone, even by my own mother, was hurtful but I didn't hold any resentment toward them.

God allowed me to still show love toward them, my abuser included. I have a kind and forgiving heart, for the most part, and I tolerated and accepted what people did or said to me. It's kind of hard to describe my personality.

Tony and I spent a lot of time together. When he wasn't at work and wasn't with me he went fishing, even got my mother involved. He would catch the fish and she would clean and cook them they did that every day for a week.

By the next week they couldn't eat any more. They both had an allergic reaction from eating so much fish from the river. It was so funny how they looked. I wish I'd had a camera at that time to take their pictures. My mother's lips perked out just like a fish. One of Tony's feet swelled up so badly that he couldn't put on his shoe.

I noticed that my mama seemed to like Tony. They got along good and I believe it was because he helped provide and share pills with her. That's when I discovered he took pills too, which was shocking to me because I never saw him high. I knew he smoked marijuana, but the pills I didn't know anything about. They didn't affect him like they did Mama. I assumed it depended on the amount you consumed.

Mama liked anyone who gave her pills. If she just met you and you mentioned anything about medicine she would ask you what kind. If it's any kind that she knows that will get you high she will ask you to give her a few. When it came to pills she had no shame to her game. All of her friends did some form of drugs, and most of them she met while going to the doctor, which was major part of her life. While we were being subjected to her drug environment she had people judging and looking down at us. Her drug habit affected my life, and made a big impact on my decision-making, whether good or bad.

I thank God that I turned out to be nothing like my mother. I took care of my babies the best way I could, with the limited resources and knowledge I had. I knew I had some emotional problems that came from all the abuse. I tried not to let if affect the way I took care of my babies. I did make some bad decisions concerning their care when I occasionally left them alone with Mama while she was high. But I did that just so I wouldn't be there to be abused. But that was a mistake I made. I was young. I tried to not dwell on what was happening to me and focus on every day living and the raising of my kids.

I sat back and watched other people go through problems. I wondered how could they cast stones, putting us down about our situation when skeletons started coming out from their glass doors. When the truth came out about a certain family situation, it was like a hurricane went thought that house; crying, screaming, yelling about how they couldn't believe what was happening.

I didn't judge. I understood when you get some devastating news how it effects your actions; when you been mislead into believing certain circumstances and then find out it was all a lie how it effects your mental state. It's devastating. Then when other family members find out the secret they start mistreating you, the teasing starts and you are made to feel like you're an outcast.

That's why I say don't cast stones at others when your house is not in order. With all that was going on at their house we were the ones looked down on.

Not everything was traumatic, though. I did have some good moments and the bad did out weight the good. Over the years I learned to adapt to what was happening to me and what I couldn't control.

Daddy tried to make some of our financial situation a little easier to the best of his ability over the years. But I would've preferred to spend more quality time with him instead. Sometimes I got upset when I would miss his visit all because I didn't want to be at home. I made sure I didn't miss anymore of his visits. When he visited us, I knew the routine: I sat in the backseat with my brother, and Amy sat in the front. I'd been doing that every sense I found out that I wasn't his biological daughter.

This particular visit wasn't all that unusual. He took us for a ride, gave us money and we stopped at the store like he usually do. I put my money away to be used for my kids. That's what I did every time I got any money. The only thing that was unusual this time was Daddy gave Amy money to play the lottery for him. He gave her a certain amount on a certain number and he gave her an extra ten dollars to put on the same number for herself.

When we entered the store, Amy looked at the money Daddy had given her. "Daddy must be crazy," she said. "I'm not going to put the whole ten on that number. It's too much."

She only played it for one dollar, and we left the store. She gave Daddy his ticket. She didn't tell him that she hadn't put the whole ten on his number. I didn't say anything either. What I didn't understand was why Daddy hadn't given my brother and I extra money. We could've played the number too.

Later that night at 7:30 the lottery numbers were being announce and to our surprise the number Daddy gave my sister to play came out exactly the way he told her to play it. She was excited. Daddy called right after the number was announced, asked my sister did she hit and she told him yes. I didn't understand why he asked her that when he knew she played it. I assumed he was joking with her. He asked her how much she hit for. She told him the amount. He asked her why so little? That he'd given her ten dollars to put on it.

"I know. I didn't put all of it on it," she said.

"That was too much money to put on one number." He said he told her what to do and if she had listened she would have had a lot of money. That was her lesson to be learned. I knew Daddy also hit, but we didn't know for how much.

Two days had past since my sister and Daddy hit the number. My sister and I and Mama, and her friend Dorty were sitting on the porch talking, laughing and enjoying the nice day when we were surprised by another visit from Daddy, which was unusual. He rarely visited us twice in the same week unless we called him for an emergency or for a financial need. Wondering why he was visiting us again, he called Amy and I into the house. My brother was already in the house.

He handed us some money. We were surprise by that because he had just giving us some two days earlier. But we didn't question him as to why he was giving us more money. We thanked him and we went back outside. He then handed my mother and her friend Dorty some money. I was surprised by that too because he didn't even know Dorty. He hadn't given Mama money in years. He then had me go get Lady H. He gave her money, too and thanked her for helping us.

Daddy was always a generous man, but this day he was extra generous. I was expecting Daddy to leave like he usually did after giving us money, but he stayed, talking with us. I didn't complain. I was happy that he was spending more time with us. But I became suspicions of Daddy's strange behavior. He kept looking down the street, which made me look too.

"Daddy, why you keep looking down the street?" I asked him. "I'm waiting' on something to arrive," he said.

Not long after he said that a big white truck slowly drove

down our street, as if the driver was looking for an address. The truck stopped right in front of our house and two men got out, went to the back of the truck and started unloading furniture, then a freezer. We were so excited and surprised! We were just all smiles.

After the delivery guy left, so did Daddy telling us that he would see us tomorrow. We looked at each other, surprised and wondering why.

The next day came and so did Daddy. He called us to the car. We looked inside and on the backseat were two big boxes filled with meat wrapped in white paper, just like when you bought meat from a deli. Daddy had bought half of a cow and had it cut up into different cuts of meat. It filled that freezer up and we had enough food to last for a while. Excited and surprised about Daddy's generosity, we talked about it for days.

After receiving all the wonderful contributions from Daddy, a week of our summer days was invaded by fish flies. Because we lived off the riverfront, they were everywhere; all over everything. They were extremely bad, so bad that we couldn't sit outside or walk because we would step on them. That "crunch, crunch" sound irritated me when you walked or drove over them. I hated things that fly.

One night while Mama was high, her munchies stage had hit her and she was craving Chinese food. She made us walk five blocks to get her some food with all those flying bugs around. When it came to any kind of creepy crawler and flying insect or rodent I was scared. I'd run if they didn't.

I was mad because we were made to go. I put on a raincoat so the bugs wouldn't land on me. She picked the wrong time to send us. We had to fight our way there and back. It was so funny, the way I behaved when it came to bugs.

My brother, Tony, and his brothers Stan and Carl worked for Robert, Lady H's male friend at his boatyard and his house off the lake. They did odd jobs for him so they would not be a prey to the street life and they would have money in their pockets. Amy's boyfriend Carl was also Diana's nephew. Almost everyone who lived on Hilliger was related to one another and Carl's family took up the majority of our block. For some reason Carl had a disagreement with Lady H and Robert that led to a fight between Tony and Carl. The whole incident was funny to me especially when Carl threw Tony in the trunk of his car and closed the hood.

Because of all the traumatic stuff in my life, I shouldn't have had reason to laugh. But that was funny. When the fight was over, their friendship was dissolved and Carl no loner worked with them. But the good thing was that no one carried on with their feuding, and no one walked around holding a grudge toward one another. It was sad because they had been friends for a long time.

The Big Day!

The day I turned eighteen, the day I could finally move out and be free, finally arrived. Something I been dreaming about for years, believing that one day Daddy would get me and my siblings out of the torture of Mama's house. That day never came, but my age is what unlocked the door and freed me. I didn't want to leave the neighborhood so Tony and I talked Lady H into letting us move into the flat downstairs from her daughter ReeRee. She talked to Robert because he owned the dwelling.

They finally agreed. When something involved me, no one did anything willingly they had to be persuaded. A week later my babies and I were out of Mama's house. Financially, I wasn't ready to move, but mentally I was. I had no financial help. From Tony's end, we were allowed to move in rent-free until I got financial assistance from the welfare system.

We moved with very little. We had a bed and whatever clothes we did have. I didn't care if we didn't have furniture. I wasn't going to do what Mama had us doing for years, which was furnishing every room in the house with other people's trash. That was embarrassing and scary, because we didn't know what bugs or germs would be brought into the house and we had to lay or sit on whatever she found.

I finally felt free physically, but not necessarily mentally free from years of abuse. My mind was damaged from all the abuse. But I was unaware of how extremely bad off I was. I was aware that I needed help but didn't know who to turn to seek help nor was there anyone to support me in finding help. I was being condemned because of my irrational behavior instead of them being aware that I was crying, reaching out for help, my cries were ignored.

I wanted anything that affiliated me with abuse to stop. I wanted the cycle of abuse to stop. I abused my sister; I abused myself, by having sex with men, thinking that if I was with a man, even for a moment that it would ease the pain of being alone or give me the feeling that I was loved and comforted. I wanted to feel that I mattered and have my emptiness filled. I was searching for something and I not quite sure what it was. And sex was not the answer, because I was never getting any pleasure out of having sex from whoever my sexual partner was at that moment. So to get something out of having sex I took whatever they had to offer me and that became my pleasure. I didn't give a damn about those other guys I was with and I could care less if I ever saw them again.

Tony was the only man that had an emotional effect on me. Losing him for any reason would be devastating to me. I loved him and I was trying to stop the pattern of people whom I love or cared about walking out my life or harming me. Now that Tony and I were together, I hoped that I was free from any more emotional trauma. That included trying to commit suicide. I was trying to change my own pattern. I thought living in my own house and being free from abuse would give me feelings of excitement and freedom. I was wrong. Tony and I hadn't been in our home long when a lot of emotional and tragic circumstances started to surface, adding more pain inside me.

Chapter Six

Dysfunctional

The bad judgment of a neighbor almost cost me my son's life. My neighbor Bill who lived in the unit behind my house, where Tony used to stay, was sitting on the porch waiting on the mailman. He asked if he could sit in my hallway or foyer, as they called it. I didn't have a problem with that, he was an old man and I knew him. I assumed the sun was bothering him. He sat in the chair and my son and daughter stood next to him and he was playing with them. I turned to go back and finish what I was doing in the other room when I heard this loud bang. I started shaking I was so scared to turn to see what it was. I braced myself, and turned around. I looked at them and they looked like ghosts.

The Bill tried to explain to me that he had the safety lock on when he let my son hold his gun. I grabbed my babies. I started feeling all over them to make sure they weren't hit by a bullet, and was relieved that they were Ok. I was shaking uncontrollably. Tony's sister ReeRee came running downstairs and his mother came from down the street to find out what happened. Bill started crying and shaking too. As he tried to explain, Lady H took him out the house. He was apologizing. Lady H came back in and we standing there looking at the ceiling and saw the bullet hole.

I started crying because of how close I was to losing my son, because of bad judgment of someone else. All I could picture was my son holding that gun. My three-year-old baby could have blown his head off. I didn't hold a grudge; I just was thanking God that my babies were Ok. I didn't let him around my kids again, though. I didn't let them out my sight.

That was the scariest day of my life. I know being raped was scary but if I had lost one of my babies, I don't know what I would have done. From that incident it caused me to be over protective of my kids.

"Circumstances like that was just the start of my emotional breakdown."

Living on my own with the man I loved and who claimed to love me and having my kids to love felt like we were one big happy family. I wanted this to be a start to my recovery and the beginning of a new life of happiness. I was supposed to be free from all the abuse that had been so much of my life. I soon found out that wasn't the case.

Living with Tony began to feel like I was still living with my mother. It wasn't what I expected because he started changing. He started complaining about everything I did.

First he started with the way I cleaned the house. I had mopped the floors and needed to rinse out the mop. I didn't know where I should rinse it out, so I rinsed it out in the tub. And when Tony saw what I did, he went all crazy, yelling at me. Instead of telling me the right way to clean the mop, he criticized and disrespected me, which led to an argument. Then his mother tried to intervene. I told them what I did was the way I was taught at home and if I wasn't doing it right, they should show me the right way and not talk about me.

Their actions only angered me and made me feel like whatever I did wasn't right. It seemed like now that we were in our own house he was spending less time at home. Causing me to continue suffering emotionally. I started arguments with him, because he was neglecting his responsibility at home. He was working long hours, not spending quality time with us and not helping me financially. He claimed his position required a lot of his time, very long hours and I got to thinking…if he was working all these hours why hadn't I seen or received any of the money?

We were surviving off the money I was getting from welfare. What little was left after paying the rent and the bills left me unable to provide everyday necessities for my babies. I was trying not to do anything to jeopardize my relationship with Tony, in fear that he would leave me. That's what all the people did to me whom I loved. I accepted what he was doing even though it was taking a toll on me. I felt what he was doing to me was better than what I had endured living with Mama.

When he wasn't complaining about things, we seemed to be doing good and we had planned to have a baby. Whenever he was home we were intimate. When he wasn't at home my babies and I had nothing to do and I started feeling lonely. I took the kids to visit friends and family until it got cold. I didn't want my kids to suffer because of my emotional issues.

One day Tony pulled up in front of the house in this car. I questioned him about the car and he said he brought it from his boss so that he could get back and forth to work. You know, those long hours he claimed he was doing? He had money to buy a car with the money he made working long hours, but he couldn't help me financially, where he lived. I was so naive to everything he did and said because I loved him. I left it alone.

He did what people normally did when they got something new: he showed off his car, drove me and the kids around, dropped us back off at home and disappeared. Well, one night while he and the kids were asleep I decide I wanted to drive. I'd never driven before. I'd held on to a steering wheel when I was younger when JB called himself trying to teach me how to drive. This only gave him an excuse to get me to sit next to him so he could play with my vagina.

Over the years I observed other people driving. I assumed I could drive too. I took Tony's keys and asked my brother if he wanted to ride with me. He got in the car and I drove off. It was late at night and traffic was very light. I had no particular direction I wanted to go so I just drove in the area I was familiar with.

I was doing an excellent job, driving like I was a pro. I was in the area of Warren right off St. Jean and we came upon railroad tracks and just when we got on the tracks the crossing rail came down in front of me. The lights start flashing, and the trains horn was blowing. I looked behind me and that crossing rail was coming down, too. I said out loud, "Oh no! What am I going to do?" I had to think fast. I wasn't about to get hit by a train and this was my first driving experience. Plus if something happened to the car I was going to be in trouble.

"What are you going to do?" my brother asked.

"We not about to die," I said I backed that car up just a little so that I could turn it around on the tracks and I got off just in the nick of time. Even though the train was going slow, that was a scary situation. We laughed after the shock wore off and we went home.

My knees were wobbly and my hands were shaking. I dropped my brother at home and I went home. I put Tony keys back where they were and he never knew what I did.

I did sneak his keys again but drove by myself with no incident.

In October the situation between Tony and I hadn't changed. It was just a week away from Halloween and I'd never celebrated any holiday growing up so I wanted to start a tradition with my babies. I discussed with Diana, Lady H and Tony's sister ReeRee about doing something for the kids. We planned a Halloween party for the kids on our block. Everybody had a part in it, from the games to the spooky house.

When the day came for the party, it turned out to be a great success. It was the best idea I'd ever come up with; the way we had things set up we had those kids so scared they broke down the dry wall that divided the basement. I was happy about the way it turned out. Christmas was the same. We were given a Christmas tree and we decorated it.

I couldn't afford to but them a lot of toys, but it was very nice for them. I accomplished what I set out to do for them without any help. Then I had good news that I was about to have a baby, finally after a year of trying to conceive. I didn't have to wait until I was five months to spread the good news like I did with my first two babies.

I told Tony's family and mine right away, everybody but my daddy. I didn't want to hurt him anymore than I already had; it meant a lot to him that I finish school and I hadn't done that.

I was eighteen, a drop out and about to have my third baby. But this time the baby was planned. I thought having a baby with Tony would bring us closer because of how he was betrayed by the other woman when he believed he was the father of her baby, a baby he hadn't fathered. Things were progressively getting worse between us.

Realizing my mental state was unstable from what I had been through over the years, I realized that I had no business being with Tony. He wasn't with me emotionally, mentally, and physically like I needed him to be. From the first day we moved in together he began to verbally abuse me. Tony was more concerned about Tony. He was immature and not handling his responsibility as a husband or father. His job was more important than we were.

Because he didn't help financially, I was unable to provide all the necessities for my other babies. This was the man I fell in love with and I chose to stay and deal with what he was handing me out of fear that he'd leave me like everyone else had that I loved. All I knew was abuse.

As I was trying to deal with our problems emotionally, other problems started escalating. I became frustrated and took out my frustrations on my daughter. One day, I was washing her hair in the sink in the kitchen, I guess she was scared of the water and I was so agitated and stressed out. My emotions didn't allow me to see that she had a problem with the water, as she continued to wiggle, and scream, fighting to get away from me. Because my stomach was kind of big, my arms were getting tired of trying to hold her tightly. I didn't want her to fall and hurt herself.

Then out of the mouth of my one-year-old baby came, "Let me go b...."

"What'd you say?" I asked as I looked at her.

"She repeated it and I lost it. I lifted her up in the air and I threw her to the floor, picked her up to throw her again, and saw a big knot on her forehead. I started screaming and crying all hysterically. I thought I'd killed my baby. I knew I hadn't meant to hurt her, and called my mother, telling her what I did and that I thought I'd hurt my baby.

Mama came over to see what happened. After I calmed down, she took Emmanuel and Toya with her to give me some time to pull myself together. I knew my emotions had taken a toll on me, and I'd tried to hurt my baby because I was suffering emotionally.

For no apparent reason my nose started bleeding. I put water on a tissue and squeezed it into my nostrils, which didn't stop it; I held my head back, that didn't work. I ran water in the bathtub, took a rag and squeezed water over my face, just like my mother had done when I was two, even that didn't work. I gave up and I let my head hang over the tub and just let the blood drip out. I stayed there for fifteen minutes and then I took more tissue and blew my nose real hard and it stopped.

As I was getting further along in my pregnancy depression set in heavily and I began neglecting myself, emotionally and mentally, as well as the well being of my babies. My daughter had injured herself and I hadn't noticed until it healed. I was washing her up and noticed she had a burn print from the iron on her hand. I asked her when did it happen, but of course she couldn't tell me. I said to myself, this little girl tough. She didn't let me know she had been burned, nor did she cry.

I wouldn't go out the house nor did I let my kids, because of my depression and my emotional problems. It affected my kids and they suffered because I was suffering. I was not going to be irresponsible and let them go outside by themselves. I made the back room into a playroom for them because I didn't want to leave my house. I didn't want responsibilities to fall on family members.

I imposed on other people to help me monetarily with my craving. The craving I had with this baby was different than what I had with Emmanuel. With him, I was addicted to milk. With this baby it was folded pizza. I was begging everybody to buy me pizza. It didn't matter; whoever I saw going to the store I would ask them to buy me a pizza. I even got it on credit when I didn't have enough money, just to support my craving.

I was four months pregnant when tragedy struck my family.

My daddy had come to visit, and he gave us some money like he always did, but I received less. I couldn't understand why because he had never done that before. He always gave us equal amounts. I called and questioned him. He told me because I wasn't in school. Hearing his reason made me cry. Rage came upon me. I got mad and wrote him this nasty letter, telling him I hated him and that he wasn't my daddy and that I never wanted to see him again.

When he received that letter, he called my mother crying, asking her why I wrote that. He told her to tell me that he loved me, and that I'd hurt him. He just wanted me to go back to school. She called me and told me all that he said. I was stubborn and emotionally upset. I didn't want to hear it. I didn't want to talk to him. I was hurt and felt betrayed by my father. I felt he turned on me like the rest of the people I cared about.

Two days passed since that phone call from Mama telling me what Daddy said, when I received another phone call from her, and she was crying. I asked her what was wrong; she said that she received a phone call informing her that my daddy had died. I instantly started crying, screaming. I fell to my knees. I went into complete shock; I couldn't feel a thing. My mother and Lady H rushed to my house. I was crying so hysterically, they were trying to help me calm down so that I wouldn't cause any harm to myself or to my unborn baby. But I couldn't stop. I loved my daddy. I said all those bad things to him, and he died before I got a change to say I'm sorry.

I regret saying those harmful things, and I didn't mean what I said. My daddy was my heart, my world, and I never wanted to do anything to hurt him. And out of anger, I wrote that hateful letter because I was hurt. I mistreated and disrespected him. I ignored his plea to talk with me, refusing to talk to him. I had an emotional outburst of anger, and was vindictive. I would never get a chance to talk to him or to tell him how sorry I was, and that I love him. How could I hurt him like that? (We have to watch what we say and do to the ones we love; we never know when we won't see them again.)

My daddy died thinking I hated him because of that letter

and what I said and not wanting to talk to him. If I had a chance to talk to him again I would say, Daddy, I am so sorry for what I said. I did not mean any of it. I love you with everything I have in me, and wherever you are, I hope deep in your heart you know that you meant the world to me, and that I never meant to hurt you. You were a good daddy and a wonderful man. I will never forget you.

At that moment, I wasn't concerned about me or the baby. I was so devastated and incoherent, in such bad shape, my mother gave me a pill, a Valium to calm me down. Tony took me for a drive, and Mama took my babies with her. We ended up at the drive-in theater. I cried and cried and cried. I stopped for a minute, got to thinking about my daddy, and started back crying. I believe that we were only there for thirty minutes when Tony asked me if I was ready to leave. I said yes; I was so out of it. I don't remember what movie we saw. Emotionless, I went into my room and lay in my bed, staring at empty space.

Mama brought the kids back and Tony was with them. That was the only time he attended to my kids. My daddy died not knowing I was pregnant or about my abuse, nor did he ever know I tried to take my own life twice. My daddy knew nothing about me. My life was a secret.

The next day I was a little better, tried to pull myself together for the kids' sake. When I called my mother's house, Amy answered. While talking with her, she told me that she and Carl went to see Daddy, and that he didn't want to see her, saying that he was sick. The YMCA was an all-male facility, and my sister wasn't allowed to go up to his room to check on him. Since he wasn't coming down, she continued talking to him on the phone in the hallway, trying to convince him to come down. Nothing worked, and that was very unusual for Daddy, not wanting to see any of his kids.

She said the manager let Carl go up to his room, and he even refused to see or talk to him, saying he didn't know him, when he did. Carl tried to explain to him that he was Amy's boyfriend. Daddy said he didn't care who he was. He wanted him to leave. Carl went back down and they left. My sister never mentioned that to us.

This experience with my daddy's death taught me to always be aware of people's actions; pay close attention to their behavior. If it's out the ordinary, out of character for them, seek help or inform someone so that they can help regardless of the situation. Don't just ignore them; don't push it under the table. You never know what kind of help they may need or when that will be your last time seeing them. The signs were there.

I told my sister that she should have told me because something had to be wrong; I said Daddy would have come down, especially to see her. Within that same hour after talking to Amy, someone knocked on the door. When I opened it, there were two police officers standing there.

"Is this the home of Ernestine Moore?" one of the officers asked.

"Yes. That's me."

"Well, a letter had been found at the YMCA residence addressed to a Samuel Williams, and it had your return address on it. Do you know Samuel Williams?"

"Yes, he's my father."

"Miss Moore, I'm sorry to inform you that he died."

"I know, Officer. Thank you for taking the time to come and inform me." And they left.

Mama, Lena, and me had to go to the hospital where he died; we caught the bus to the South West Detroit Hospital on Michigan Avenue. I'm assuming my mother had to sign papers for them to release his body to the morgue. I was not sure. She came out with some of his personal belongings. I was still in disbelief that my daddy was gone and that I would never see him again. I missed my daddy so much.

While we were there, we found out that he died of pneumonia, the same illness Mama had. Things were not adding up. I questioned why he hadn't survived. My mother said my daddy didn't like going to the doctor. She said he probably thought he could let it run its course, thinking he just had a cold.

We left the hospital to catch the bus downtown to the

morgue to identify his body. Inside we were taken to a little room that only had a TV monitor mounted on the wall. We were in that room for a while when the monitor popped on, and on the screen was my daddy, lying there like he was sleeping. I lost it again, falling to my knees.

"Oh my God! That's not my daddy! That's not my daddy!" I didn't want to face the fact that he was gone. I knew it was him; it didn't look like him, but it was. I couldn't handle it, seeing my daddy like that. We left and went home.

Mama had to make the funeral arrangements. I was at home cleaning the house, trying to occupy my mind, and trying to get comfort or moral support from Tony. He paid no attention to me. He was inconsiderate, unconcerned, not showing me any compassion. He acted nonchalant about my grieving. It was obvious to me that this man had been showing me he really didn't love me or care about me.

We were in the kitchen and I was doing the dishes. I asked Tony if he would take some time off work to be home with me in my time of need, especially when it came to the day of the funeral. I was going to need some support while I was grieving. He said that he wasn't taking off work. This angered me, and we got into a argument.

"Tony, will you please stay home with me?" I asked him again.

"No," he said and turned and walked away from me.

I was very angry because of his emotionless attitude and just like with my sister my emotions erupted. I grabbed a knife and while his back was toward me, ignoring me, I snapped. I hesitated for a second, and before I knew it, I had stabbed him in his shoulder. I did it so fast; I couldn't believe that I had stabbed him. After pulling the knife out I saw blood and thought I'd hurt him badly. That's when I began screaming.

I called my mother, crying hysterically, and screaming. In my state of mind, I thought I'd killed him. She hung up and a few minutes later, Mama and Lady H came running into the house. Mama took the kids to another room, and Lady H went to check on Tony in the kids' playroom in the back of the house.

She convinced him to go to the hospital because he didn't want to go. And when they left, I was scared. I didn't know how badly he was hurt and I thought the doctor was going to send the police to the house to take me to jail.

I was so scared; I didn't want to go to jail. Mama and Lady H took the kids with them when they left so that I could calm down. Later that night, Mama brought them back. Tony got home right after she left and showed me his stitches.

"Why did you do it?" he asked.

"I did it out of anger, Tony, because of your unemotional behavior concerning me. I'm grieving right now. And you act like your job is more important than me and you're putting it ahead of your family."

I walked away. I didn't care anymore; I had been doing things on my own, so why stop now?

My sister and my bother and I went to the funeral home for the family hour, to view the body. Amy and I were standing at the door, staring at Daddy from a distance as he lay in that casket, still in disbelief that he was gone. Tears were rolling down my face. I walked over to the podium, and signed the guest book when other people started to arrive, packing that small room. As I was standing there looking, I was so amazed at all the wonderful people there to pay their respects.

I whispered to Amy, "Look at all these people."

"I know," she said.

We both said we didn't know why Daddy had been telling us all those years that he didn't have any friends. What would he have called this? I continued standing next to the guest book when two guys were standing at a distant from me, talking. I overheard one man say he wondered if I was his ex-wife. I looked at them with an attitude.

"No, I'm not his ex-wife, I'm his daughter, and furthermore, he was still married." I said.

They looked at me and said, "Oh, we apologize, we didn't know he had a daughter."

"Well, yes. He has three kids," I said. Daddy had kept us

a secret just like he kept his family and friends a secret from us. We didn't know anything about his family, we knew nothing about him, or about his childhood, nor did we know if he had siblings. We didn't even know his mother's name or where his people lived—nothing. His life was a mystery. His father, we knew his name because he was Samuel Williams the First and Daddy was the second, and my brother the third.

The only thing we were ever told about my father's past came from my mother. She said that he had run away from home and joined the Army when he was sixteen. He was discharged when they found out his real age, and that's all we were ever told. My daddy didn't know me, and we didn't know him, I thought. After those guys walked away, guests were still arriving; and just before the family hour was over, those same two guys along with another man approached me, offering me their condolences once again.

They started reminiscing about the time they spent with Daddy at work, laughing, saying what a kind, good, caring man he was. The two men informed me that they owed him some money and asked me if I could give them my address so they could drop the money off. I said sure, and I gave them Mama's address because I knew I would be there. I thanked them as the tears rolled down my face.

My heart filled with so much gratitude. I wondered what my daddy was talking about, saying he had no friends. These guys didn't have to tell us they owed him anything. They could have kept that between themselves. We would never have known.

We left immediately after family hour was over, heading home. I dreaded going home to my empty house where there was no emotional support. All I was going to have was silence, and my mind was going to my daddy and the time we did get to share with him. I put the kids to bed, and I lay in my bed crying, knowing the next day would arrive fast. I finally dozed off. When the sunlight was hitting me in my face, it seemed like I had just gone to sleep.

I wasn't mentally prepared for this day; this funeral was

going to be the hardest day of my life. I was already traumatized by the fact that I wasn't ever going to see or talk to my daddy again, and how I disrespected him and that was something I never did before. My behavior was the effect of all the years of abuse I withstood. It had me behaving outside my true personality, outside of who I was deep down inside of me.

I am a good, kindhearted person, but I let the abuse I suffered and anger control me and my actions. I had a man I loved who was not concerned about giving me any moral support. I didn't know if I was going to make it through this. We were getting dressed for the funeral. I took a chance and questioned Tony one last time.

"Are you going to go to the funeral with me?"

"No," was all he said in his unpleasant voice.

"Ok," I said and I left it at that. Arguing with him would have only done more damage to my mental state. There would have been tragic consequences if I had let him take me to that point; he left. The car from the funeral home arrived to pick up the family. My heart was beating fast, my stomach felt nervous, and my knees were trembling. I did not want to go.

We arrived at the funeral home. Once inside, seeing my father lying in that casket, knowing that this was going to be my last time seeing him, became overwhelming for me. Crying, I clutched my babies' hands, wanting to fall to my knees. I couldn't because I didn't want to risk harming my unborn baby. There was so much emotion going on inside of me, it was hard to explain. I loved my daddy tremendously, and I had so much guilt on my heart over the way I treated him out of my anger.

As the service was about to start, there weren't as many people as there were at the family hour. Looking around at the people that were there, all were crying except my brother. I didn't question his handling of his grief. Everybody handled grief differently. My mother was even crying. I was shocked because I didn't think she had any kind of feelings toward Daddy.

Our neighbor and friend, Ella who lived upstairs graciously sang all the songs, singing them so beautifully, touching our hearts.

I couldn't stop crying. After the condolence cards were read, we were led back up to the casket; we just stood there. I was staring at my daddy, trying to memorize every moment of his life with me, knowing I wasn't going to see his face again. My daughter didn't know what was going on and she tried to climb into the coffin with my daddy.

I grabbed her and said, "No, baby, you can't get in there with him."

We were then led back to our seats. I had no idea what was about to happen. When I looked back toward the casket, I saw the funeral director and another man closing his casket. I lost my mind. I started screaming, jumping up and down, about to run and stop them from closing it.

"Don't do that! Don't close my daddy up," I yelled at them.

I kept saying, "Please don't close my daddy up! Please, Daddy, come back." I yelled, "Daddy, I love you. I'm sorry." I was saying everything over and over, jumping up and down. My pleading went unanswered; they closed it, and I could not see my daddy anymore. I looked around the room; my attention was then focused on my brother. He had tears rolling down his face, staring back at the casket.

A few more words were spoken, and our neighbor sang another song. We were escorted out of the building, following the casket. Everyone gathered outside giving their condolences, and the director walked around, seeing who was going to the burial site. My mother, sister, and brother didn't want to go. The kids went with Mama and Lena, and I went. Three cars went; a short recession. I stayed at the end. Before we left, I asked the guys if they were going to bury him in his casket? One said yes. The reason I said that is because I heard about a scam someone was doing with caskets; they switched your loved one to a box and resold the casket. They assured me that was not true; he would be in the original casket.

As we were leaving, I kept looking back. I wasn't satisfied with their assurances because we weren't allowed to see the actual burial. People were gathering at my mother's home, sitting around, talking about my father. I was sitting, wondering how this happened. I couldn't understand why my daddy died. He was stricken with the same illness that Mama had survived.

The two men who approached me during the family hour stopped by Mama's house like they said and gave me the money they owed Daddy. One man handed me a card from him and some of his coworkers. I opened it, and there was money inside. He said they took up a collection at work. I said thank-you, and they left. I gave the money to Mama. After everyone left, Mama split the money that she received from all the well-wishers between us, which wasn't much, and my babies and I went home to an empty house. Tony did not come home to give me any kind of support.

The next morning, my babies and I walked to Mama's house. We started going through Daddy's belongings, and we found out that he put everything in my sister's name. He had stocks and bonds that were made out to my sister and brother. I received nothing. We came across some paper that listed my sister as the beneficiary of his estate. My mother had to be her conservator because she was a minor.

I kind of understood why I wasn't chosen to be the beneficiary because I wasn't his biological daughter, nor was I responsible for handling business affairs. My sister handled all that, and she knew how he conducted his business. Whenever Daddy gave us money, he divided it between us, and he assumed she would do the same. Well, that didn't happen when the money started coming in. I was left out. Whatever money they received they went shopping, and Mama came back with a floor model television.

Mama had told what they were about to receive to all her so-called friends, her pill buddies. Lena was sticking real close to Mama, making sure they were well supplied with pills, making sure Mama stayed high. All her drug buddies were coming around more than usual. They had lots of pills to sell her.

A few days later, another installment of money was received. I believed it was money left over from Daddy's lottery winnings, not sure exactly how much it was, though. I was excluded from knowing that part of the business affairs. I knew it was a few thousand dollars from what Mama divided between them and the amount I received, which was six hundred dollars. I was disappointed, hurt, and angry about the amount I received. I didn't say anything; I just took that money. I shouldn't have expected anything. I wasn't his biological daughter. Why should I be included in receiving any money now that he was not alive?

  I assumed Mama felt I had no rights, and she took advantage of the situation. I was already ousted from the other money they received. I knew she was wrong because that money was supposed to be divided between us kids. Mama wasn't supposed to receive anything. Her bragging resulted in a tragic situation.

  Mama's friend Poochie and a man I had never seen before came over to sell Mama some pills. I stayed at Mama's house all day, watching her while Amy and Carl went shopping. Like I said, Lena was sticking to Mama like glue. Mama decided she wanted to go to the store, and Lena and the kids went with her. Mama staggered all the way as I walked halfway with them to my house. I was going to wait for them. I took the money I received and put it up. I put twenty dollars in my pocket and put the rest in my dresser drawer.

  As I sat at the house waiting on them to return, I called Tony at work to tell him how I was mistreated and what I received. He really didn't have any encouraging words. After hanging up, I figured I had missed Lena and them because it didn't take that long to go to the store. I walked back to Mama's house. I always peeked through the little window to the side of the door when I get on the porch, and that's what I did this time. I wanted to see if they'd made it back. I saw my babies sitting on the floor in front of the table coloring. I knocked on the door, and when it opened, I stepped inside. A gun was pointing in my face. I looked toward my family, and a gun was pointing at them, too. I knew when I looked through that window I'd only seen my babies and Mama. If I had seen those men, I would have ran and called the police.

They must have heard me coming on the porch and hid. The gunmen escorted me into the dining room with the others. As we entered the room, I saw Lena sitting on the arm of the chair by the window and Poochie standing next to another gunman. I sat down in the chair next to Lena. The third gunman, who I assumed was the leader because he was giving all the commands, I recognized as the man who came to the house earlier with Poochie. He was pointing his gun at Mama and my babies.

I was furious, outraged, and distraught over the fact that I couldn't do anything to protect my babies. Part of me was scared for our lives. I was sitting there, observing their actions, and I noticed Lena and Poochie were too calm. They didn't have the look of fear upon their faces. The leader was pacing back and forth, demanding that Mama give him the money. Not once did I see him ask Lena anything.

Mama responded to his demands, reaching in her hiding spot, giving him what she had. After he collected the money from Mama, in an intimidating voice, he asked who else was in the house. No one responded. He started searching the house. He went straight to my brother's room, which was suspicious to me because he didn't search Mama's room, nor did he search the other rooms. He went straight to my brother in his bed; he was asleep.

"Wake up!" he said. "You got any money?"

"No," my brother answered.

"Get up outta bed!" Then he said, "What was that?"

"Nothing," my brother said, but he was trying to put something behind his bed.

"Give it to me," I heard the man tell my brother.

My brother was silent as they walked into the living room. The gunman had him sit next to Mama while he went through my brother's wallet and took all the money he had, which was thirteen hundred dollars. Anger was boiling inside of me. I was about to explode, and before I knew it, I started cussing the gunman out and Poochie too, because she was the one who brought this man to the house earlier to transact some business.

She played a part in this robbery, and I believed in my heart that Poochie and Lena set Mama up because of the circumstances of the robbery. Seeing that they got all the money, the one who I said seemed to be the leader told the other two gunmen to take the floor model television Mama had just gotten a few days earlier. They picked it up and walked out the front door. Poochie was right behind them.

I was still cussing at him as he followed right behind them. As he was walking toward the door, pointing his gun at us.

"You better not move," he said that. "If I see any one move, I will shoot you."

When they were out the door, before he could close it all the way, Mama moved, trying to get up. The door flung back open!

"What did I tell you? Didn't I say not to move or I'll shoot you?" The leader guy yelled.

We screamed at Mama to sit back down and don't move. He closed the door. And we sat there, less than three minutes when the door opened back up. We thought it was the gunmen coming back in, thinking somebody else moved. My heart started beating fast, thinking we were about to be shot. But it was Amy and Carl.

We yelled at them, "Did you see them? Which way did they go?"

They were like, "Who?"

I said, "Those guys that just ran out the house with Poochie. They just robbed us." Knowing that they didn't take any money from me, but they robbed me of my security. Carl ran outside to see if he could see them, but he ran back in saying he didn't see anybody. I assumed they had a getaway car in the alley.

We called the police. I was thinking that they would have arrived fast, seeing how the police station was right across the street. They arrived an hour later. When they entered the house, they started asking questions. Before anyone could answer, I spoke out, taking control (that was the Leo side of me.)

I explained, in anger, the whole situation in full detail. I gave the officers Poochie's real name but didn't know where she lived, nor did I have any information on the robbers.

"What all was taken?" one officer asked.

"A few hundred dollars from my mother and thirteen hundred from my brother," I said. After I said that, they stopped writing, looking stunned at what I'd said.

The officer asked, "Why does a fifteen-year-old boy have that much money?"

I said with an attitude, "My father just died, and that was what he inherited." And he looked back down at his pad and continued writing. He told us to take precautions, basically telling Mama to get a shotgun, and they left. We just sat there, trying to calm our nerves, discussing what happened.

My brother described what he heard. He said he was awakened by a loud commotion, and he just laid there, pretending he was asleep just in case they came into his room. Not having time to react, he said he heard what the guy was saying before he came into his room. He tried to push his wallet behind his mattress, which was on the floor. But he hadn't pushed it far enough, still pretending to be sleep when the guy entered the room.

I could tell by the look on his face that he was mad. I know I was, and this time, Daddy wasn't here to replace what was taken. I know he had to be mad at Mama just like I was for putting us, especially my babies in this dangerous situation for some pills and from all her bragging. I was still shaken. I got my babies, and we went home.

As we were walking, I was checking my surroundings, hoping that the robbers weren't following me home. I was so scared that they would come to my house because I knew I was going to be alone. When I got home, I locked the door and called Tony as I was locking up. I was still shaken, telling him what happened. I don't know why I did that. I already knew he wasn't going to be concerned. I was right, he tried to rush me off the phone, showing me that he was not concerned about our safety. I checked all the windows to make sure they were locked. I cut off everything that made noise, even the aquarium that I bought with the other money I was given. I wanted it to be so quiet I could hear a pin drop. I made the kids keep quiet until they fell asleep.

Tony didn't come home until three or four in the morning. I felt uneasy the whole night, scared to go to sleep. I was scared because I was pregnant; how was I going to defend myself and my babies if someone broke in?

Mama had gotten the floor model television that was stolen as a rent-to-own purchase from the Rite-Way Rental Center. The next day I went with her to show them the police report about the robbery. The manager told her that she still had to pay for the television. She paid it off and got another one with no problem. When we got home, I was feeling resentment toward my family because I watched them spending all that money. They still had money left after the robbery and they were buying clothes and anything they wanted. And I'd only received six hundred dollars. I distanced myself from them because I felt like I wasn't part of the family. I was treated like I was a friend visiting sometimes, being ignored. Why stay around and be treated as if I didn't exist?

The next day out of anger, I took my money and my son, and we caught the bus to K-mart, and I bought the kids some clothes. I found an outfit for my son, a Michael Jackson jacket and leather- like pants. My baby looked like Michael Jackson, and I let him pick out what else he wanted. I spent the whole six hundred on my kids, only buying myself a camera. I took pictures of Emmanuel before we left the store.

That's when I started my tradition of taking lots of pictures to have memories as they grew up. I was hurt that I was an outcast from my family, treated like I wasn't related to them.

The lawyer handling my father's estate informed my mother that she should apply for my daddy's social security for all three of them. She couldn't file for me because I wasn't his biological daughter. Amy and my brother had to go to court to change their last name to Williams in order to receive benefits. Now I really felt like I wasn't part of this family, and when they started receiving their checks, I was excluded. I was never offered any financial help. It would have been good assistance for my babies and me.

It wasn't a secret that I was not receiving any financial help from Tony. I couldn't afford to buy anything for the new baby. I was waiting to see if Tony would wise up and be a man, handle his responsibility by giving me some financial support to buy things for our new arrival. That never happened. After not receiving any kind of support from Tony or my "distant" family, I became depressed, occasionally leaving the house to visit friends. And every time I went to my mother's house, I got upset, watching them spend money, buying whatever they wanted, and didn't show any concern for my needs.

And of course, Lena would be over 'cause Mama made sure they had enough supply of pills. I believed she was stealing from my mother to support her own habit. I knew Mama would buy or give her pills, but that wasn't her only habit. With Mama high all day and every day, we wondered how would she know if her money was missing? So whenever Amy left the house she started taking Mama's money and hiding it, just leaving enough out to get something. When my sister would return home, Mama would ask her for some more money, and would hide the rest. We knew Lena was a moocher.

I don't know how all this came about, but a few months after my daddy died, my brother and cousin started selling drugs for Carl. An altercation took place between Carl and my brother and cousin after Carl and Amy came home. We were all standing on the back porch, just finishing barbecuing; Carl confronted the two of them about some money and drugs that was missing. I was in disbelief over what was taking place. He was supposed to be my sister's boyfriend, and he was trying to fight her family over money and illegal product.

I didn't say anything because I wasn't quite sure what was happening. I had distanced myself. I knew nothing. My brother and cousin didn't answer Carl about the missing cash or product. He got angry and very quickly hit my cousin in the face. He cussed and threatened them, saying what he was going to do to my brother and cousin.

My brother didn't give him time to hit him; he ran. I looked at my cousin. Seeing the blood pouring down his face, I lost it. Enraged, I started cussing out Carl. My mother and Amy were standing there, not saying anything. I was pregnant, but that didn't discourage me. I continued to cuss him out.

When he slapped me, that made it worse and I became more outraged. I picked up a fork that was on the table that we had just finished using while barbecuing, and I was about to stab him when somebody grabbed my arm. Then he started calling my mother bad names. I was still cussing at him; I was angry.

"How can you disrespect your girlfriend's family like that and hurt them over drugs? What kind of morals do you have?" I yelled at him. I looked at my sister; she was standing in the doorway, not saying anything to Carl about his irate behavior toward her family and disrespecting her mama. I walked over to her, and I started cussing her out too, and she said nothing. She was scared of him.

I was led away to calm down, and my sister and Carl left. My brother didn't come back home for a while. After the whole ordeal, no resentment was held between them, and they continued to sell drugs for Carl.

I was five months along with my pregnancy, getting big as a house, still begging people to buy me pizza. I was so big; I was bigger than my two previous pregnancies. The doctor had me take an ultrasound as a precaution, checking on the development and well-being of the baby. Tony went with me because we wanted to know the baby's sex. The baby was growing fine, and we were told we were having a boy. After we left the hospital I was excited, and so was Tony. We both smiled all the way home. He wanted a boy so he could have a junior. And I was finally going to have a baby named after him.

After learning the sex of the baby, I took what little money I had left after paying the bills and brought a few baby clothes. I couldn't afford to buy a baby bed. My brother's friend

Tee approached me, saying that he could get me a baby bed for twenty-five dollars. I accepted his offer; to me that was a deal I couldn't turn down, with the limited financial support or resources I was receiving. I knew he was about to commit crimes to get the bed because that's how he made money. At that time, I had no alternative. He informed me to look out for him at a certain time. I agreed, and he left.

Later that night, exactly around the same time he told me to expect him at my house with the baby bed, I heard a police siren. I looked out the door and saw a helicopter circling around the area he said he was getting the bed from. That's not good I thought. I just knew he'd gotten caught. I walked back in the house and closed the door. I didn't have a chance to sit down when there was a knock at my door. It was Tee, out of breath. He didn't have to say a word. I knew the police were looking for him because we didn't have really bad crime in our neighborhood that I knew of. If someone's house was broken into, we knew who was involved.

When he was able to talk, I asked him what happened. He said he was almost caught by the police when he broke into the school. It was TAPEC the same school for pregnant teens that I attended when I was pregnant with Emmanuel. He said he escaped from the roof. He said he hid the baby bed and would go get it when the police situation cleared, and he did. I paid him, and I felt a little bad at the extreme measures I had to take to get things for my baby. I took this desperate action because I still wasn't getting any monetary support from Tony.

Tony surprised me one day when he came home with a bag of baby clothes he purchased by himself, leaving me home. But we continued to argue over his not being at home and not supporting me. My babies and I were always home alone because we had no money and no place to go, and I was in no condition to travel. I was so depressed. I loved him so much I couldn't understand why he was mistreating me the way he was. He knew all I had endured in my past; it was obvious he didn't care. I was trying to make everything between us better, hoping that one day he would open his eyes and love me like I loved him. I wasn't going to give up on us. I accepted what he and everybody else did to me just to receive partial love.

This pregnancy was different. Medical complications started to arise. I was suffering emotional trauma and the lack of family or financial support. On top of that, I'd gained a huge amount of weight. I was so huge that I could not bend down to tie my own shoes, barely able to walk. I became clumsy, falling up the stairs because I missed a step, hurting myself, but laughing because I was embarrassed at how clumsy I became in my eight months. I developed preeclampsia and had to be put in the hospital for observation. The doctor was concerned that I may lose the baby if I didn't get medical treatment.

Of course, hearing that really upset me because I was concerned for the baby's safety. I had to stay in the hospital for a few days then was sent home on bed rest. I had so much difficultly with this baby; I wanted to deliver him sooner. I tried to make myself go into labor. I drank two bottles of Castor oil—that didn't work; it didn't even make me have a bowel movement like it was made for. I walked up and down the stairs over and over again. But I gave up on trying a home remedy. I was only making myself sick and tired.

I was now in my ninth month, and I still showed no sign that I was ready to deliver even after trying all the different remedies to make this baby come out. One night when Tony was home, we had sex after not having had sex for a long time. Afterward I fell asleep, but was awakened in severe pain around 6:00 am. I took a bath just in case it wasn't a false alarm. I waited before I said anything to Tony to make sure I was in labor. Thirty minutes later, in constant pain, I was sure it was real labor.

Still in the tub, I yelled out to Tony, "It's time, help me!" He jumped out of bed and helped me out of the tub, and helped me get dressed. I called Mama; she came and got the kids and we returned to St. John Hospital, hoping to deliver my baby this time. Tony was right by my side, holding my hand. I was relieved and joyful at the same time because I didn't have to deliver this baby alone. I was hooked up to a monitor, going though the same procedures as I did with my others babies.

I was in labor for ten hours, and finally it was time to deliver. I would soon be relieved of this agonizing pain. The doctors and nurses were preparing the room; the doctor told me to start pushing. As I was pushing, I looked up at Tony and saw emotion on his face for the first time; there were tears rolling down his face, and for that moment, I felt he cared about me. The doctor said push one more time, and out came the baby.

"It's a girl!" the doctor said.

Tony and I looked shocked.

"What did you say?" I said

"It's a girl," he repeated.

"It can't be. Look again."

He said, "I assure you. The baby is a girl."

I explained to the doctor that when I took my ultrasound, the technician told me that I was having a boy.

"Technicians do make mistakes," he said.

I was shocked because I brought all boy clothes, and the baby was supposed to be named after Tony. To me what was a joyful occasion turned out to be an inconvenience, another setback. I didn't have a name for a girl picked, nor did I have any money to go purchase her any clothes. I was upset. The doctor laid her on my stomach for a second to cut the umbilical cord before handing her to the nurse.

Not believing the doctor, I checked and sure enough I had a girl. Her vagina was swollen, making it seem like she had testicle.. While he was stitching and cleaning me up, the nurse handed the baby to Tony, who had this joyful expression upon his face. I was more concerned about his feelings than my own. I thought he would've been disappointed because he was expecting a son and instead he had a daughter.

He gave her a kiss and handed her to the nurse; and the nurse took her, wiped her off, and weighed her. She yelled out her weight, seven pounds and fifteen ounces, born on July 15, 1984 at 12:14 am. She was then transported to the nursery to be cleaned up. Tony leaned over and gave me a kiss and left. As I lay there, the nurse finished cleaning me up. I was trying to figure out what I was going to do. I didn't want my baby to go home in boys' clothes. I wasn't expecting any help from Tony. I had never seen or received any of his money.

An hour later, Tony returned. He had my sister and his sister with him. They came to see the baby, saying what people usually say when they see a new baby. Then Tony said, "Let's go." He had to go to work. After they left, I was trying to get some rest but couldn't because the nurse brought the baby back to my room.

"I thought the baby was going to stay in the nursery," I said to the nurse.

"No. Babies stay in the room with the mother now," she said. I wanted so desperately to get some sleep.

The next day the baby was taken to have her picture taken. Another nurse came in the room and said she needed me to fill out some forms for her social security card and birth certificate. I named her Chrissy Nicole Moore. Two days later, we were discharged. As I was getting her ready, about to put her in the boy outfit I'd brought, Tony entered the room. To my surprise, he had a girl's outfit for her. I put it on her. She was so cute. I was happy that she did not have to leave the hospital looking like a boy. She was a gorgeous baby, just like my other two babies were. She had a unique look; chunky, with a big face, looking like a Chinese baby doll with her puffy slanted eyes.

There were more baby things when we got home from the hospital. I was happy. I later found out Tony borrowed money to buy what she needed. Tony was walking around, acting like a proud father, smiling from ear to ear, extremely happy. We started receiving visitors. Lady H was first to arrive. I was sure she was coming to see if this baby was Tony's. I assumed it was because of my promiscuous ways and because he was misled before, thinking he was the father of his ex-girlfriend's baby.

In the past I used my promiscuity to self destruct. I was hurting and out of control. I had stopped being promiscuous when Tony and I became a couple. I didn't want or need to be with another man. I was with who I wanted.

Lady H finished examining my baby.

"Yes, that's my granddaughter," she said. She picked her up, holding her. Other family members started arriving to see our new addition. And Chrissy looked just like her father and Lady H. There was no way he or his family could deny her.

Everybody decided to leave all at the same time, including Tony, saying he had to go to work. I was left alone with no physical or emotional support. There I was, just home from the hospital with a new baby, and two children who needed my attention; they didn't understand Mommy hurting. They had to be taken care of, had to eat, take a bath. And physically, it was difficult because of my pain and stitches, but I couldn't neglect them.

I was emotionally overwhelmed, but I said to myself, I'm strong. I can do this by myself. I was already handling all the responsibilities on my own, why should I expect any help now? I did what I had to do. It was a slow process, but I took care of my babies by myself.

I was home for only two days when I rushed my baby to the clinic, telling the nurse that something was wrong with her eyes, complaining that the nurse at the hospital didn't clean her eyes good enough. The nurses at the clinic knew me well. Nancy came rushing to me. I was hysterical, over-dramatic. She took the baby, and Sharon told me to calm down. I was scared.

Nancy said she would clean her eyes again just for me. I was convinced something was wrong with her eyes, that they looked like they were going to close. I was panicking. When Nancy brought her back to me, her eyes still looked puffy. Nancy assured me that she would be all right. I calmed down, realizing that I did all that panicking for nothing. Her eyes were supposed to look like that; her grandmother's eyes were puffy too, but hers was extremely puffy. She looked like a China doll. It was funny to me afterward.

I experienced another funny moment that following week. My babies and I were at home, alone as usual. Chrissy and I were lying on the bed, and Emmanuel and Toya were in the back room playing when I heard a loud noise in the back part of the house that frightened me. I thought someone had kicked in the back door. I jumped up in sheer panic. My first thought was to grab the baby and yell to the kids to run. That didn't happen.

I reached for the baby, but my body froze, and fear wouldn't let me pick her up. My hands were touching her, but I just couldn't

pick her up, and I ran. As I was running, I was trying to tell the other kids to run, but it wouldn't come out my mouth. I ran, leaving the baby on the bed and the other kids running behind me, asking me why I was running. As I was running, I was laughing at the same time out of fear. Once outside, realizing I reacted out of fear, I started crying, wondering what kind of mother was I, leaving my babies behind all because I was scared. But I wasn't going back in the house.

I sent for Lady H. She came to the house as fast as she could. I told her what I suspected and that the baby was in the house. We both went inside the house. I grabbed the baby off the bed, and we went in the direction of the noise. During our investigating, we found out that the noise I heard came from the window on the back porch that we raise when the kids played back there. It had slammed shut for no apparent reason, leaving me to think someone was breaking in. I wasn't thinking that my neighbors would have known if someone was breaking in because they were sitting on their porch. I just thought how could somebody break in? I was scared.

I was supposed to protect my kids. Instead, I ran like a scared child. After Lady H left, I lay back down. After the fear wore off I started laughing as I thought about what happened. Then my laughter changed to crying. I broke down. My baby was within hand's reach, and I couldn't pick her up, and I could not tell my babies to run.

Chrissy was two weeks old when I started receiving clothes from my cousin, Emily, Lena's sister, who lived in Ohio. She'd had a baby girl a year earlier. She found out that I didn't have baby clothes for my daughter. As I was looking through the clothes, they were in such perfect condition, almost brand new, as if her baby had never worn them.

When I called to thank her, for the clothes, I asked, "Did your baby ever wear any of the clothes or go outside? Did you ever let her crawl around because those clothes don't look like they were ever worn?" She told me yes. Then I received a little support from Lady H, who brought a few other necessities, while her no-good- son brought nothing for his baby. I didn't understand his methods; how he could support another woman with a baby who wasn't his but didn't even help me with our daughter?

Now that he had his own biological baby, he had abandoned her. When he would come home, we continued to argue over the same issues: finances, responsibility, and his never being home with his family. Whatever I was saying to him went in one ear and out of the other; nothing changed. We saw him only when he decided to come home.

Tony came home unexpectedly the night the Detroit Tigers won the championship game. He said he came to get us and take us around town to celebrate with all the other people. My hair wasn't combed because I was in my depression mode, and I didn't care. I wasn't concerned about my appearance. But I was ecstatic to see him, and that we were going to spend time with him. As we were driving around, I was pretending that I was enjoying everything, when actually I didn't like any sport. When it was over, we went home and he left. I did not see him until he decided to come home again.

Because of my emotional problems and dealing with the issues between Tony and me, my depression progressively got worse. Emotions started taking over me, and what little joy turned to anger and into fights. Our fights became real violent. There was the time he had to go to the hospital when he broke his hand while hitting me on my shoulder. In another violent fight, I was cut on my shoulder when he pushed me into the glass window at the back door. I didn't seek any medical treatment.

Sometimes Lady H had to intervene, coming to control me because of the physical rage I had inside of me that would explode. I would lose control. I was like a mad woman, roaring like the lion that I was. I was on an attack, taking a two-by-four, knocking holes in walls, breaking what little things I had. After we would have one of our heated arguments and I calmed down, I realized what I had done and had to replace everything I damaged. Suffering with physical, emotional, mental abuse, I had no business being with Tony. Mentally, he was adding more stress to my already-stressful life. When I was pushed the wrong way, I would explode and try to hurt myself, or others.

When Chrissy was one month old, we had another surprise visit from family members from Ohio. They wanted to let my grandmother travel for the last time; she was getting too old. It was my Auntie, Uncle Lee and my cousin Emily, who sent me the clothes, and her husband. An hour after their arrival at Mama's, Uncle Lee came outside where I was standing talking with my neighbor. He started flirting with them. They laughed, not reacting to his flirtation, and then he looked at me.

"Where's your husband?" he asked me. "He at work."

He said, "Come on, let's go to your house and you give me a little bit."

I looked at him and walked away. I couldn't believe he was still trying to have sex with me.

"Dirty old man," I said. I didn't cuss him out 'cause he was family, and I didn't want to hurt my Auntie. This time I didn't cry. I overlooked him and went on and continued visiting with the rest of my family. I was a survivor. I stood up to his sexual advances.

Later that day, I asked my cousin's husband if he could take me to the five-and-dime store to get some cups. We didn't have any cups for our guests to drink out of, and it would have saved me some time from catching the bus. My cousin Emily went ballistic, accusing me of wanting her husband and trying to fight me. I was looking at her confused. I couldn't believe her irate behavior toward me. I didn't respond. I just stared at her in shock, thinking how do these people keep saying that I am their favorite cousin and at the same time they betray me? I walked away crying. If I had stayed, I don't know what would have happened.

She'd accused me of wanting her husband, and she knew I was living with my boyfriend. Emily and her husband got in an argument, and the next day they decided to leave early. And without any apologies for her irate behavior toward me, she stopped sending me clothes for the baby, and she stopped contacting me.

A month after that incident happened, Emily's husband called Lena and said that he left Emily and had taken custody of their daughter because something was wrong with Emily mentally. I talked to my Auntie; she told me that Emily went to jail for driving down the highway naked. I asked what was wrong with her; she said she was diagnosed as a paranoid schizophrenic after they took her to seek treatment following the highway incident.

Another family member told me that Emily had had a baby at a young age and had tragically witnessed her baby being tossed into the furnace. I don't know how true that information was, but I do know something happened that made her psychotic.

Shortly after our unforgettable visit from our family members, a man from our past surprised us: JB, my mother's ex-boyfriend and my molester. We were not aware how he found out where Mama lived; he just showed up at her door. Seeing him was awkward, knowing what he had done to me. I didn't show any anger toward him; he didn't stay that long. After he left Amy and I and her godmother were sitting on the porch. I started talking about him, confessing my secret about him molesting me. Then I was shocked to hear my sister say he molested her as well. I told her that I thought I was the only one he was doing that to.

"Our secret was kept well. It goes to show you how good a predator can manipulate someone into keeping a secret," I said to Amy. I got to thinking, he was the reason why I didn't like oral sex or hearing about it. Sometimes I would hear Amy and her godmother and Mama talking about it, and I would get up and leave the room.

We confided to Mama what happened to us. She asked us why we didn't tell her when he was doing this to us. We told her because we knew she wasn't going to do anything about it. We knew all she cared about was her pills. We told her we felt that keeping us out of any dangerous situation was not her concern.

A few days later, I was standing at the store, talking to Sam, the guy who worked there. He was Mark's brother, the man I would have sex with in the back of the store for money when I was being promiscuous or sexually seeking attention. JB walked in and I assumed he didn't like how Sam was flirting with me. Before we knew it, JB punched Sam in the face, and a fight erupted, spreading outside.

I was screaming for JB to stop. The police were called and came running one by one across the street, heading for JB and Sam, trying to stop the fight. JB started beating up the policemen, hitting them all as they approached him. Police were everywhere, arms swinging. When there were a lot of them, they surrounded JB, managing to subdue him. They carried him across the street to the police station.

I was screaming and crying, not sure why, but part of me cared about his safety. Later that night, they released him. He was not charged with the assault. They had let him sleep off the drugs he was on that made him hallucinate. That was the last time we saw him.

Sympathetic, and naive, I was robbed because of my generosity. A man I'd met who was walking door-to-door in our neighborhood was seeking financial assistance because three of his family members had been tragically killed in a hit-and-run accident. We stood on my porch and I told him I would I help him out of his tragic situation with a donation. But I didn't have any change and I couldn't leave the house because Chrissy was sleep. And I was not going to leave him at my house alone with my kids.

I was being too trustworthy and I sent him and my son to the store to get some change. I told him to let my son pick out something for him and his sister and he could to take out what I was giving as donation and send the rest back by my son. That was the only way he could get change. I stood on the porch, watching him and my son until they were no longer in my eyesight. After ten minutes passed, I started getting worried. My heart was beating fast, about to panic because my son had not came around that corner, and it shouldn't have taken that long. We lived right at the corner.

I went in the house to check on Chrissy and Toya and was about to walk to the store to see why my son had not returned home. When I went back outside and was walking down the stairs, my son came running around the corner. I was relieved. All kinds of bad thoughts were going through my head when my son

approached me. I started questioning him; he said the man brought him what he wanted and left him at the store, not giving him the rest of my money.

What that man did was heartless. He took advantage of my kindness, because I was too trusting. I put my son in a dangerous situation, and I swore that I would never do that again. I thought I was going to have to experience another tragic situation. That was another of life's lesson learned.

I was lying in my bed when I received a phone call from Lena.

"You have a brother and sister," she said.
"I know."
"No. You have a brother and sister."
"I know," I said again.

"No. Your daddy had a son and daughter by someone else," she said. She went on to tell me my brother lived in Ohio and he's her sister-in-law son. He is six months younger than Amy, born on February 16. That's Mama's birthday. And our sister is by Shirley, her friend, who stayed with us, and she is six months older than Chrissy. My baby has an aunt that is six months older than she is.

"You can't ever tell her you are her older siblings because Shirley is married, and her husband thinks he's the father," Lena said.

I felt that part was wrong 'cause we will be missing out on having a relationship with her. We were being robbed of that. I was OK with the news that I had other siblings. But when I talked to Mama about it, she was furious. She said she didn't ever want that baby coming around her. We told her she was wrong, the baby didn't have anything to do with what happened. She said she don't care; she didn't want the baby around her. And Mama ended her friendship with Shirley.

At first I didn't understand why she was so angry because she and Daddy separated but were still married. I know now Shirley had crossed the boundary line because they were friends. It kind of shocked me because I did not think Daddy was involved with someone, especially someone who claimed to be Mama's friend and someone she helped. I said OK, she could tell me more about my brother another time. Mama had known about him all along, and she kept him a secret from us. She was wrong for doing that. Anyway, I was dealing with my own emotional problems.

Tony and I continued having problems, arguing over him not being responsible about caring for his family. I was trying to raise my kids without any help or support the best way I could. Plus, I had taken in my goddaughter, Womp, whose mother's addiction put her and her brother and sister in dangerous situations, and their living environment was unsafe. I felt bad.

My heart was hurting because I couldn't get her siblings. Because of my situation, I couldn't handle any more. I went to friends to seek any assistance I could get from them, and I got her some clothes. I did the best I could for all of them with the limited resources I had. The emotional problems I was suffering from started to affect the way I treated her and the other kids. I took my anger out on her. When Toya had a bowel movement in the tub and was playing with it, and I yelled at Womp, asking her why would she sit there and watch her play with that mess. And I made her get out and go to bed. I know she didn't intentionally let her do that, but the problem I was suffering allowed me to think that, and my reaction was harsh.

She was already being sexually and mentally abused at home, and I didn't mean to add more trouble to her life.

That same week I had another physical and emotional outburst. Tony and I had another violent altercation. I was screaming and crying hysterically. I had a two-by-four in my hand. I was about to damage the wall or him with it. Hesitating, I turned my head toward the door, thinking in anger, and when I turned back toward him he sucker punched me. I became dizzy and the punch also resulted in a big knot on my head. This time, I was the one going to the hospital. Once there, I wasn't questioned about how I obtained my injury. I admitted to myself he got one on me by catching me off guard. I was usually the one sending him to the hospital, but he got one on me that time.

Chapter seven

Emotional and Mental Issues

Because of emotional and mental issues that I was suffering and the violent outburst I couldn't control, I had to send my goddaughter back home to an abusive, dangerous, neglectful, unlivable environment with me checking in on her when I could. I didn't want her to be exposed to any more violence from my irrational behavior. Every time I got a chance, I prayed to God that He protect her. Because of the love and compassion I had for her, I was trying to take her from an abusive situation, only bringing her into my emotional and unstable environment. My mental state wouldn't allow me to be available to her or tend to the other children's emotional well-being because of the situation I was going through with Tony.

After our last altercation, he stopped coming home. And once again, my unstable mental state made me use bad judgment. I used my baby to try and get him to come home. I would do all kinds of crazy things like catching the bus to his job with my babies, getting into a verbal altercation with him in front of his coworkers and customers, cussing him out, putting all our business out in the open. I was telling him he needed to be a man and a daddy; how worthless he was. He just stood there with this stupid grin on his face because he was embarrassed.

I wanted to know where he was when he was not coming home; he didn't give me an answer. In another incident I used bad judgment when Tony wasn't spending time with his baby. We were at McDonald's and out of anger, I sat Chrissy on top of the counter, and I ran out the store. He caught up with me, and we started fighting. I was being dramatic, trying to get some attention. I started crying; this ignorant, irresponsible, non-appreciative poor excuse of a man sat our baby on the curb and walked away with no regard for her safety. I caught the bus home, crying because I couldn't understand why he was treating us so badly.

That was just part of my irresponsible behavior. I was trying everything to get this man to come back home and work things out and be a family. But when he would treat me the way he did my anger would emerge. He ignored my pleading. I had pursued this man for years, trying to convince him to be with me because I believed he was my soul mate, and we were supposed to be together. Our relationship turned out to be a disaster.

When everything I did failed, I stopped trying. I became extremely depressed, withdrawn from my family and friends, only coming outside to go to the store. I kind of withdrew myself from everyone. One night, I was looking out the window and saw Lena at the corner, sitting on the step of the abandoned building. I went outside to see what she was doing while my babies were asleep.

It was midnight; men from the factories were on their lunch break, going to the store. One worker approached us. He started talking to Lena. They stepped to the side. I couldn't hear their brief conversation. Then they stepped back to where I was.

"Is she down?" he asked her.

"Naw. She not like that. She not down. She's my cousin," she said.

"Oh," he said, and walked away.

I asked her what did he mean by am I down? She said nothing, but I knew. Like I said, she thought I was stupid. I observed everything. I said to myself let me go back in the house before someone else thinks I'm doing what she's doing - prostitution. I went inside the house, returning outside, occasionally visiting family and friends.

Mentally I could not handle seeing my family spend money when I had little finances, barely surviving, and no one offered me any assistance. I was also hurt and disappointed because my mother had shown favoritism between my sister and I. She allowed Amy to move out at the age of seventeen, and I had to stay until I was eighteen to suffer all that abuse.

I was surprised with the news that my sister was

pregnant. I couldn't celebrate hearing her wonderful news when I was mentally and emotionally unstable about my personal circumstances.

I saw Tony occasionally through the months. On January 30, 1985, I was lying in bed when he came home on one of his occasional visits. He came in the bedroom and sat next to me. I was looking at him. I didn't say anything about his disappearing and neglecting his responsibilities, his malice, and emotional cold hearted abuse toward me.

He looked at me and in a soft voice he asked, "How would you like to change your last name?"

"Huh, what are you talking about?" I asked.

"How would you like to have my last name?" he said.

I sat up in the bed and I said, "Yes. I would like that. How?"

"We can go to Ohio and get married," he said.

I was happy and excited. I quickly forgave him for all the abuse he'd inflicted on me because I loved him, and that was all I ever wanted. As we were lying in the bed talking, something we hadn't done in a long time, I was massaging his back when I noticed he still had those stitches in his shoulder, and it had been almost a year since I stabbed him.

"Why you still have these stitches in your shoulder?" I asked him.

"I been scared to take them out," he said. "You wanna do it?"

When I took them out, he had small holes from the stitches

being in there to long. As we talked further he confessed to me that

he'd been cheating on me and that the other woman wanted him to marry her. He said he didn't want to marry her. I shouldn't have said yes because I was second, and he only wanted to marry me because he didn't want to marry her.

I was hurt; naive, not having a clue that he was cheating on me. But the love I had for him allowed me to forgive him. That night we had sex. It was the first time since Chrissy was born five months earlier. Thursday morning we got up early to get ready. He went to his mother's house to call the Ohio City Clerk Office, seeking information about cost and the required documentation and directions. He rushed back to tell me that we had to be there before twelve noon.

I called my best friend Eden, telling her the good news. We both started screaming. I asked her to be a part of this special occasion, to go with me to be my witness, maid of honor. She said yes. We did everything together; I told her what time to be ready. Emmanuel asked me if he could go and I told him yes. I got him ready, and dropped Chrissy and Toya off with my mother.

The drive to Toledo, Ohio was going to take forty-five minutes to an hour. Once we entered the freeway, I started getting nervous and excited because I would finally accomplish what I set out to do, and that was getting Tony to be my husband. I was checking the time, worried that we weren't going to make it by twelve because we didn't leave quite on time.

Once in Ohio, we got lost; he stopped and asked a police officer for directions. I had a sigh of relief when we made it there at eleven forty-five. Once inside, we had to wait in the hallway for our turn to see the clerk to fill out the form for our marriage license. Sitting there waiting patiently, at 11:55 am. they called, "next."

Tony walked ahead of me. I had the jitters. I started shaking as I filled out my part of the form, and after we completed all the necessary information, he turned in the forms and paid for the license. We were directed back to the hallway where the ceremony would be performed by the preacher. Standing at the door, he gave the preacher the license. We had to stand according to where he wanted us and he performed the ceremony.

"You may now kiss your bride," he said. After we kissed, I was stricken with emotion; tears started rolling down my face. I hugged Eden and my son. On January 31, 1985, I became Ernestine Howard.

As we turned to leave, the preacher said, "Hold it. You have to pay me."

I knew Tony didn't have any more money; he'd borrowed what he did have from his mother. Tony said, "We don't have any more money, and they didn't say I had to pay you when I called.

The preacher replied, "I don't care what they didn't tell you. Didn't I perform a service for you?"

"Yes and I apologize," Tony said.

The preacher was mad, and he told us to go ahead and not to do that to anybody else when somebody rendered their services. We left; I felt bad, but we didn't know. I was afraid he wasn't going to turn in our license and we weren't going to be officially married. When we got outside, we weren't walking together. He acted like we weren't just announced husband and wife. He was walking ahead of us.

I wanted to take a picture to remind me of what was supposed to be a joyous occasion. He didn't seem to be involved. I saw a man walking. I said, "Excuse me, sir, can you take a picture of us, my son and Eden and I?" When I looked at that picture, it was ugly. I looked like I went to a funeral instead of a wedding. I was thinking as we were headed back home that we had no business getting married. It was doomed from the start. He was marrying me because he didn't want to marry another woman that he was cheating on me with. I thought about how I was chosen second, and I don't do second. I should have been first; and secondly, we had no money, he had to borrow; and third, I had no clothes, I had to wear the dress that I wore to my daddy's funeral, which was all black; and fourth was his ignorant behavior toward me.

When it came to Tony, I was so naive. I let love blind me from reality, that's why I say our marriage was doomed. Once we got back home, we were standing in front of Lady H's house. He was showing everyone the license, acting like he was happy. He said he was going to go show it to his friends at his job, but I didn't want

him to take it because I wanted to show it to my friends. Plus I had a bad feeling about him keeping it.

We started tussling over it, and it ripped almost in half. I got mad at his irrational behavior. I let it go before it was damaged any further. He took the license and Chrissy and left while I was standing on the sidewalk with his mother, embarrassed and mad. Instead of spending time together so we could celebrate what was supposed to be our happy union, he left. I talked with his mother briefly, and then I went home, spending time with my kids.

He returned home late with Chrissy, leaving again, not returning home until the next morning, February 1, 1985. We never consummated our marriage. I started questioning him.

"Where were you?"

"I was with Paula," (the other woman).

"How can you do this to me? How can he be with her on our wedding day?" He didn't answer me. Then…

"I'm leaving you," he said, finally.

My heart sank, and I lost it; I started screaming hysterically. "How can you do this to me? Please don't leave me! Don't do this to me," I begged. I reacted the same way I did when I lost my daddy.

"Why did you marry me? Why did you waste my time? How do we get married one day and you leave me the next day?" I asked him. He was packing his belongings and left with no regard to my begging. His mother came to calm me down, and Amy came and got the kids and took them to my mother. Emotionally distraught, I could do nothing but cry. I cried all day long and well into the next day, neglecting the needs of my children.

Suffering emotionally from the entire ordeal, I was also still grieving over losing my daddy. I fell deeper and deeper into depression, totally isolated myself from everyone again. I almost missed the birth of my niece. I went to the hospital with Carl to see Amy when she went into labor, but didn't stay that long because my depression made me anti-social. Carl took me back home.

Amy was in labor for two days, then the doctor gave her a C- section, realizing she could not deliver normally. Mentally,

I could not enjoy the special occasion because of the harsh treatment I received from them. My niece was born on February 14, 1985, 366 days after the passing of my father. She looked just like her father, like he delivered her instead of my sister.

After they'd been home a little while, Mama called telling me my niece had stopped breathing, and they were running her to the fire station. Once I arrived, Mama tried to explain what happened. Carl returned to the house with the baby; he explained in detail what happened and how he panicked and ran her to the fire station instead of waiting on EMS to arrive. The fire station was three blocks away. They got her back to breathing, and he came back home. She had to see her doctor to see what happened, and I went back home.

Womp reminded me of another time I displayed irrational behavior. It was Easter and I'd caught the bus with all the kids to Tony's job, and argued with him, trying to convince him to come back home because I loved him. He gave the kids something to eat, and after they were done eating, he ran out the door like a scary bitch across Gratiot. I was right behind him with my baby on my hip and the kids running behind me right into that busy main street. I disregarded the safety of my children, chasing after him. Cars could have hit us all, but God was with us because my mind wasn't.

There are usually a lot of cars, and thank God at that time, there weren't. I don't know why he was running. I hadn't threatened to attack him. When I couldn't catch him, I stopped running. I was out of breath. I got my kids and we caught the bus back home, not realizing how irresponsible I was toward my kids. I used bad judgment and it affected my decisions and responsibilities.

And my kids were suffering from my emotional behavior. I allowed my depression to control me, taking over my mind. I didn't come out of the house, nor did my kids. I don't remember how I went to the grocery store. Part of my life is blank because it was so scrambled. At the time, I didn't remember what happened from one day to the next.

I remember at times I asked Lady H to bring me items

from the store. When I saw her walking past, my heart and soul were shadowed with darkness. I let myself go, neglecting my appearance, not caring about my hygiene. I started being paranoid; it felt like the walls were closing in on me. I would not leave the house. To control the fear of the walls closing in on me, I changed rooms. I put my bed in the living room to see a change of scenery, plus I could look out the window without getting out of bed.

Then I started seeing things. At first I thought it was a figment of my imagination, but I saw it again. Big cat-sized rats were actually invading my house. I sat and watched them lift up a metal plate that was screwed to the floor. They were walking around the house like they were human, and this was their house. My babies and me were on the couch, screaming, watching them when they came near us. I was petrified of anything that was not human. I yelled out loud for Tony's sister. She came running, scared because of the way I yelled.

"Call your mother! There are a lot of big cat-sized rats in here. Tell her to come now so she could get rid of them," I said. She went and got lots of big rattraps, almost immediately they were being caught. I had to call her to come take them off the trap and reset them. I called her when it came to rodents; I was scared.

Still feeling like the room was closing in on me, even though there was lots of space, I changed rooms again. I moved my bed to every room of the house except the kitchen. That was how emotionally disturbed I was.

Summer had arrived; we still hadn't emerged from the house. My mother and Lady H came to the house concerned because it was summer, and I hadn't let the kids come outside. My mother made a comment about my son's skin color. She said she was taking them with her. She said her grandson needed some sunlight, that he was pale as a ghost. They were unaware that they were freeing my kids from my emotional destruction. I wasn't free quite yet.

Every day, Mama came to get the kids to let them play. I slowly started coming out the porch. I learned that my brother was the young loan shark of the neighborhood. Friends and family members went to him to borrow money. He was tight with his

money and he charged interest; a dollar on a dollar. To get out of paying interest, some people tried to use how long they knew him; some used that he had a crush on them at one time; another used the "we family" line. But he was tight. If you wanted his money that was what you had to give back. He was a smart young man, but it was funny though. I never borrowed from him because I knew I couldn't pay him back. If I didn't have it, I didn't need it.

The Spell.....

Lady H came to the house. "Have you ever heard of voodoo?" She asked.

I said, "No, what's that?" She explained that she'd received a phone call from Paula, saying that she and her mother put a spell on Tony and me. I was astonished, wondering why and how and what to do.

I received a phone call from Paula herself; she had the nerve to call me. She told me what her and her mother did and said I need to be careful about where I leave my things. Hearing this made me more heated and puzzled at the same time, wondering what was she talking about. How did she get something of mine? Did Tony steal something of mine? And I knew she hadn't been in my house.

I told her she was a liar; she didn't have anything of mine. She mentioned my comb that I left in Tony's car. She said it had some of my hair in it.

I told her, "Who cares? When I see you, I'm going to beat your ass." And I hung up on her. She called me back. I asked her why she was still calling me.

"Don't you have my husband?"

I said, "What? You mad that he didn't marry you?" And I hung up again. I believe she was mad that he married me and not her, but that was stupid. He left me for her. He consummated our marriage with her. I believed what she said about the spell because of a situation I had one night.

In the middle of a deep sleep, I felt excruciating pain in my stomach. I was sweating profusely. I had gotten up to go to the bathroom. While sitting on the toilet, everything turned black, as if I went blind. I tried to shake it off without success; then I started getting nauseated. Not able to see, I had to feel for the bucket to vomit in. I was scared. I was alone, and I didn't know what was wrong with me. Then all of a sudden, everything stopped, and I was better. I went back to bed.

I started searching for more information about curses and how to remove it and I slowly started resurfacing into the outside world. I also found out that a lot had changed in my neighborhood; friends had moved, and new people had moved into the neighborhood. Nessa was one person I met when she was walking from the store with her son. When she stopped and asked me a question, she invited me to visit her.

Our friends who lived upstairs from Mama also moved, and there were new people living there. When I met them, they said they didn't know who I was or that I even existed. They didn't know my mama had another daughter, saying they thought my kids were my mama's kids because they never saw me. There was a lot I had missed that I found out when I resurfaced back into the world. I learned about the severity of my niece's illness, her being taken back and forth to the doctor, then she was diagnosed as having sickle cell anemia, and she had to be put on a heart monitor. They had to take classes on caring for her, concerning her condition and knowing what to do to help her if she had a medical crisis. I wasn't involved because I couldn't help care for her because I was trying to care for my kids alone and trying to handle my mental issues.

Amy was about to turn eighteen in a month and a half and would soon be receiving the money from Daddy's life insurance that she was supposed to divide between us. Instead I was given a car that I didn't want or like. It was a man's car that they used to race. I took the car. I had no choice. The money was left to her. She knew what she was supposed to do with it; but she was naive to love like I was. At the time, I didn't see it, and I blamed her for letting Carl convince her into making the decisions she made about the money.

She knew how Daddy divided things between us, but I was dealt a bad hand before because I wasn't his biological daughter. So I accepted this bad hand too. I didn't have money to purchase license plates for the car. I drove over to Eden's house. I mentioned it out loud that I didn't have plates; one of her brothers said he had a license plate. I could have it but it didn't have a sticker on it. Her younger brother mentioned how we can get one but we had to wait until it got dark. I said Ok, that I'll be back then and I left.

I returned when it got dark. He said we had to take the sticker off a car. I drove two blocks from their street, and we parked behind this car. He told me what to do; I was scared. I convinced him to do it, and I'd be the lookout. We made ourselves look obvious. A man came to the door, talking loud to whoever was in the house with him when he spotted us.

He yelled at us, "Hey, what are you doing?" We jumped in that car so fast, and I took off laughing. I dropped him back off, and I went home.

First thing I wanted to do now that I had plates was drive to Tony's job, and try to convince him to come home. I wasn't experienced yet with the rules of driving, and I was following behind the police, and I saw this sign that read No turning between

3:00 pm. and 6:00 pm. Something told me not to turn.

I had on my turn signal, hesitating, but when I saw the police turn, I turned behind them. I got a strong feeling that I shouldn't have done that. They let me pass them up just a little and flicked those lights on, pulling me over. I said, damn, I should have followed my first thoughts. The officer approached the car, asked me for my license and registration. I told him I didn't have a license. He lectured me about not having my license, and he said he couldn't let me drive the car. He gave me a ticket, and I got the kids out the car, and we started walking.

I sat on the curb just a few blocks away where I could still see the car. I waited until they left and were out of sight. I waited for about ten minutes before I walked back to the car. I got in but just sat there just to make sure they didn't drive back around and catch me. I then drove to Tony's job. I let him see his daughter and was talking to him, trying again to convince him to come home. That still didn't work, and we left.

A couple days later, Tony came by the house to retrieve the rest of his belongings. He also took the fan that Lady H gave us, and that was the only fan in the house. I started arguing with him, asking him how could he come and take something out of my house that we were using, including his own daughter. He was being insensitive about our welfare. I couldn't stop him because it was his mother's. She didn't tell him he could take it, but once again, I felt I had no right when something wasn't mine. He added more insult to my emotions by taking something from my house to give to another woman.

Nessa became my new associate. She lived in one of the apartments in the four family units from where Jack and Linda and Marianne and Eddie had moved. Nessa had come to my house to visit me, as I was in another phone confrontation with Paula that had me enraged. I told her before I hung up that I was coming to beat her ass. She laughed like I was playing. She assumed I didn't know where they lived, and I really didn't, other than the information that Tony provided me with, saying they lived in an apartment across the street from Henry Ford Hospital.

Nessa said she would go with me. I took my kids to Mama, making up an excuse about where I was going. I drove to the area of the hospital in search of the apartment building on West Grand Boulevard across from Henry Ford Hospital. There was only one building that sits directly across from the hospital.

Once inside, I started searching for her name on the mailbox until I found it. I waited until somebody went in, and we walked in behind them straight to her door. At first, I knocked on the door, calmly asking for Tony to try and retrieve my fan. Paula came to the door. She refused to let me see him. I became belligerent, She closed the door and Nessa grabbed me.

"You don't go in nobody's house like that. You don't know what they got," she said.

"I don't care." I wanted to hurt them. I started banging on the door, cussing at them, telling them to bring their scary asses out.

Nessa said, "Let's go before somebody call the police."

"I don't care. Fuck the police." I yelled though the door at Tony, "Just give me my fan back so I can go." Those cowards. I was still trying to get that curse off me. I took what little money I had and paid this guy who claimed he could remove spells and return my loved one home. The man was kind of creepy, but he didn't try anything sexual with me. I went a few times. When nothing he was doing worked, I figured he was a fraud.

My kids and I were suffering from the heat, and I had no money to buy a fan. Well, I kind of did have money but my priorities weren't right because my mind wasn't. My family wasn't concerned for our well-being; their money was to benefit them. I started getting furious because I had no help and no one cared. and Tony had taken the fan, and he knew my financial situation.

I grabbed a butcher knife and got my babies and went back to Tony's apartment. I parked right next to his car in the back parking lot. I put the kids in his car to play just to be vindictive, feeling like I had the right to because he was my husband. We had been there waiting for thirty minutes when Tony and Paula and her daughter came outside. I had the long butcher knife in my hand, waiting for Paula to come out for another confrontation.

I demanded Tony go get that fan. He refused, walked to his car, took the kids out of the car, including his own daughter, and told Paula and her daughter to come get in the car. I went ballistic. I was a scorned woman. I started swinging the knife, trying to attack them.

Paula, in a frantic voice, yelled, "Somebody, help! Call

the police."

"Call the police! This is my husband," I said.

Her daughter started crying, saying "Daddy." When what she said registered in my head, my rage was fuming.

I said, Bitch, that's not your daddy." I looked at him and said, "How do you have her calling you Daddy when this is your daughter, your only baby right here and you can't be a father to her?"

He made Paula and her daughter go in the house and he got in his car. I said, "Wait, I just wanted to talk to you." I jumped in my car. He took off, and so did I, right behind him. I drove through these thick yellow poles, damaging both sides of my car. At that

I was trailing right behind him. He tried to elude me by driving onto the John C Lodge freeway. I was right behind him like I was the police. We were doing speeds up to hundred miles an hour.

He exited, went around the bend, and so did I. He then reentered back onto the freeway, going the opposite way. I was right behind him, speed still topping at hundred miles until my car started slowing up, causing me to pull over to the side of the road. I started crying because I couldn't continue to chase him. I was angry. I was going to hurt him.

I knew he saw me pull over and that he didn't have the morals to see if something had happened to us. He showed no concern for our well-being or for his daughter at that time. I wasn't either. Even if not for my kids and me, she should have been the main reason he stopped or came back. We sat at that roadside for ten minutes when a car pulled up behind me and an older gentleman came up to the car. He said he saw me and thought I might need help. He said he exited the freeway, came back around.

"What's wrong?" he asked. "Are you having car trouble?"

"I ran out of gas, and I don't have any money," I said.

"Do you have a gas can?

I shook my head no and he told me to wait right there, which was funny: where was I going? He was gone for ten minutes. I had thought he wasn't going to come back. He had a gas can.

"This is what I want you to do after I pour this gas in. I want you to follow me to the gas station. This is just enough to get the car started," he said.

I did exactly what he told me to do and he put more gas in my car. I thanked him; I appreciated what he did for me. He didn't have to stop to help me. He was my Good Samaritan. I thanked God for letting me run out of gas and sending this man. Who knew what the outcome could have been? Probably tragic because the way we were driving and the anger I had inside of me had me thinking unclear. I wasn't thinking of what the tragic consequences would have been because of my irrational rage.

I thanked him again, and we left, went our separate ways. When I got back home, everybody was looking at the car damage, asking me what happened. I told them in full detail. That was an example of more of my irresponsible behavior.

A week had passed since my altercation with Tony and Paula when Lady H came to my house. She said Tony was in the hospital because Paula had her brother's jump on him. They beat him badly with a baseball bat, severely injuring him. He continued to be with her. When he wasn't fully recovered from that injury, he was injured again, sending him back to the hospital with third-degree burns from the waist down. He told his Mama that he accidentally knocked a pot of boiling hot water on himself. When I heard that story, it sounded suspicious because I knew he was lying.

Lady H said he wanted to see Chrissy. I said he had the nerve to ask to see her after his neglectful treatment toward her. I was debating on if I should let her go. I said she was not going without me, and I definitely wasn't going to let her be around Paula.

"If you go, please don't do anything," she said. "You know, Paula's going to be there."

"Ok, but she better not say anything to me when we arrive at the hospital." Lady H pleaded with me not to start an altercation.

I said, "Ok, I won't."

We entered the hospital and stopped at the information desk, asking for his room, and we were given a pass. As we entered his room, Paula was sitting next to him, holding his hand like she was concerned about his well-being. First thing I noticed was his injury from the baseball bat attack. I walked over to the bed to take a closer look.

"Man, they f*** you up," I said. I was walking around the room like I had the authority; like I had a lot of privilege because I was his wife, daring her to say something so I could beat her. I could see Lady H was feeling uncomfortable because she kept looking at me, making sure I wasn't going to try to attack them.

Every time Paula said something or touched my baby, I got mad, ready to jump. But I promised Lady H that I wouldn't. I asked him what happened; he said the same thing, that he knocked the boiling water on himself when he tried to lift it. He looked at Paula.

"Isn't that right, baby?" he said.

I was fuming when he said that. I said, "Right. I know what happened." And I left it alone.

Lady H was ready to go, and so was I. After sustaining both of those assaults as the result of her doing, he stayed with her. This led me to believe she had put a spell on him because of his unexplainable behavior.

When Tony got well, he would come over to see his daughter. I questioned him again about his incident; he continued to deny Paula's involvement. I continued to seek out so-called psychics, hoping that they could remove the curse; hoping that whatever they were trying would work. I just wanted him back home, to be a happy family. I wanted him to love me. I knew I couldn't afford it but I just believed that they could really help me.

I allowed those psychics to manipulate me into buying items, like a comforter set that I had, to send it to one lady who said she needed it to remove the curse. They had me burning candles and other rituals where people thought I was practicing witchcraft; they were scared to visit me, thinking I would put a curse on them. I just wanted this curse off me and to get my husband back. I was naive; I believed they could help me.

Every time Tony would come see Chrissy, he would verbally abuse me, criticize me; saying I was ugly and other derogatory comments about me. He would say that no man was ever going to want me because I had too many kids. I fell for his degrading comments, believed him. He knew that he could only hurt me with words. He was scared to physically put his hand on me because of my violent outrage. I relapsed back into extreme depression.

Amy turned eighteen, receiving the money from daddy's life insurance. She gave my brother his money. He didn't let them do him like I was done even though the money was never split between us. He was given just enough to get a car. I received nothing; my sister was in love and naive, trusting her man just like I was. She believed Carl had her best interest at heart only to manipulate her out of her money. He got her to purchase a house and put it in his name. Carl was a good provider so she had no reason not to trust him monetarily. But other women? That's a different story. They moved into their house, and it was completely furnished.

My brother wasn't happy with what he received, neither was I. I was taken for granted. I didn't have a choice in what I received. I rarely spoke out when I was being mistreated. I accepted what was being dealt to me. I didn't want or like that car Amy gave me, but what could we do? I was made to believe I wasn't part of the family. Besides, we thought she would do the right thing and do what we thought Daddy expected her to. Like I said, love blinded us.

My brother bought a Dodge Colt, I believe. He wasn't of legal age to drive or experienced, but he and his friends were hanging out. "Joyriding" When they came back home, they told us what they had just experienced, driving to Flint, Michigan to meet some girls. They described what happened, and the story they described sounded like a scene right out of a movie.

They were in a conversation with some girls who were friends of his friends when they got into a verbal altercation with a group of guys; guns were pulled, the chasing started. They said they were running, jumping fences, ran in the back door and out the front door of somebody's house. They hid out until they weren't in any more danger then hit the freeway all the way home. We laughed hysterically. I told them that's what they got for messing with somebody's girlfriend.

I was trying to heal and overcome some of my abuse I was suffering from, when I was hit with traumatizing news from Tony. He said he and his mother were going to seek custody of Chrissy, saying I was an unfit mother. I got mad, but didn't let him know I was. I started laughing.

"Go ahead, do it. No judge is going to give you my baby," I said. "Prove I'm unfit when you haven't taken care of her financially nor spend time with her. You work all the time, and Paula is not touching my baby."

I was not physically neglecting my kids; I took care of them to the best of my ability, though sometimes making irresponsible judgment. I loved my babies. They were all I had.

"Do what you and your mother have to do but you're not getting my baby," I told him. 'You're not even the daddy."

He laughed, he knew I was lying; she looked just like him. I was mad, and he left. I couldn't believe what they were trying to do.

Hearing what they were trying to do devastated me. I felt betrayed by someone I cared about and who I felt cared about me. Lady H was the only one who had supported me. Not sure what he was going to do, I packed a few of our belongings, and we went to Eden's house. I told her what transpired between Tony and I and that he threatened to take Chrissy away from me. I also informed Eden's family of his threat just in case he came over to their house.

That night, Tony showed up at her house, saying he wanted to see me. Her daddy denied him.

"I came to get my baby," he said.

Eden's daddy grabbed his shotgun and said, "Mister, you have two seconds to get out of here. You are not taking my granddaughter nowhere."

In fear, Tony got out that house; we laughed. We went upstairs. Eden comforted me, gave me moral support. Her brother cared for the kids. We stayed up all night talking. I knew they already considered the kids and me as part of their family. She wanted to help me to stop dwelling on my emotional and traumatizing circumstances that seemed to continue to intrude on my life. She planned for us to do outdoor activities like we used to do before I started isolating myself.

With little or no money, we started back going to festivals, concerts, trying to lift my spirits, keeping my mind off my problems. We visited with each other so I wouldn't be alone. That helped a little. Reality set in when I would have to be alone, especially through the winter months. I was miserable; upset at all I'd had to go through all my life, wondering why this was happening to me. As the winter was upon us, I rarely visited her because I didn't want to constantly drag my babies out in the snow or cold.

As spring approached, I started visiting Nessa occasionally.

Her neighbor, who lived in the front apartment, was pursuing me, even though he had a girlfriend whose name also was Nessa. I knew he had a woman, and I ignored his advances. I wasn't trying to betray another woman because I had been betrayed.

There was another man who showed interest in me.

Nessa's Uncle Rob made advances toward me. At first I wasn't interested in him even though I liked the attention I was receiving. One night while hanging out with them, I was having a nice time laughing, and joking—something I hadn't done in a long time. Then they started drinking and smoking. At first, I didn't participate. But after awhile, I became a victim to the peer pressure, allowing them to talk me into joining them in their kind of fun.

We got very intoxicated. Someone came up with the idea to go to the park. Instead of going to the closest park, we went to Belle Isle. We were just observing the view and continuing to drink. No one was in any shape to drive back home. I knew I wasn't going to trust my life with them even though I had no life. I was the one basically more aware of what was going on and in control. Laughing and joking as we got in the car, I opened my eyes wide, trying to make sure I drove correctly so I wouldn't draw any attention toward us. We arrived safely.

Not having sex in a year was driving me insane. I took alternative measures to relieve my urges by taking a cold washrag, and putting it between my legs to cool down. Instead it instantly turned hot. I thought that would help. I didn't want to commit adultery nor had the desire to be intimate with another man just in case Tony and I might get back together.

I felt that I would be cheating on him even though he was cheating on me with Paula. As I got to thinking about what he was doing to me, that feeling soon ended, and I mentally gave up. Now I was ready to take revenge. When I had enough, I resorted back to my promiscuous ways. I didn't care about who I destroyed along my path, including myself. Dan, who was the other Nessa's boyfriend, convinced me into letting him come over my house. I told him what time so my kids would be asleep.

He showed up at the exact time I told him. He barely got in the door when he was all over me, kissing me. I felt no attraction or excitement toward this man, but I let him continue because I needed to relieve my urges. While this man was touching me, it made me feel disgusted. Sitting on the couch, he took off my underwear and started performing oral sex on me. I wasn't feeling any pleasure. It felt disgusting. I pulled him up on top of me so we could get into the sexual act. He fumbled around with his penis, trying to stick it inside of me. He started humping, moaning like he was enjoying himself.

I was lying there, waiting to feel something. I couldn't feel a thing. He was still humping and moaning. I felt nothing, and that angered me.

"You can get up," I told him.

"Why?" he asked.

"Because," was all I said, not really telling him why. "Just get up. You have to leave," I said again.

He looked stunned. "Why are you making me leave?"

I said, "Because you have to."

I made up an excuse about me not knowing if my husband was going to show up. I said to myself, this nigga wasted my time. With the anger I had inside of me, he was lucky I spared his feelings, not outing him about his small penis. .I kept my encounter with him a secret from Nessa because I knew she liked him.

When my encounter with him wasn't successful, I moved on to my next victim, giving Nessa's uncle a chance. He wasn't any better, but at least I could feel him slightly. He made a big mistake, though and I wasn't taking anybody else's cruelty toward me. He tried to disrespect me in front of his family, criticizing me. I got mad and I told him to shut up before I tell everybody about his small penis. He became embarrassed when they started laughing. Once you disrespect me, I have nothing else to do with you.

We had new neighbors that moved on the block right next door to Nessa. It was a big family who I predicted were troublemakers from their wildly out-of-control behavior. They were showing off as they were moving in. They had not been living on the block long when a big family street brawl occurred between them and some of Carl's family. Jealously arose up between Diana's daughter and the girl in that family. Seeing them fighting reminded me of the big street fight we had when I was younger. All of a sudden, they all stopped fighting and went their separate ways, still arguing as they walked away. They held resentment toward one another.

The atmosphere in the hood was thick, not knowing when another altercation would happen. I didn't know if I should be friends with them, thinking Carl and his family would think I betrayed them by befriending the family who they considered their enemy. That wasn't my intention. I'm a friendly person that likes to meet people, and I was trying to make friends with them.

I stopped being concerned about how I thought they felt about me. When I saw the other brother of their now enemy, he wasn't quite my type; his complexion was too dark. I normally didn't like dark-complexioned men. I made an exception with my preference because he was fine. I became infatuated over him, became mischievous, spiteful, in a way. I tried to persuade him to be my man, unconcerned with other people's feelings.

I began to act like the people who had hurt and betrayed me. I didn't care that he had a girlfriend. He was aware of my attraction toward him, and I would have done anything for him so he would know I was serious about me wanting to be in a relationship. He was in desperate need of a place to live. He asked me if I could rent my back room out to him and his girlfriend. I felt vindictive and heartless.

"You can move in, but your girlfriend can't," I said. I wanted him to move in and be with me.

He said, "I can't move without her, she don't have a place to stay, and that's my girlfriend."

"Too bad. She can't stay," I said. Then he said he'd have to find somewhere else to live. I said Ok, and that was that.

Whenever I saw him, I flirted with him. I would take a shot at it, still trying to convince him to dump her and come be with me. He declined, never disrespecting me. We remained friends, me flirting with him when I saw him, and he would flirt back with a smile.

Out of desperation and out of control, I did the unimaginable. I had sex with his brother who was making sexual advances toward me. I was vulnerable and unstable and vindictive. I knew he was young, just reaching his teens, and I was twenty. I didn't use good judgment. I let him come over after telling him what time to come, and we had sex, and I made sure he knew it wasn't ever going to happen again.

Mentally, I was trying to convince myself that Tony was wrong when he criticized my looks, saying I was ugly; that nobody would want me. I wanted to prove he was wrong, and I did things I regretted at my lowest moment. I wasn't caring about myself or others, as I was proceeding down my path of destruction.

I met this man who said he was visiting a friend that lived in the neighborhood. He asked me to follow him to his friend's house to have sex, and I did. The house was the same house Joe Bob used to live in. I had never seen his friend whom he said lived in that house, which made me doubt him about who lived there. He had a key. And inside clothes were thrown all about the small-framed house.

I knew somebody lived there, and we had sex without me knowing anything about him. Our second sexual encounter was even more degrading. I allowed myself to show my lowest self-respect when I had sex with him at the front door of an elementary school. We were on the ground out of sight from people. After we were done, we went our separate ways. He returned a few more times, saying how good I was, and he wanted to continue our sexual encounters. I refused and had a nonchalant attitude, because of how I allowed myself to degrade myself like that. And I wanted to be more then someone's sex toy. At that time, once I had sex with you, I had no desire to continue having sex with you. Being vindictive made me feel like I was in control.

Eden's brother GP came to my house; it was shocking to me because he'd never came over before. We sat on the couch, talking, and I could tell something was up.

"I'm curious about why you're here," I told him.

He did this slight laugh, and was hesitant about saying anything. Then, "I like you, and have for years," he blurted out.

Hearing that shock me because I had no idea. I never saw any signs that he was interested in me in any kind of way.

"Why are you telling me now?" I asked him.

"You were off limits," he said. "I was forbidden from getting involved with any of Eden's friends, especially you because of all the trauma you been through."

Eden knew I was vulnerable, and I was; she was trying to protect me the best way she could, and she didn't want him to play with my heart or emotions. Defying her wishes, we started secretly having sex. Keeping the secret from Eden was hard because we told each other everything. We did everything together, even putting ourselves in dangerous situations.

There was the time we went to the show and a group of guys approached us and we stood there, talking. Then we decided to leave with them, ending up at their house. We had no idea where we were at, spending the night with them. We only had sex with the one that we were kind of attracted to. Their other friends thought they were going to have sex with us. The guy I was with thought we were going to switch partners. We told him we don't play that. They came up with an excuse for us to leave, saying their sister would be home from work soon. It was kind of funny because we had to catch the bus home, and we didn't know where we were. They had to tell us what bus to catch and lucky it was one bus straight from there.

We did things spontaneously. I was not as close to any of my other friends as I was with Eden. We were like sisters and at times, that's what we would tell people. This shocked them because she was white and I was black. When those guys didn't believe us, we laughed and said we had different fathers.

Wherever we went we had fun, and we didn't have to have money to enjoy ourselves. We would catch the bus downtown to the festival, only having bus fare. We got there and didn't do anything special, just walking around, enjoying the scenery, music, and meeting guys. When guys approached us, they were more attracted to her, some being so aggressive as to walking off with her, leaving me standing there like I didn't exist. This made me fell like I was the third wheel. And at times she did not like the guys; she was with them for what they had to offer her, treating her like she was a queen, showering her with all sorts of gifts and money.

And here I was, passed by when I was looking for a man to for companionship and love. Being treated like that made me think Tony was right that I was ugly, that no one would want me as a girlfriend. I felt worthless. I had been for years, leaving me to degrade myself by having sex with a man that showed me some signs that he was interested in me sexually. That seemed to be the only way I could receive attention, even if it was or a moment.

Eden and I were spending so much time together that everyone became concerned about our destructive behavior, staying out late, sometimes not coming home at all. Her daddy abruptly interrupted our friendship when he pulled his shotgun on us, the same one he pulled on Tony. He forbade us to continue our friendship, giving us no explanation as to why. I was devastated by the betrayal of someone who considered me part of their family. I felt that someone else I loved and cared about was taken away. But our separation was temporary.

Eden sent GP to the house to give me a message to meet her at the bus stop on Jefferson and St. Jean. That night, when we met we hugged each other like we hadn't seen each other in years. We were happy. After sitting and talking for almost two hours, we decided to go home. We made plans to meet at the same time the following night. We did that every night until her father found out we were secretly meeting each other. He, then allowed us to continue our friendship. What's sad was how he stopped our friendship in the first place, and we were in our twenties. We were supposed to have a bond that no one could come between, and because her daddy tried to separate us, that incident caused me to distance myself. I do that when I feel I had been treated unfairly.

While sitting on Mama's porch talking with Neicy, Mama new upstairs neighbor and her aunt, I started talking about feeling ugly and that no men wanted me because I had kids.

"Who told you that?" they asked me.

"Tony."

They both got upset.

"Listen… don't listen to him. He's just trying to bring you down. Don't let anyone ever do that to you because you are beautiful and you can get a man. And we'll prove it to you," they said.

They invited me to one of their many parties they

had every weekend. The people that were there were family members, who I noticed were alcoholics. As they introduced me, instantly one of her family members showed interest in me. He really wasn't my type, nor was he attractive, but I talked with him because he showed interest. Of course we had sex.

    I attended more of their parties. I was attracted to another family member of theirs. I flirted with a man to see if he's interested in me. If he showed interest back, I would take it further, and I flirted with him. He never acted on my advances; he just smiled graciously. So did the other guys.

    Neicy wasn't through showing me that somebody would want me so she took me to a bar. When we sat at the bar, the first thing she said was for me to never leave my drink unattended. When she said that, it reminded me of my family member who'd died when someone spiked his drink. Sitting there for about five minutes, we were approached by this older guy.

    He was sitting beside me, smiling, and he bought us drinks. I smiled and told him thank you. As I was doing that, I was saying to myself, I hope he doesn't think something is going to happen because he bought us a drink. I wasn't attracted to him because I wasn't interested in older men.

    Then the right man came along. I was geeked; he was my type with a light complexion, and very, very good looking. We planned to meet the next day to have sex. He came and picked me up, and we went to his house. We had continuous sex all night, and it was wonderful. Not just satisfying but wonderful. We had one more sexual encounter and I never saw him again.

    Neicy and her auntie were right; guys were interested in me but not for a relationship. I was only good for having sex. I never dressed provocative because I had no clothes, nor did I portray myself as being promiscuous. I don't even know if I had been describing my sexual behavior correctly because I didn't have sex with a lot of guys. Promiscuous means loose, having sex with anybody and everybody. I described my entire sexual encounters as sporadic.

    One of Neicy's brothers came to visit her. He became interested in me. I had no interest in him because he wasn't my type, nor was he attractive to me. I had the nerve to be choosy when I didn't have a man in my life. I didn't want any man that was uglier than me. I was not that desperate. I had to be attracted to him. I had problems with letting someone that I wasn't attracted to touch me. It felt disgusting and eerie, and that's how I felt when I let him kiss me. Plus he was married. Nothing was going to happen, not even an affair. I talked to him just for convenience.

Neicy had another brother who came to visit. He was her baby brother who had just moved back to Detroit. We both started flirting with each other, and it turned into a few sexual encounters. One was unforgettable. We were in the back room of Mama's house on the bed; we were making too much noise. I suggested we get on the floor. The feeling I was getting was intense, becoming really rough. We both were humping so hard I thought if we humped any harder, we were going to fall through the floor.

I was trying to get him to make me reach that ultimate climax, something I'd never had because of the severe damage I suffered internally as the result of my rapes. He was unsuccessful. I felt embarrassed when Mama said she heard us. I thought getting on the floor would silence some of the noise. I laughed it off. I had no remorse being involved with two brothers. I didn't care; the older brother was mad because he said he really liked me. I didn't feel the same way about him, plus he was married.

I also accomplished fulfilling something I had tried to do when I was thirteen, with Chicken whom I was infatuated with, but our sexual encounters weren't successful. Because I was seeking attention from him, I had been brutally raped by a man at his house.

Chicken stopped me, once on my way to the store. I had not seen him since that rape. Neither of us mentioned anything about the incident. I told him how hurt I was to hear him having sex with Lena that time at our house, and I was mad that I couldn't say anything because of our age difference. I smiled at him, saying how I wanted to have sex with him to see if he can penetrate now. I figured since I had three kids, he should be able to.

Well, that night, he came over just like we discussed. Not taking him inside my place, we went in the backyard. I laid a cover down; he pulled his pants down and started to penetrate me. I couldn't believe it! There was still difficulty and tremendous pain but I didn't stop him; I let him continue and blocked out the pain. I was still amazed at how well endowed this man was. He succeeded with half of his penis inside of me, which made it impossible for him to lie down on me. Every time he pumped, the more pain I would feel, then we were rudely interrupted by my sister's godmother Dorty and my son. And instead of her leaving and getting my son away from the door, she made him leave and she stood there and watched after seeing what we were doing. She knocked on the back door to get our attention. I already knew she was there. I got mad, told him to continue after he was done, and he left. I asked her why she did that. She laughed. I didn't think that was funny, and that day was the last time I saw him.

Winter was about to arrive, and circumstances surrounding my life hadn't changed. Tony continued to mentally and verbally abuse me, and I continued to seek companionship to help heal my loneliness along with other things that was taken away from me mentally. I couldn't handle any more of Tony's threats about seeking custody of my baby or his criticizing me. Out of desperation to escape the abuse, I decided to secretly move. I searched for a house quickly, finding one that was far from where we lived. I told his mother, I was moving, telling her the reason why.

We moved what belongings we had in my car. Eden helped along with my brother and his friend, Chris. I told them not to let Tony know where I'd moved. Well, that plea went unanswered. He showed up with my brother and his friend when they brought the last of my belongings, defeating the purpose of me moving.

"How did you find out where I stayed?" I asked Tony. He didn't say anything. He just stood there looking for Chrissy.

"I told him," Chris said.

"Didn't I specifically tell everybody not to tell Tony where I moved?" I said.

Chris said, "Oh, I didn't know you were talking about him."

"You dumb!" we all yelled at him.

After everyone left, Tony included, I knew I was going to be alone in a new neighborhood I knew nothing about. I asked Eden to spend the night with me because I was scared. I never experienced living alone where I didn't know anyone. I would take her home and spend the day at her house or Mama's. When nighttime came, I asked Eden to spend the night again, each day, doing the same, just so I wouldn't be alone.

Then I ran into my childhood crush Chuck and gave him my address so he could visit me and we could catch up. My intention was to see if we could accomplish what we tried to do when we were younger. Eden and her boyfriend stayed. I disliked her boyfriend because he was jealous of our bond—he was devious, trying to come between our friendship. I tolerated him because of her. I put the kids in bed, leaving Eden and her man in the living room.

Chuck and I didn't do any foreplay, going straight into having sex that was successful, no complaints. It was not that painful until he slipped, humping fast and forcefully, he hit my anal area. I jumped up knocking him to the floor.

I yelled, "What you doing? That shit hurt."

"I'm sorry, it slipped," he said.

After he got up off the floor, we continued after the pain eased up. The next day he left, saying he would return.

I stayed at Mama's house, doing my same routine. Only this time Eden wasn't allowed to spend the night. Her family was complaining that she was spending too much time away from home. (Yes, she was grown.) I had to go home alone. I was so scared; I put the kids in bed as soon as it got dark.

I turned on the television, had it turned down low so I could hear. I was scared to go to sleep, waking up early checking on the kids and the house. The next day in the afternoon,

Eden's boyfriend came over looking for her. She wasn't coming over until later, and I believe he knew that because he had to pass her house to come to mine. He then asked me where my friend was. His odd behavior made me feel uneasy and suspicious.

Then he started making unwanted sexually advances, acting all nice when we both knew we didn't like each other. He was saying he knew I wanted to have sex with him and was trying to come into my house. I was trying to stop him. I knew I had to do something to get him away from my door because the way he was acting scared me. I didn't let him know I was, but I started having flashbacks of my brutal attack. I got angry and told him he had to leave. His irate behavior and what he was saying to me was getting out of hand.

When Eden arrived later that evening, I immediately sat her down and sat next to her. I told her what he tried to do and I told her he had no business coming over when he knew what time she would be at my house. He came back over while she was there and she confronted him. He denied it. We got into an argument because he said I was the one making sexual advances at him, but she knew he was lying. She knew I didn't like his ugly ass and that I would never cross that line. But she loved him, and she didn't know what to do. She said she would keep him away from me, and from that decision we saw less of each other. She was spending her time with him. If I went to visit her and he was there, I would leave.

My friend Chuck came over to my house and asked to borrow my car. I let him. He told me what time he was going to return, and when that time came and passed, still no Chuck. I started getting mad. Day one passed, day two, day three, and still no Chuck. Now I was angry, because he was my friend, and he betrayed me like this. I was left in that house, having no money or a way to get to Mama's house. I was stuck until I got my check.

My kids and I walked to the store, cashed my check and caught the bus to Mama's. That night, my brother took me home and I got my belongings, and I moved back into Mama's house without asking. That same week, Amy and her daughter moved back in, too. Carl had assaulted her and put her out of her own house. And to add insult to that, he took her car and moved another woman into her house. And there was nothing legal she could do because she let him manipulate her into putting the house and car in his name.

I knew she was hurt, and I knew how she felt dealing with all that I had dealt with. I was devastated at how Chuck did this to me. My car was not found until a month later on the shoulder of I-94 freeway. Carl asked me if I wanted the car. I said no, and he took ownership back, and I still had not heard anything from Chuck to explain why he betrayed me like that.

Christmas time came and all the money I received was used for my kids to have a nice Christmas. They had so much stuff and combined with my niece's stuff, the living room was filled with nothing but presents. I bought my niece and Chrissy a brown rocking horse and got them a red-and-yellow table to sit at because they were so close in age. Seeing how excited and happy my kids were with their gifts made me happy.

After Christmas, Amy and I got into an argument, for what reason I can't remember. But I know I got angry, ready to fight her, but I didn't. We just kept fussing at each other. I took my gift back from my niece, and I stopped speaking to my sister. The tension in that house was so thick with anger. I held everything in me so I wouldn't fight her. I believe our feuding lasted for a week or two and then we apologized to each other. I gave my niece back her horse. I don't know why I took her gift from her in the first place. She had nothing to do with what was going on between her mother and me.

I was trying to move back into my old house, the one I'd lived in with Tony, but Lady H and Robert refused me because of all the damage I caused. My sister asked if she could move in. She discussed it with Robert, and she was allowed to move in. My brother moved in with her, not wanting to live with Mama anymore, who no longer had money, especially to pay bills and buy pills like she use to.

Amy was no longer in a relationship with Carl, but

he thought he could still control her, forbidding her to be in a relationship with another man. She was scared to see another man because of his threats even though it was all right for him to be involved with their woman.

Amy liked, Pat, one of the brothers from the family that Carl had had that big brawl with. She secretly invited over. My sister and I were both infatuated with men whose complexion was fair to light. They were in the house; somehow Carl found out, came over, and kicked the door in. Carl and Pat had an altercation that almost turned violent. Amy ended her relationship with Carl for good, keeping a friendly relationship with him because it was good for the sake of their daughter, and he was a good father and provider.

Tony and I had another sexual encounter, but I vaguely remember how the circumstances arose and where it happened, but I know we had sex again. I thought we were going to reconcile because I still loved him. I quickly forgave him for all the abuse he afflicted me with, only to have him traumatize me by deceiving me again. I found out I was pregnant. I thought Tony was the father because I'd had sex with Eden's brother, GP the prior month. I told Tony when he came to see Chrissy.

"I don't want no more kids with you. Get an abortion," he bluntly told me. I refused. I didn't believe in abortions. He continued to harass me about having an abortion every time he came to visit his daughter. He criticized me, emotionally stressing me out. I laughed at him, not letting him know how he was affecting me emotionally. I was trying to make Paula envious.

I went to the grocery store, running into Eden and her brother, telling her my good news. She had some good news of her own. She also was pregnant. We stood there for a while talking. I told her I would visit her, but I didn't right away.

In March of 1986, I struggled to raise three kids by myself. I was vomiting every day and miserable. I didn't have the finances to support myself. I was mentally distraught all day. I was tired of Tony pressuring me to have an abortion and my mother agreed with him. She said I should consider it, that I wasn't financially able to take care of another baby.

My situation was no different from my other pregnancies; mentally, I'd given up when Eden told me her plans to get an abortion. She wasn't ready for a baby. She wanted to finish school, and like I said, we did almost everything together. We went to the abortion clinic for consultations and to set up an appointment. We returned on the date they gave us. Before we arrived at the clinic, I had second thoughts about doing this, but I knew I was mentally unstable, and just tired. I also knew I was making a bad decision.

We had to fill out papers; we were given a pill that was supposed to relax us. We started conversations with the other women, listening to their problems and why they were having an abortion. One girl was on her double digits' abortion, said that was her birth control. Eden and I were both called at the same time. I said we did things together. I was put in one room and Eden was in the room right next to me.

The doctor started asking me routine questions. I was given another pill to relax me, and then he had me to get into position. I was nervous and scared, hesitant about going through with it. He took this long clear tube that was attached to a big machine, and he inserted it inside my vagina and turned it on. I was scared; the noise was loud, sounded like a vacuum cleaner. I immediately felt pain.

"Stop! It hurts. You gotta to take it out," I yelled out. And he took it out. I got up, and put my clothes on. When I opened that door, I heard Eden; she was telling the nurse not to touch her.

She said, "I heard my friend, let me out of this room." They were trying to calm her down.

I couldn't go through with it. There was too much pain. But then I started bleeding before we left the clinic. The doctor had ruptured my bag, and I didn't want to take the risk to bring this baby into this world and have all kinds of serious health problems. So the doctor gave us another option where we could be put to sleep and have same-day surgery at the hospital.

"What have I done?" I cried. He had the nurse set up immediate appointments for both of us. I had to use my brother's car. Eden's boyfriend, whom I despised, had to come with us to drive us back because of the medicine we were going to be on. I wasn't going to be in any condition to drive. When it was over and I woke up, I cried. I'd made the biggest mistake ever. We left the hospital and recovered at home. When I was well, for some reason unknown to me, I distanced myself from Eden again A month after my abortion, I met this man while I was sitting on the curb, crying because of what Tony been doing to me. His name was Don. He was Nessa's friend. He wasn't my type. He looked like a monkey, but at that time in my life, my pain and feeling the brunt of all my abuse, I just wanted to continue hurting myself. I did not care. I went with him over to the house he was staying at, not knowing anything about him. He said the house was his sister's house. We sat and talked really about nothing, and then we had sex. I explained and told him that whatever he did not to let his sperm go inside me, to take it out because I'd just had an abortion.

When we were finished, I got out the bed and felt something running down my leg.
"Did you cum inside me?" I asked him. And when said yes, I became outraged. "You stupid motherfucker! Why did you do that? I told you not to. You stupid bitch! Now, you better get prepared because you're going to be a father." I was mad and I left.
I told Nessa what happened. I didn't talk to him again, and I was right. The next month, I didn't have my menstrual cycle. I knew for sure I was pregnant. I went through all that pain and suffering only to get pregnant a month later. I was already traumatized by my decision and the guilt of what I did, and it was for nothing. Every time I saw that man walking down the street, I cussed him out.
"Leave him alone," Mama said. "You just as at fault."
I said, "No. He is stupid. I told him what not to do."

Over the months, more circumstances arose. Tony continued to harass me when he came to visit his daughter. He defended Paula when I would talk about her, telling him he should have left me for a woman that looked better than me. He would get mad. I asked him why was he defending her when I'm his wife. Knowing something was about to happen, I went in the kitchen, got a small knife to defend myself.

I continued to talk about Paula, shaking the knife around, holding it close by my face. In anger he hit my arm, and the knife went inside my nose, and I started bleeding. When I saw the blood, I went crazy. I ran to Mama's room, grabbed her shotgun. Tony started running after me and he hit me, and ran for the door. I ran after him, but my brother and Stan, Tony's brother grabbed me, trying to take the gun away from me.

I said, "Let me go." Then, "That bitch is going to die." But when I saw they weren't going to let me go, I changed my threats.

"I'm not going to shoot him. Please let me go. I swear I won't shoot him," I said. They wrestled with me over that gun until I was exhausted and gave up. They took the gun away from me. Tony was standing on the sidewalk in front of the house, laughing and taunting me. I ran to the kitchen, still cussing, and grabbed Mama's big cast-iron skillet. I ran out to the porch. Tony started to run across the street, I threw the skillet at him, but I missed.

Something was wrong with him; he was acting ignorant. He got in his car, and drove past the house.

"Please give me the gun," I told my brother. "I'm not going to shoot him. I'll just shoot the tire." But they wouldn't let me.

Days later, while we were sitting on the porch, we believed my brother's friend Tee broke into Mama's house though the back door, stealing that same shotgun. We didn't see him do it, but like I said when he stole the baby bed for my daughter, if somebody's house was broken into, we knew who did it. Because of his reputation, we knew he did it.

Due to mama's inconsistency in handling her financial obligations, her heating provider turned off the heat due to nonpayment. Lena offered to let my kids and me stay at her new house until Mama resolved the issue. We only stayed there one day because that morning, I overheard her and Jo-Jo arguing because Chrissy cried all night. I'd taken her off her bottle and was potty training her. What I'd overheard made me angry. When the kids woke up, I packed our bags and called for my brother to come pick us up. We'd just have to deal with the cold. I dressed them in lots of clothes and used a heater, and we did just fine. We survived, and I knew summer was going to be arriving soon.

The City of Detroit and Chrysler were buying up a lot of property on the east side to expand the factory, build new homes and other big commercial projects. Some families were unhappy with the idea. Some weren't. The big controversy was people were thinking they were doing this to move all the black people farther north so all the white people could move to the riverfront. Part of me wanted to move so that I could have a better place for my kids to live. We didn't want to move out of the area and miss out on what they were offering. We were going to wait until the fall to see if I could get the heat turned on in my name at Mama's house.

Amy and Tony's brother, Stan were in a relationship. It was shocking because I had no idea he liked Amy. He'd had a longtime girlfriend that we were all friends with. Those two were inseparable. I guess with all I was going, though I missed knowing that they had broken up. Now he and Amy were inseparable from the beginning. Over time they started having problems due to his jealousy issues that made them argue, breaking up and getting back together.

As we were dealing with our issues, Mama went missing for a day. When she didn't return from the store, we started panicking because we didn't know where she was. The next day, as we searched the neighborhood, one of Mama and Lena's pill buddies told us where she was. Amy went to retrieve her because I had the kids. When Amy and Mama returned home, Mama smelled like she had been in a fire.

Amy said she was laid up with this eighty-year-old man

in a storefront where the man had made his home and was burning wood to keep warm. She was high, very incoherent. We were yelling at her like she was the kid. We were mad because she always used bad judgment because of her drug addiction. The next day, she had to be taken to the hospital because of severe pain. When she arrived back home, she said she had a bad infection. The old man had given her worms. I don't know if that's possible. We were furious because we had to look after her for years because of her irrational decisions. She risked her health, her life and ours for pills.

In August, I was four or five months pregnant when I leaned something shocking about the father of my unborn baby. He came over to the house and knocked on the back door. I thought he

wanted to see me. Instead, he asked for my brother. At that time, he was still selling drugs.

"I wanna buy a rock from your brother," Don said.

Looking at him in shock, I said, "Aw, man! Don't tell me you on drugs." He didn't answer, but I knew. He was standing next to me, rubbing my stomach, asking me how his baby was doing. I knew his concern was faked because he had been denying that he was the father of my baby from the day I told him. He believed my husband Tony was the father when I knew in fact that Tony wasn't. At that time, he was the only guy I had sex with since I had my abortion.

I was distraught over learning about his drug habit. I told him that he could never see my baby. I may have made the wrong decision, but at that time, I was concerned about the well-being and safety of my baby. That day was the last day I saw him. I could not contact him because all I knew about him was his first name. I went back to the house he'd taken me to, and it was vacant. I asked Nessa, if she knew how to contact him. She claimed she didn't know, but I believe she did. She moved, and I lost contact with her.

Tragedy struck our neighborhood weeks after Nessa

had moved. Bob, an older white man, moved into the apartment Nessa moved out of. He was a loner, not harmful to anyone. We would only see him when he went to the store. I was watching television when I started hearing police sirens. They were getting closer. I got up, went to the door, and checked to see where they were. As I looked out the door, police cars were everywhere. They were at the apartment where Bob stayed.

I went outside. Being nosey, I asked someone what happened. They said some old man was just shot. Within minutes, I learned it was Bob. He was beaten and shot when he returned to his apartment from the store. He was transported to the hospital and died. Police started searching the area for his killers. The helicopter was hovering around to help with the search.

A witness identified the killers; hearing who it was shocked me. It was Larry, the man who violently raped me when I was thirteen. The other man's name I did not recognize. Both killers were captured later that week and were convicted and sent to prison. Larry was killed not long after. I felt he got what he deserved in the long run, after committing violent acts toward helpless people.

For me, the lesson was don't think you can do something bad to somebody and think you've gotten away with it. You will get your turn in the long run. God will handle it.

Since living in that neighborhood, I knew of five tragic deaths that occurred; two were the result of another person's vicious act. One was when we first moved into the neighborhood, at the corner in an abandoned building, an older homeless man froze; the second one was a seventeen year old boy who drowned in the Detroit river; the third was a lady we knew who froze to death clinging to a fence when her father denied her access inside the house due to drug abuse; the fourth one was the older lady who died as the result of her house being firebombed; and Bob was the last. Times had changed what was once a safe and quiet neighborhood.

My brother stopped selling drugs as the result of two Detroit police officers threatening him and my cousin one night.

The officers took them to the river and told them they would come up missing and no one would know who did it. They were trying to get information on who they were selling for. I believe they were trying to use a scare tactic. They brought them back home when they didn't get the information they required. They scared my brother; he stopped. My cousin continued.

School was about to start, and due to my not having enough financial assistance, my son was not going be able to attend school. I was hurt already because he was previously unable to attend kindergarten. Diana came to my aid. She asked me if he was going. I told her no because of my financial situation. She told me to enroll him in school that she would help me, and she did.

I went to the school, thinking he would be put in kindergarten. The lady in the office told me no, he would be in the first grade.

"But he didn't go to kindergarten," I said. I was told that didn't matter; he would be in the first grade because he would be six. I was worried that he wasn't going to do good because he had no previous education.

I was very grateful to Diana for all the help she had given me over the years. Because of her help, I had that boost to get ahead, and I was able to provide for my other kids. I never told her how much I loved her.

Winter was going to be approaching soon, and I could not bring a baby into a cold house, nor could I let my kids continue to live in that situation. I had to start looking for a place for us to live. But I didn't want to move out the neighborhood because I didn't want to miss the opportunity to receive financial help from the city to relocate. I found one, and how ironic that it was the house where Bill used to live, where I conceived Emmanuel. I talked to the owner. He told me what it took to move in.

When I went to take him the money, I was involved in a verbal confrontation with his wife. She didn't want me to rent the house because she thought that her husband and I were having an affair. I told her that we weren't and that I didn't like her husband. This old lady was furious. I didn't understand why she had so much hostility toward me. I didn't know her.

She finally calmed down, and I explained my situation to her. I convinced her that I was no threat, that my mother was moving in with us and she let us move in. I had no choice at the time. That house was the only one available. I did not want to live in that house because I knew it was infested with mice when I visited Bill. I thought over the years they had taken care of the problem. When we moved in, I soon found out that they hadn't.

The first night we were there, I made a pallet on the floor because that's where the kids said they wanted to sleep. In the middle of the night, I was awakened to screaming. It was Chrissy. I jumped up to see what was wrong. I kind of suspected what happened. When I picked her up, she showed me her hand. It had two marks on her finger that were bleeding a little. I cleaned her finger and put a bandage on it and put them on the couch.

I had to make other sleeping arrangements. There were so many mice that when I walked in the kitchen to get something or went to the bathroom, they would be everywhere. I would yell at them to "get" or bang on the wall. They would look at me then turn back and continue what they were doing. I was the one to "get". It was like that when we took a bath. They would be running all around under the tub, and I was scared for us to take baths. When we did, we had to hurry up and run out.

I started having trouble with my next-door neighbor's kids. I'd known their parents for years. They were like the children of the nursery rhyme, There Was an Old Lady Who Lived in a Shoe - she had so many children, she didn't know what to do. I mean this lady continued to have baby after babies, so many that the state refused to help provide any more financial and medical assistance to the kids after her eighth child was born. Her boys didn't like my son; they were jealous.

When Emmanuel would get off the school bus, they would chase him home, trying to beat him up. They couldn't catch him. I would be in the kitchen window yelling at them that if they put their hands on him, I would come beat their asses. They would walk away and go home, but they would try to fight him when he was outside playing. They didn't listen to me that much.

Every day after school, when he got off the school bus at their stop, they continued to chase after him. Every day I had to go talk with their mother. I was trying to control my anger. If I had gotten a hold of those kids, it's no telling what I would have done to them. I'd had enough. I was tired because I was pregnant, and I had to go up and down stairs again and again. I went outside, walked over to their house, politely asked their mother to get control of her kids, and told them to leave my son alone.

"If they don't leave him alone, and they touch him, I'm going to beat their asses," I told her. She said OK, but she had so many kids, she couldn't control them. They controlled her. She didn't know what her kids were doing, and they continued to chase him. Even the bus driver would tell them to leave him alone.

When what we said didn't work, I wobbled my butt to the bus stop and stood and waited on Emmanuel. When the bus pulled up to the stop, to my surprise the driver was Brice's mother. We carried on a short conversation and talked about those boys trying to bully my son. She said she would tell them that they better leave that boy alone. She said she did not know that he was my son, nor did she know that Toya was my daughter. She had only seen her once in a picture.

She said that she would keep an eye on him so they wouldn't bother him while he was on the bus. When she picked him up and dropped him back off, I was standing at that bus stop. They always tried to bother him when he got off the bus. A few days later, the bullying stopped after I talked to Carl and told him what they were trying to do to my son. Carl talked with their daddy.

There was another incident that happened involving my kids when I let them outside to play on the porch. I was sitting on the couch, and they started screaming for me. I went outside to see why. My son told me an old man had called him to his car and offered him candy. When he went to his car, the man had his pants pulled down and his penis in his hand, trying to grab him. My son got a loose and ran yelling for me. The man drove off. I explained to them the danger of approaching a stranger's car. This was something new for us. I never had to explain to my kids what to do when a stranger approached them. We ad never experienced that before because we considered our neighborhood to be safe. We used to be able to stay out all night and no one bothered us… another lesson to be learned.

That year, my kids' Christmas was not as good as the two previous years because I was the only one receiving money. I had to pay all the bills and try to buy baby clothes before the baby was born. Mama took whatever money she was getting and spending it on pills. And in an effort to get a little extra cash, Mama's on- again-and-off-again boyfriend, Raymond, asked me if he could stay with us. His mama put him out. I told him he could, but he had to pay fifty dollars a week; he agreed.

He brought over what little belongings he had. That Friday, he paid me. But the following week he bailed, called himself moving out, but didn't take his belongings. Then he came over trying to retrieve his belongings.

"I come to get me stuff," he said.

"You can't get them until you pay me my money," I told him. I

should have never trusted a drug addict.

He said, "OK. When I get paid, I'll bring the fifty dollars to you."

Payday came, no Raymond. That same night, after we went to bed, somebody trying to kick the door in awakened me in the middle of the night. I went to the door.

"Who is it? I yelled. As the kicking continued, I grabbed the phone and I called Amy and told her that somebody was trying to break in. I got a butcher knife out the kitchen.

"Who is it?" I yelled again.

"I want my TV and my other things," Raymond yelled back. "You ain't getting anything until you give me my money!"

My kids were screaming.

"Now get away from my door, or I'll call the police," I told him but I didn't. I heard another guy talking, saying they weren't leaving until they got his stuff. When he kicked the door again, it opened. I went to close the top door. But before I got it closed, I saw Raymond and two other guys.

I was concerned for our safety. I was pregnant, and my kids were scared. How was I going to protect us? They couldn't get through the top door because it was secured with a two-by-four. They knocked on the door, saying they wanted his stuff.

"When I get my money," I told him again.

Amy and my brother were taking a long time to come. I took the two-by-four off the door so we could try to get them out the house because they had my babies scared. When I opened the door, Raymond and some guy I had never seen before were standing there.

"I'll leave if you give me my stuff," Raymond said.

"Give me my money then," I said. "Or you going to leave without it."

He was trying to get in. I told him, "If you don't leave, I'm going to stab you." My hand was shaking. I was hesitant about doing it. I was trying not to because he was Mama's boyfriend, and I thought I would go to jail. In my mind I was going to stab him, but my attention was focused on the man that was with him. He kept talking, saying what he was going to do. They were high.

Mama had come to the door and out of anger she pushed one guy down our twenty-three stairs. That man literally bounced back up when he hit the bottom. He walked right back up the stairs and Mama pushed back down. He did the exact same thing, like he was made out of rubber. But Raymond decided they should leave, seeing they were not getting what they came for and before somebody got hurt. And I was angry because he did this and wasn't concerned for the safety of my babies.

Mama and I walked behind them; we were outside. I was still cussing them out. After what seemed like forever, Amy and my brother finally arrived at the house, asking what happened. I said Raymond and the two other guys broke into the house; they denied it. The guy who mama pushed down the stairs said he didn't kick the door in. Out of rage, I lifted the two-by-four and was getting ready to bash his head in. My brother blocked the blow.

After defusing the situation, Raymond said he would bring my money when he got paid on Friday. After they left and we calmed down, it was funny because I started thinking about the way Mama pushed that man down the stairs and he bounced back up as if he was a ball. To secure the door, after Amy and my brother left, we had to take a smaller two-by-four and place it between the door and the bottom step. Friday came, Raymond brought me my money, and I gave him his property. I told him that's all he had to do and not try and use me. He knew me too long, and he knew what I was capable of doing when someone crossed me. The man Mama pushed down the stairs was killed not long after they broke in our house.

Mama was hoping that one of her grandkids would be born on her birthday. She almost got her wish. One day when I was sitting on the couch, watching television, I heard a commotion coming from outside. I got up to look, and I saw Jo-Jo beating up Lena. I yelled for Mama and I went outside to stop him from hitting on her. He already had beaten her badly with a chain before this incident, and her eye was swollen shut. In the midst of the excitement after getting her in the house, I started having labor pains, and I was taken to the hospital. It was premature labor, and I was given medicine through my IV to stop my contractions. All of a sudden I started shaking like I was having a seizure. My insides felt like they were being burning.

"What did you do to me?" I yelled. The nurses were holding me down while one nurse put a cold rag on my forehead. I was given a shot. After five or ten minutes, I calmed down. Amy and I were panicking because we didn't know what they'd done. I overheard the doctor say that was a side effect of the medicine. I think they over-medicated me. I was released later that evening. When I got home, Mama was a little disappointed that the doctor stopped the baby from coming on her birthday, February 16.

The following month, on March 1, Lena called the house. I was the one who answered the phone.

"Girl, you haven't had that baby yet?" she said.

"No, not yet," I said. She inquired about the rest of the family, and we hung up. And as soon as I put the receiver on the phone base, I started having labor pains. I said to myself, I need to stop talking to her. She jinxes me. I went into premature labor because of her, now labor pains came again. I called Amy to get a ride. When she and Stan pulled up, he was driving; they were arguing. I noticed that he had taken the long way to St. John Hospital, and he was driving two miles per hour.

I interrupted their argument. "Excuse me, do you want me to have this baby in the car?"

"No," he said.

"I'm in pain. Speed up! You driving too slow," I said. The pain was unbearable, and he was driving like a turtle. We entered the emergency door and I was taken to the fifth floor labor and deliver room. I was in labor all night, and at 6:25 am., March 2, 1987, I heard, "It's a boy!"

I said, "Amy, what do he looked like?"

"Like the daddy," she said in a low voice.

I said out loud, "Oh my God! My baby is ugly." After I said that, the nurse and doctor looked at me in shock. Amy looked away; she didn't want to tell me he was ugly. The nurse held him up. A frown instantly came on my face. He looked ugly; he looked just like a baby monkey. His legs were in the position like one, and he had hair all over his body. They took him away, and I was stitched and cleaned up and taken to the recovery room for an hour and then to my room.

I was in the room getting myself situated, when the nurse entered the room with the baby. I was on the phone with Mama. I looked at him.

"Whose baby is this?" I asked the nurse.

She looked at our armbands and said, "Yours."

"That can't be. That's not the baby I delivered." I was telling Mama how ugly my baby was. I said, "Mama, oh my God, this baby is cute! This can't be the baby I saw when I delivered him." They had cleaned him up. I was wondering if they had shaved him. He looked like a different baby.

I looked at him and I said that if I had another son, I would name him after the guy I liked at school that never knew I liked him. I just liked his name, Von. So I named my baby Jyvon Dorrell Moore. The day we went home, Mama was all over my baby just like she was with Emmanuel, only different. She couldn't tell me what to do with him. Mama would come in my room and check on him to see if he was OK because he was a good baby. He didn't cry, and I would have to mess with him to wake him up just to feed him.

Three days at home, an old friend named Norm cam to see me. I'd had crush on him from the first day I met him. He was a friend of my goddaughter Womp's mama, Darlene. He had this walk about him that turned me on. He was one of the guys I would flirt with, and he would graciously turn me down and smile at my advances. He came to me, needing a place to stay and asked if he could stay at my house for a while. I told him he could, although I really didn't have the room. I was glad he was at the house. We talked and talked; he slept in the bed with me and the baby at opposite ends. He didn't want to have sex with me and I was upset because I had been trying for years to get this man in my bed to have sex.

I started feeling sad and emotional, not myself again. I didn't know why. At the time I never knew or heard anything about postpartum depression. I now believe I was attacked with it. Angrily, I cussed at him and put Norm out for eating a hot dog and not asking me if he could eat my food. I told him that food was for my kids. He said he was sorry, and left. I knew he had to eat when I allowed him to move in. I didn't know what was wrong with me.

I ran into GP at the store across the street from where I lived. I told him to relay my good news to Eden because I hadn't seen her since our abortion. I learned even in our separation we still did things together and thought alike.

"Tell Eden I had a baby," I said. "She did too," he said.

"I had a boy on March 2," I told him to tell her.

"She had a boy, too. He was born in January," he said. "Tell her my son's name is Jyvon."

He laughed. "That's her baby's name, too."

The coincidence surrounding this circumstance was unbelievable. How could we unknowingly give our babies the same name, just spelled differently? When we told people, they believed we'd previously planned on naming our babies the same name. In actuality, we had no idea that either of us was pregnant. Again, that was just the closeness we had and how we thought alike, even in separation.

I told him to tell her I would visit her soon. When I did finally decide to go visit her, I learned that she and the baby's father were no longer together, again. And we were inseparable again. We started hanging out but not as much as we used to. When it comes to anybody doing anything for me, I had to be the one to always initiate.

While we were waiting on the city to get to our area to start the slow relocation process, our neighborhood started to look like a ghost town. Some of the people started moving out and drug dealers started moving in. That's when the trouble started and we became concerned for our safety. As soon as spring arrived, we had our first causality as the result of drugs and the fighting over turf. I almost became a statistic.

I'd started having sexual relations with a drug dealer named John whom I had very little attraction to because he was ugly. I was with him for convenience and for the sex and the money and material gifts he was providing me. I had never been with a bad boy and I liked the idea that I was with a drug dealer. Carl was forbidding me to see him because he was their enemy. Carl and his partners said John was trying to come in the neighborhood to take over and steal customers from the other drug dealers. He was staying in the apartment where Bill, the older man, was killed and where Nessa had moved from.

The entire apartment building was empty, except the apartment he took over. No one knew I was in the apartment with him because I was forbidden. We were in the room having sex when we heard a loud noise and glass breaking in the back apartment. We got up and went to investigate and saw flames at the back door. We ran and got dressed. I wasn't so scared. But I was a little concerned. How were we going to get out the apartment? Whoever threw the firebomb planned to harm whomever was in that apartment.

I asked him what we were going to do? If we went out through the back, we could burn. Or they thought we were not going to take the risk of going through the fire and they'd be waiting in the front for us to run out and start shooting. We waited, trying to figure out what to do because whatever we were going to do, we had to hurry up before the fire spread. He peeked out the door to see if it was safe for us to leave. When it was safe, I left first, going straight home. I kept checking my surroundings until I entered my house. John came thirty minutes later. I was a little worried, thinking something had happened to him, but was relieved when I saw he was safe.

I never found out who did that violent act, nor did I tell anybody about the unthinkable incident. John and I continued our sexual affair until he disappeared. I ran into him months later, not able to talk to him because I was with Lady H. After me and John nodded hello, I ran into my childhood best friend Deanna. I tried to keep in touch with her since our reunion, only to learn she was the victim of a severe case of domestic abuse by the father of one of her children.

I was not in a position to provide assistance or advice to her in any way because of my situation and all the abuse I had endured and accepted. I could only talk with her and give her moral support; not tell her to do something when I hadn't it done myself. She had to make her own decision concerning her and her children's safety.

It was amazing to me how I was dealing with my own abusive situation and now being surrounded by other people and their abusive situations. Lena finally got the courage to leave her abuser, Jo-Jo for good only to be with another man that also abused her. We had to come to her aid. He beat her badly when he thought she was consuming more drugs than him. She continued to be with him until she was tired of the beatings.

When Mama was involved in a knockdown fight, I kept my promise I made when I was younger when I tried to defend her from JB's abuse. At that time I was only to be betrayed by her when she allowed him to beat me. I'd vowed never help her again if she was ever in a violent or similar situation. And that's exactly what happened.

Mama and her pill friend, Poochie, who had set us up to be robbed, were involved in a fight in front of the store. The reason for them fighting was unknown to me. I was standing there, watching, just to make sure it was a fair fight and no other person joined in. They fought until they got tired, and when they were done, they went their separate ways. Mama did not see Poochie again. That was a funny scene: two old women fighting. I still don't know why they were fighting. But knowing them two, it had to be over pills. Or Mama blamed Poochie for bringing that guy over to the house to rob us. I don't know. The pills were the only things they had in common. And I kept my word; I didn't help her.

My kind heart allowed me to let another male friend move in with us temporarily, at first. This is how I met him. His name was Benny. Neicy came over to the house and told me to come outside. I had to see these guys who were friends of her sister's boyfriend. Neicy was so impressed and excited with their dancing, she wanted me to see them in action. And when they started dancing, I was excited right along with her, even growing attraction toward one of them.

I would go over Neicy's house just to see them dance. After knowing Benny for two weeks, he needed a place to stay. And since he knew I was attracted to him, when he asked me, and I let him stay with us. My intention was to persuade him to sex with me. My family was concerned, telling me not to have sex with him because of their concern with his sexuality. They believed he was gay because of his feminine behavior. I suspected he was, but my state of mind had me not caring.

He had to sleep in my bed because there was no place else for him to sleep. I tried to entice him by sleeping in the bed naked; rubbing my butt against his penis, with no reaction from him. He just ignored my advances. He started staying in the kitchen with the mice, gossiping on the phone all night instead of coming to bed. But I didn't stop pursuing him. I don't give up so quickly.

Finally, all my persistence worked and we had sex, though it wasn't really enjoyable. He wasn't putting any effort into trying to please me. He wasn't interested in having sex with a woman. He humped just enough for me to feel his penis, and he got up and got on the phone. Two days later, he moved. I did not tell anyone of our half sexual encounter. Neicy had gotten her money to relocate, and she moved, and I had no idea of her location. I wasn't too worried. I knew I would find out where she lived one day.

Jyvon was two months old when Mama's ex-boyfriend Raymond had the nerve to come over to my house to visit Mama. After the trauma he'd caused us. He tried to explain his actions, but I didn't want to hear it. He was a crack head punk anyway. He didn't come to see me after what he had done to us. I still tried to give him respect because he was Mama's friend. He tried to play it off, being fake, trying to play with my baby. Jyvon looked at him and started screaming. Raymond walked away; Jyvon stopped crying.

I noticed right away, my baby didn't like him. I told Raymond to walk back so I could see something. When he started talking to Jyvon, he started crying again.

Raymond said, "He don't like me."

"He knows you tried to harm us when I was pregnant with him," I said. Jyvon only did that with Raymond. I believe babies are aware of a lot of different things before birth. And that was the last time we saw Raymond. We had no idea where he relocated. We heard he was in a relationship with Dorty's sister, who was also a drug addict more severe than Mama.

Jyvon was involved in a scary situation when he turned five months. I told the kids to always keep the top door closed because Jyvon was in his walker. The first place he would go to was the door. One of the kids forgot to close the door once. I was standing in the living room, talking to Mama when we heard something tumbling down the stairs. I instantly got scared, knowing it was my baby falling. I was too scared to go look down those stairs, thinking my baby was not alive. He'd stopped crying or making any kind of noise.

"Mama, go look."

"I can't," she said. She was scared too. I was terrified, my heart racing, scared of what I might see. I slowly walked to the door and peeped around the corner looking down the stairs. I saw my baby and his walker upside down. He was kicking his feet, and I knew he was alive. I ran down those stairs as fast as I could I, grabbed my baby out that walker, and held onto him. I checked him all over his body to see if he was OK. He appeared to me to be fine. But to be on the safe side, Mama had called 911. When the EMS technician arrived, and examining him, I told them I thought he was OK. He asked me if I wanted them to take us to the hospital to be on the safe side. I told him yes because the way he was in that walker, it was amazing that nothing was wrong with him. He could have broken his neck. God was with him, and I provided extra precautions.

There was a lot of controversy arising with the city about how they were buying the property for development. Some residents felt deceived because they weren't receiving a fair deal. Some homeowners were offered less money, meaning that if they found a house, they would have to start paying mortgage again. Some were too old to start over, and some of the tenants were receiving enough money to pay for their house in full.

The homeowners held out. They were not moving until

they received a fair settlement. I also felt what the city did wasn't fair. I got $5,000; Amy got $6,000. Some of our friends who were tenants received twice as much. I had no choice but to accept what they were giving me. I felt we were being cheated, but that was something I was used for years. Why should anything change now?

We all had the same Realtor. I said to myself, she made a fortune off us. I was shown three houses. I found one I really liked: a beautiful five-bedroom house. It was in an area where there were mixed races. Amy found a house too. I didn't know what area she was relocating to, nor did she know where I was relocating to because we weren't familiar with the area. We had to wait for everything to be finalized.

While I was waiting for my house to be finalized, the table was turned on me. Instead of me pursuing someone, this older man named Buddy was pursuing me. He was another one of those older men I said would seek out young females for sexual activity in exchange for money. He would always approach me, and I would refuse him because I was not attracted to him. I wasn't attracted to dirty old men.

I should have kept it that way, but I let Lena, Mama, and Dorty press me into having sex with him to get money. I felt so nasty, disgusting. I was glad he didn't last long. He gave me money, and he left, and I said to myself, I am not doing that again. And I tried to erase the memory of that encounter from my mind.

Eden and I were on our way home from downtown when I noticed the bus driver was staring at me. I gave him my number before I got off the bus. I knew what he was interested in doing what I was only good at—sex. He called me when he got off work and he arrived at my house around 4:00 am. We went right into having intercourse, not knowing anything about each other. When he was done, he didn't get up and put his clothes on to leave; he lay on my bed, talking. Then he started scratching in his penis area; he continued talking. When he said something bit him, he asked me to turn the light on. He looked through his pubic hairs and pulled something off.

He said, "Oh my God! You gave me crabs."

I didn't know what crabs were. I instantly became frightened. I didn't know this man or what he was capable of doing to me. He could harm me, and no one would have known.

"I'm sorry," I told him. I explained to him that I didn't know anything about crabs or how you get them. "I don't have crabs."

"Yes, you do," he said. He began to look through my pubic hair, and he pulled one off me. I was shocked because I didn't know I had them. I did notice that soon after I had sex with Buddy, I started itching, and I didn't know why. He saw I was scared. He assured me that he wasn't going to harm me.

"I am mad," he said he. "You need to be careful about who you have sex with." And he got dressed and left.

Man, was I scared and mad because I let Mama, Lena and Dorty talk me into having sex with this man, for money. He ended up being nasty, and look at the price I had to pay? Knowing I had those bugs on me felt disgusting. I was uncomfortable. Because it was dark outside, I had no way to get to the doctor at that time. The first thing I did when I woke up was go straight to the emergency room, seeking treatment. I was given a prescription to kill the bugs and I went back home.

"I will never let y'all talk me into having sex with anybody ever again," I said when I walked in the house. "Your friend gave me crabs, and I gave it to someone else." I said, "The next time y'all know he offering money, you have sex with him!"

I had seen the bus driver again while catching the bus and it felt awkward. My heart started racing as I entered the bus. The way he acted made me believe he did not recognize me. I wasn't sure. I sat at the back of the bus, and when I reached my stop, I exited from the rear in, fear and shame.

I had some doubt about the treatment the doctor had prescribed for me. When Eden informed me she found a bug on her after she was bitten, she asked me do I think she could have gotten it when we were in the Jacuzzi together at her male friend's uncle's apartment. I told her I didn't know. I knew nothing about these bugs. I didn't think they would survive in water, but we were in hot water. Anything was possible.

Because I wasn't sure, I went to the pharmacy to find alternative treatment to get rid of them. Even though they weren't attacking by them anymore, but just the thought that they still might be on me made me feel me creepy and irritated. I was going to use anything that would help me get them off of me. This experience prevented me from being interested in having any sexual contact with any man for a while.

Chapter Eight

Reminiscing

Carl's mama, Vivian and Diana planned a farewell party for the neighborhood. It was being thrown in the vacant lot next to Diana's house. As they were setting up everything, I was talking with the neighborhood drunks when I noticed this guy we called Bigfoot had a hole in his pants. As he was squatting down talking to me, his penis was hanging out, touching the ground; I remembered what Dorty told me about him. He'd put his girlfriend in the hospital for damaging her vagina because of his huge-sized penis.

I didn't think anything would happen to me because all the other guys were there, and it was daylight. I'd been in that same situation before, when I was raped. But I didn't have any fear of these men. I didn't want to take any chances and assume anything. I did that before when I got raped, and there were other guys there, too. I made up an excuse to leave, and I walked away from them real fast.

I went home to get myself and my kids ready, waiting for the party to start. When we arrived at the party, there were not a lot of people. Several neighbors had moved, and their residences were unknown so we couldn't have invited. But there were enough people to still have a good time. I sat there looking and thinking this may be our last time seeing one another.

I was going to miss my friends and the neighborhood. I reminisced about the things that happened while living in this neighborhood. Like when we first moved on the block and we started meeting people. An incident came across my mind when Amy was in an altercation with one of the boys who lived next door. He liked her and he got mad at her. But he'd made her so mad she went to drop kick him and both of her legs flew up in the air. She dropped and hit the ground, hurting herself. When she landed on the ground, it was funny to us. We were wondering how she did that.

There was another funny moment when my sister called herself being a girlfriend to one of my brother's friends, and he tried to tell her what to do. She loudly said, "I quit you." And we started laughing because that was the shortest relationship I ever saw. That morning, he asked her to go back with him, and she dumped him that night.

Even while I was going through my entire tragic, emotional trauma, I did experience some good times. My dark outer appearance overshadowed any good feeling I had inside of me. Once, I experienced a funny moment when I took a shortcut through Lady H's backyard, as I always did. Two geese were kept in a cage back there, and I'd entered the yard not checking to see if they were in their cage. Out of nowhere, Benny started making noise. It sounded too close. When I turned to look to see where he was, I saw he was flapping his wings and coming straight toward me.

In fear of being attacked, I started running. Benny was right behind me, almost catching me. The gate to exit was closed and it seemed like it was far away. Benny was on my tail. I exited that gate and locked it as fast as I could, sitting on the porch, trying to catch my breath and laughing. I became wise from that incident. If I was going to take a shortcut through Lady H's backyard again, I was going to make sure I checked my surroundings.

I didn't laugh that much because of the sadness surrounding my life, so when the opportunities arose to smile, I enjoyed them. I remembered when my goddaughter, Womp's mother got into a fight with a Hispanic woman while under the influence. I didn't intervene because I knew them and I had no problems with them, plus she started the altercations. Whatever she was on led her to believe she had a lot of courage to start a fight. I believe she thought she was a famous fighter and she was unbeatable. Other people broke it up, and everybody went their separate ways.

I was never the type to start any altercation. I had a good, kind heart, and I endured a lot of pain. But God kept me to be who I am and had me survive for a reason. As more people start arriving at the party, I started talking with them, and seeing them reminded me of things I saw and heard about them.

Like Dorty, my sister's godmother who used to be an alcoholic who quit and started having medical problems. She struggled to beat the odds and survived. She did it on her own. We would have to go check on her because we would not see her, but once a week. She got on the right track and started working. That was a lot better than the stories I'd heard about what she did while under the influence, passing out on the grass and had to be taken home. I wished my mother would have followed her and given up her habit.

I remember when we got into trouble when my little cousin went missing when he was two. He was left in our care while Mama and Lena went pill hunting. We were in the house, cleaning, and we locked the screen door. Somehow without us knowing, he unlocked the door and left. We had no idea where he was. We started panicking. We searched, and searched all around the house. We just could not find him until one of Mama's friends called and said that the police had him and told us where to go.

My sister and I ran to Jefferson and saw Mama's friend on the next block, standing with my little cousin. We ran to them. She said the police put him out the squad car and left him with her because he was crying, and they couldn't get him to stop.

I said out loud, "How could the police officer do that to a baby?" That showed me how unprofessional and uncaring they were.

It seemed like we would get in trouble for anything. That was why I tried to stay away from home. Doing this led me to experience things I should not have experienced. Just so I could escape the abuse, I tried sniffing glue, smoking marijuana, and drinking not to cover up pain to cause pain. I did not use what was happening to me as an excuse to do any of those things. I did them out of curiosity and so I would fit in. I didn't experience that stuff again; that was not the lifestyle for me. I used sex to cover up my pain.

There was always something going on in our neighborhood. I remember when I would walk around meeting people and visiting. I would see Carl's car parked on the next block with a different girl from the neighborhood. On different occasions Tonia and my sister would secretly meet him at that spot. I knew where to find them, and when Lady H and Mama would ask about their whereabouts, I would go get them before they were caught. Tonia eventually put her interests somewhere else. Amy and Carl became a couple.

I missed a lot being away from home. When I would talk to someone about the past, everyone shared a story. I might say I didn't know how I missed that. But I would have to remind myself I was hanging out in the street to escape the abuse, which was why I sometimes didn't know what they were talking about. I missed the gang activity and I wondered how I missed that. I was on the street in the midst of everything and missed it all.

I know one thing I didn't miss was the abuse. I was surrounded by it. It started with me, and went on to my sister-in-law who was constantly abused by her husband, to my childhood best friend, and my cousin. Two different men were beating Lena. The abuse my niece suffered was different. She was the abuser. She hasn't taken no shit from any man. She was beating her kid's father. She was so short, and you had to wonder how this little woman was abusing this man. She would throw him down the stairs. It was funny, not the abuse, but we would be sitting around the house, and all of a sudden you would hear something tumbling down the stairs. And before we would go see what it was, I would have figured it out.

If you knew her, she didn't seem like she would do that; she didn't look or portray herself as mean or cruel to anybody. Maybe it was just toward him. We were kind of alike. She took care of her kids before she took care of herself. I remember walking with her in deep snow ten miles from our house to go get her kids some clothes. The store sold clothes we could afford. We were good friends to each other. When I was someone's friend, I was a true friend. I would go beyond my duties as a friend. But I didn't always get that in return.

I barely had anybody do anything for me out of the kindness of their heart. Rarely was anything even done for me unless I asked for something. I never complained about anything. I graciously accepted what was presented to me whether good or bad. Abusers surrounded me.

I was reunited with a man that violently abused and raped me when I was twelve. Pookie approached my sister and I as we were walking to the store. We stopped and talked to him, carrying on a short conversation like we were friends. He said he had just left a family member's house. He pointed to the house I used to live at and where Amy stayed. Just in that short period, he abused me again, violated me mentally.

As we stood there, talking, he was making seductive eye contact with me then at Amy. He said that he should have raped her instead of me. I was hurt by what he said even though it was wrong. Like others had, he implied that I was ugly, too ugly, to be raped. Not only did he finally admit he raped me, he was also saying he regretted raping me because I wasn't attractive enough to for the act.

My sister, in anger, said to him that he was wrong. I didn't say anything because I was traumatized by what he said. She said, "Come on, let's get away from him."

As we walked away, I turned and looked at him. He had a smirk on his face. When we returned to the house, I found out that he was some kin to Chrissy's auntie by marriage. That was the last day I saw or heard anything from him. I often wondered about him; how his life was; had he changed, how he looked. I wondered if he had not raped me, would we have had a relationship? I never told anybody that I had fallen in love with him. Because of all the abuse I endured, I seek aggressive men or abusers because that's all I knew. That was how I felt they loved me. That was the only way I felt loved. Call me crazy for loving someone that robbed me and hurt me in every way imaginable. I did not understand why myself.

I endured many traumatic situations, and God allowed me survive. When I was going though all the abuse, I never called on

God. I knew he was with me, guiding me every step of the way. Just like I knew he was guiding my goddaughter Womp through all the trauma she had to endure at such a young age. Because of my emotional issues, I could not physically, mentally, emotionally rescue her like my godmother tried her best to rescue me.

My goddaughter lived and watched other people's kids in an uninhabitable living condition. It hurt me to see her and those kids staying in such bad conditions, and I could not do anything about it. I could not legally take them. When my sister and I walked out of the door, I prayed for them. I believe God provides us with a good mind to take care of ourselves at such a young age. The only difference between my situation and my goddaughter's situation was she had to care of babies from infant to toddler. I was kind of relieved when Protective Services rescued them. God was watching over them and me. We survived.

No matter what I experienced living in this neighborhood, I loved the people I was close to. I was going to miss everything and everybody. I remembered when we first moved in the neighborhood, how safe it was. We could sit outside until four or five o'clock in the morning, and no one would bother us. I remember when the city recreational department had a mobile swimming pool that would come to your neighborhood upon request, block off the street so that we can swim. The drag racing—Carl and his friends would drag race up and down the street. I was going to miss that even though it was dangerous. The car Carl raced with was the same car he gave me.

He used that same car to try and teach Mama how to drive. It was so funny because he did not get in the car to tell her what to do. He stood in the street in front of the house, and I was at the end of the street in the driveway of the factory, trying to give mama instructions from my end. She was driving very slowly before she reached my end. That was the day someone came outside and said that the news just announced that Marvin Gaye was shot and killed by his father. That day was April 1, 1984.

We were devastated by the news. Mama's driving lessons stopped after that news. We sat on the porch in sorrow as if we'd known him personally. We felt like we did because we listened to his records all the time. I was very sensitive. I loved and cared about other people even though they didn't feel the same way about me. What could I do? I had to be who I am.

As I looked at the people attending the party, I visualized the memory of each person that played a part in my life. If it was good or bad, it will always be etched in my mind. My experience with rodents was also etched in my mind. They had invaded my life and I petrified of them and I would run out of the house when I would see one. I almost hurt myself jumping off the porch, never touching a step.

I remembered when Tony would chase me out the house with one of those cat-sized rats that was caught in the trap. And then I move into a house invaded by different-sized rodents that tried to eat my daughter and almost got my baby when he fell out my bed. I quickly grabbed him before they could get to him. Some of my experiences with them were funny, but I couldn't wait until we moved. I was tired of running from them and seeing and hearing them everywhere.

I had to stop reminiscing because if I didn't, I was going to miss the party as it neared the end. I had someone take a picture of me holding Jyvon and Mama standing next to us. I was wearing jeans for the first time. I had taken advise from Carl who tried to talk to me from a man's point of view. He told me about how a woman is supposed to look, saying I needed to clean myself up, take better care of myself, buy myself clothes, that my kids are not going to be neglected if I did something for myself. He told he that I would be attractive to somebody. I don't know if I should have taken that as a criticism, but I took his advice and got some clothes.

I had been neglecting myself because of my emotional issues. I felt my kids came first and deserved to be taken care of before me. It was getting late, and I enjoyed myself. I found myself still reminiscing. But I had to stop. There was so much to reminisce about I could go on and on.

I gathered my family, and we said our good-byes to everyone; and we went home. We waited on the day we were supposed to move. And in the summer of 1987, we moved. We said our good- bye to our friends who stayed behind, waiting on more money. And when we moved, I did not know where any of my friends or my sister relocated. We moved with nothing more than our clothes and a couch Mama found in the alley.

You can contact Ms. Ernestine Moore at
emooreablewriter@yahoo.com

Or visit her website at
www.ernestinemoore.com

RESOURCES

If you are in immediate danger, please dial 911 to reach your nearest police department.

National Domestic Violence Hotline: (800) 799-SAFE (7233)

TTY for National Domestic Violence Hotline: (800) 787-3224

From anywhere in the U.S. call the National Sexual Assault Hotline at 1-800-656-HOPE(4673) or call 202-544-3064 to reach the RAINN (The Rape, Abuse & Incest National Network) business office.

National Suicide Prevention Lifeline
With Help Comes Hope
1-800-273-TALK (8255)
www.suicidepreventionlifeline.org

www.ingramcontent.com/pod-product-compliance
Lightning Source LLC
Chambersburg PA
CBHW031239290426
44109CB00012B/368